TRANSFORMING LEADERS

THINKING | DESIGNING | PLANNING | CHANGING

Lester Massingham
Clive Smallman

IIMBAS Publishing

Published by GLK Knowledge Ltd (trading as the International Institute of MBA Studies)

First published April 2021

GLK Knowledge Ltd
1 Malcolm's Place
Wrea Green
Preston PR4 0LT
United Kingdom

ISBN (eBook): 978-0-6451824-0-8
ISBN (Print): 978-0-6451824-1-5

Edited by Mary Haropoulou
Produced for the Publisher by Kindle Direct Publishing

CONTENTS

TABLE OF FIGURES

ABOUT THE AUTHORS

Professor Lester Massingham, *President, International Institute of MBA Studies*, is a vastly experienced management consultant and academic leader, having taken global academic leadership of in-house and public MBA and DBA programmes for thousands of executives. He holds and has previously held Adjunct Professorships in European and Asian business schools and universities. He is an examiner for leading professional bodies and has co-authored best-selling textbooks.

His career as a management consultant spans Europe, Asia and the Middle East, designing and implementing strategic solutions for governments, multinationals and SMEs. His clients include Commerzbank, NCB Bank, National Westminster Bank, Standard Chartered Bank, Bank Negara Iinceif), ING, Zuellig Insurance, Gleneagles Hospital, Durdans Hospital, Ministry of Higher Education, Najran State Government, Makkah Development Corporation, Philips, Toyota Distributors, Lotus Cars, Schlumberger, Nippon Oil & Gas, Leica Geosystems, DHL, Stanley Tools, TV3, ICAC, EAC, TYCO.

His expertise as a strategist is to influence top management mindsets towards new value creation through impactful strategy determination for financial value capture, culture change and incremental stakeholder value. This formula for leading transformational change is achieved by challenging existing business models for 'relevance' to thereby enable organisational strategy realignment for financial sustainability. Not surprisingly, Lester is the originating designer and author of IIMBAS's Certified Transformational Leader award.

Professor Clive Smallman, *Vice-President (Academic), International Institute of MBA Studies* is an experienced higher education entrepreneur, executive and advisor with over 30 years-experience in business and executive education, spanning Europe, the West Indies, the Middle East and Australasia. He is presently Dean, Higher Education Leadership Institute, and formerly President of Asia Pacific International College, Founding Dean of Business and Assistant Vice-Chancellor, Western Sydney University, and Professor of Business Management, Lincoln University, New Zealand. He remains an Adjunct Professor, Western Sydney University.

Clive also has prior commercial experience in artificial intelligence and machine learning and in large scale project management. His commercial clients include Royal Bank of Scotland, Halifax Card Services, Coca Cola, Ford, General Motors, Shell, PGG Wrightson, the Bank of England, Philips, ING and the British Safety Council.

Clive has taught on MBA and DBA programmes worldwide, including Europe's leading programme at the University of Cambridge, Judge Business School, where he was James Tye/British Safety Council Senior Research Associate; he was also Isaac Newton Trust Teaching Fellow and Director of the Management Studies Tripos, Hughes Hall.

His professed expertise is in strategy, risk management, and higher education learning and teaching. He has supervised well over 100 MBA projects as well as 16 doctorates. He is a widely published author with over 100 peer reviewed papers and book chapters to his name, as well as four books. His co-authored article 'Process studies of change in organisation and management: unveiling temporality, activity, and flow' is one of the most widely cited articles in the *Academy of Management Journal*.

ACKNOWLEDGEMENTS

We are like dwarfs on the shoulders of giants, so that we can see more than they, and things at a greater distance, not by virtue of any sharpness of sight on our part, or any physical distinction, but because we are carried high and raised up by their giant size.

Bernard de Chartres

We jointly acknowledge the role of our friend, colleague and business partner, Professor James Kirkbride in bringing us together.

Lester's giants are a collection of influential groups who have provided powerful opportunities to learn from permitting me to "stand on their shoulders" ,their significance is immeasurable.

In particular, international consulting clients, multinational corporation leaders and SME owners have provided application insights to transformation enablement which remains, for many, a major stumbling block.

Teachers, mentors and bosses have guided and coached me how to think both analytically and critically. This, in turn ,has honed a leadership mindset for transformation strategy design to thereby impact and accelerate business outcomes.

Politicians and global statespersons have provided the opportunity to observe, to witness and to assess high level transformation in action and to then realise that without political sponsorship at organisational level, nothing moves!!

The literature has and continues to have a substantial impact upon my own research ,writing and understanding of the strategic change imperatives required to achieve effective leadership for transformation. In this respect I strive to design new conceptual frameworks, with executives at different managerial levels, for workplace application.

Students provide inspiration for creating innovative ways to communicate the message of transformational leadership; moreover, their understanding ,adoption and confident application will transform lives and livelihoods.

Networks, good friends and family are *the* giants without which transformation leadership ambitions will stall before they get started.

Indeed, these are *the* influential group who have anchored my own professional transformation internationally.

Collectively, these 'Giants 'allow transformational leadership competence and capacity to flourish

Clive's giants include some people that I've never met, some no longer with us, some still here, but all of whom inspire me, and I cite them in this book. I acknowledge the influence on my work of Dr Viktor Frankl, Dr Stephen Covey, Dr Gerd Gigerenzer, Prof. Martin Seligman, Prof. Mihály Csíkszentmihályi, Prof. Shelly Turkle, Thich Nat Hanh, Dr Alex Osterwalder, Prof. Yves Pigneur, Prof Kim Chan and Prof Renée Mauborgne.

We have been building the material for this book over quite some time. During that period, Clayton Christensen passed way. Prof. Christensen was a scholar of great prominence in innovation and strategy. His achievements are a model for all students of leadership.

Other giants who I've met or know well and who similarly inspire me include Prof. David Weir, Prof. Steve Letza, Prof. David Kolb, Prof. Dame Sandra Dawson, John Williamson, Dr Wilf Jarvis, Rhonda Hawkins, Peter Graham, Dr Suzy Green, Matt Church, Peter Cook, Lisa O'Neill, Chris Freeman, Oscar Trimboli, Dr Peter Ryan, Gary Greig, and Dr Greg White.

My family of giants include my mom June, sister Dr Jane Smallman, brothers-in-law Prof. William Allsop and Andreas Haropoulos, sister-in-law Thekli, my sons Christos and Nikos, and my wife of 31 years, Dr Mary Haropoulou.

Thank you all for allowing us to perch on your shoulders.

Singapore and Sydney, May 2021

1. TRANSFORMATIONAL LEADERSHIP

"The challenge of leadership is to be strong, but not rude; be kind, but not weak; be bold, but not bully; be thoughtful, but not lazy; be humble, but not timid; be proud, but not arrogant; have humour, but without folly."

Jim Rohn

1.1 TRANSFORMATIONAL LEADERSHIP DEFINED

Transformational leadership is a theory that explains how leaders work with teams to identify required change. Such leaders create an inspirational vision to guide that change and execute it working with committed team members.

Whilst transformational leaders have existed through history, Downton (1973) first recorded the concept. Burns (1978) refines the definition, viewing transformational leadership as when

"leaders and followers make each other advance to a higher level of morality and motivation".

Through strength of vision and personality, transformational leaders inspire followers to change expectations, perceptions, and motivations, working towards common objectives. Burns (1978) further describes transformational leaders as those who move followers up Maslow's (1987) hierarchy and beyond their interests.

1.2 A REVISED FULL RANGE LEADERSHIP MODEL

Transformational leadership is one of three leadership types in the full range leadership model (Avolio & Bass, 2002; Bass, 1990, 1999, 2000; Bass & Riggio, 2005). We revise this model to include two types created by Whicker (1996) and further refining the defining dimensions (Figure 1).

We'll return to transformational leadership shortly but first, let us consider the dimensions of leadership and other forms of leadership defined in the revised model.

1.2.1 PRODUCTIVITY

In its original form, the full range leadership model defines leadership in terms of engagement (from passive to active) and efficiency. In our revision, efficiency is replaced by productivity, combing efficiency and effectiveness. Productivity runs from destructive to high-performance. The original model also offers two sub-types of transactional leadership, the leftmost of which we have redefined as transitional leadership. We've also added toxic leadership to the model.

Figure 1: A revised full-range leadership model

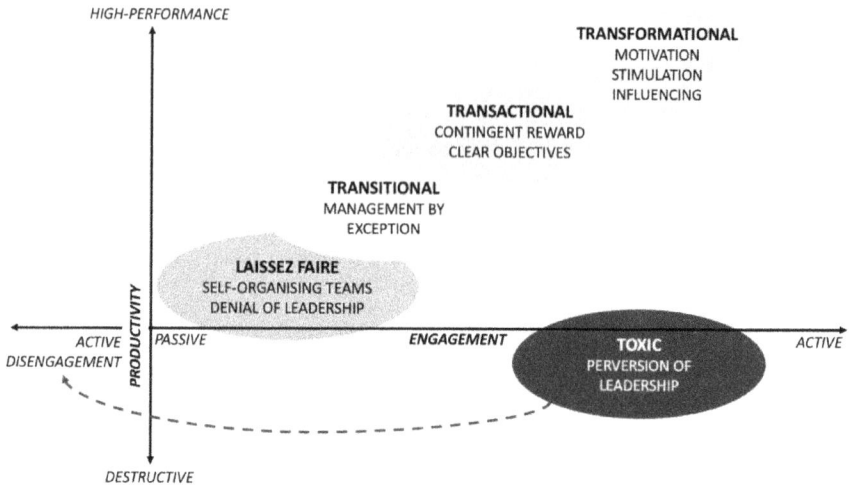

An inevitable consequence of toxic leadership, destructive or toxic productivity equates to decreased employee work effort of about 48%, a decrease in work quality of about 38%, and an association with about 73% of employee turnover (Laguda, 2020, p. 20). Drawing on a range of highly credible sources, Laguda (2020, pp. 20-21) notes an extensive list of individual physiological and psychological negative impacts of toxic leadership, supported by a range of other authorities (Bhandarker & Rai, 2019; Boddy & Taplin, 2017; Boddy, 2015a, 2015b; Boddy, 2017). Amongst these impacts, arguably most troubling is the number of suicides in the United States military and the nursing profession.

Organisationally, Laguda (2020, pp. 21-22) cites evidence that toxic leadership is negatively associated with group cohesion, job satisfaction, productivity, organisational trust, and organisational commitment. Reduced organisational performance, unit cohesion, team spirit, dysfunctional group behaviours, and reduced organisational health and survival similarly link to toxic leadership. Laguda (2020, pp. 21-22) further finds that toxic leadership is associated with high absenteeism rate, reduced personnel efficiency, negative cost-benefit relationship for organisations, and increased personnel transfer and groupthink. If left unchecked, Laguda (2020, p. 22) cites further evidence that toxic leadership impacts organisational growth and output, harming overall profitability.

At the other extreme, high-performance workplaces promote improved, sustainable organisational performance (Appelbaum et al., 2000; Appelbaum & Berg, 2000; Becker & Huselid, 1998; Boxall & Macky, 2007; Gospel & Wilman, 2003; Ramsay et al., 2000). There is no agreed definition of high-performance workplaces, but organisations that fit this model have common characteristics. First among these is the ability to recognise the need to adapt to the organisation's surroundings. High-performance organisations quickly and efficiently change their operating structure and practices to meet requirements. These organisations focus on long term success while delivering on actionable short-term goals. These workplaces are flexible, customer-focused, with staff able to work highly effectively in teams. As well adaptability to the environment, the culture and management of these organisations support flatter hierarchies, teamwork, diversity, which contribute to the success of this organisation type. Compared to others, high-performance organisations spend much more time continuously improving their core capabilities by investing in their workforce, leading to increased growth and performance. High-performance workplaces are sometimes labelled high commitment organisations (de Waal, 2007; Holbeche, 2005; Wood, 1999).

1.2.2 ENGAGEMENT

Employee engagement is workplace jargon widely used but not widely understood. Employee engagement is, in fact, a metric that calibrates the extent to which employees are fully involved in their work and that they are committed to 'on the job' performance for their employer. It is synonymous with terms like 'employee experience' and 'employee satisfaction'. An 'engaged employee' is fully absorbed by and enthusiastic about their work and takes positive action to further the organisation's reputation and interests. Engaged employees have a positive attitude towards the organisation and its values. In contrast, a passive or disengaged employee does the bare minimum at work ('coasting'). Worse, an actively disengaged employee will actively damage the company's output and reputation (Crabb, 2011; Hardy &

Phillips, 1998; Harter & Blacksmith, 2009; Harter et al., 2020; Kahn, 1990).

Consequently, organisations with high employee engagement usually outperform those with low employee engagement. In July 2020, the highly influential Gallup global survey of employee engagement recently found that[1]

> *'The percentage of 'engaged' workers in the USA (those who are highly involved in, enthusiastic about, and committed to their work and workplace) reached 38%. This is the highest it has been since Gallup began tracking the metric in 2000. However, their measurement from June 1-14 (following the killing of George Floyd in late May 2020 and subsequent protests and riots on top of a pandemic, unemployment, and attempts to re-open some businesses) finds that 31% of the working population are engaged. Taking into consideration three Gallup measures of employee engagement this year, the overall percentage of engaged workers during 2020 is 36%.*
>
> *The percentage of workers who are 'actively disengaged' (those who have miserable work experiences and spread their unhappiness to their colleagues) remained at approximately the same engagement level. It was 14% in June compared to 13% in early May. This drops the ratio of engaged to actively disengaged employees from 3.0-to-1 to 2.2-to-1 in the U.S., the lowest ratio since 2016.'*

We'll return to this critical construct later.

1.2.3   TOXIC LEADERSHIP

Toxic leadership has almost certainly existed for as long as homo sapiens. Exercising a perverted form of leadership, Toxic leaders are "maladjusted, malcontent and often malevolent, even malicious" (Whicker, 1996, p. 11). They engage in destructive, counterproductive behaviours and exhibit dysfunctional personality characteristics, both to the extent that they inflict lasting and severe harm to their followers, organisations, society, or the natural environment (Cohen, 2016; Kellerman, 2004; Lipman-Blumen, 2004).

A vibrant metaphor characterises toxic leadership as poisonous, destructive, virulent, metastasising cancer scarring both those in its path and others seemingly unconnected to the leader concerned. It

---

[1]   https://www.gallup.com/workplace/321965/employee-engagement-reverts-back-pre-covid-levels.aspx, accessed 10 May 2021

consumes individuals, groups, and left unchecked, organisations (Laguda, 2020, p. 20).

Toxic leaders' success comes through destroying others and their works. Their mission is to suppress followers, while simultaneously holding them in thrall. They seek to control, relishing conflict and protectionism (Davis 2016). In short, they induce disorderly entropy in individuals (Csíkszentmihályi, 2008, pp. 36-38) and organisations (Anheier & Moulton, 1999, pp. 274-279). They promote the vices of ignorance, fear, inhumanity, injustice, impulsiveness and subservience (Jarvis, 2004; Peterson & Seligman, 2004). They fail to provide coherent direction or structure, leading to disabling (if often sub-conscious) self-doubt in their followers. They undermine followers and opponents alike through offering opaque or perverse feedback on actions taken at their behest (whether they work or not), further 'de-structuring' rationality. Most have clinically undiagnosed but readily observable personality disorders (American Psychiatric Association, 2013). At best, they are self-absorbed narcissists, and at worst, they are murderous psychopaths (Boddy & Taplin, 2017; Boddy, 2015a, 2015b; Boddy, 2017; Fennimore & Sementelli, 2016; Michalak & Ashkanasy, 2018; Nai, 2018; Neo et al., 2016).

Toxic leadership ultimately creates decreased performance, productivity and output at best. Nevertheless, where such 'leaders' are allowed free rein, while they might superficially generate significant returns for investors, more often than not, they are purely self-interested "natural born opportunists" (Fennimore, 2017). All too frequently, any supernormal returns they generate are often short-lived (Laguda, 2020; Lipman-Blumen, 2004; Whicker, 1996). As Cameron (2012, p. 9) notes, organisations managed by toxic 'leaders' are prone to be unprofitable, ineffective, inefficient, error-prone, and unethical, built on internal and external relationships that are 'harmful'. When under external or internal stress, they struggle to adapt owing to rigid adherence to the toxic leader's vision of how things should be. Individuals within such organisations are commonly prone to a higher incidence of physiological and psychological illness. At worst, such organisations may impact society more generally (Kulik et al., 2020).

Toxic leaders typically are more malevolent than transitional leaders. They are self-obsessed and typically narcissists (American Psychiatric Association, 2013). Functional territorialism and emotional or psychological stressors targeting non-followers express these characteristics. Toxic leaders are always on the defensive, seeking actual or creating imaginary attacks. Their favourite leadership metaphor is commonly 'warfare', with co-workers, subordinates and superiors identified as 'the enemy'. While their ruthless pursuit of personal gain might incidentally drag an organisation with them, over time, they will stimulate decline, exacerbating and compounding dysfunction and disruption (Whicker, 1996, pp. 59-68).

Whicker (1996, pp. 59-68, 116-172) defines three toxic leader styles:

1. As in the case in broader life, *Bullies* are at odds with everyone and everything, pugnacious and fundamentally angry. Their jealousy of others, particularly those who 'beat' them is unbounded. Their routine mission is to diminish or invalidate others anywhere and anytime. Their malevolence is commonly grounded in bitterness over past personal failures; denigrating others is a proxy for admitting their shortcomings. They are overly emotional, frequently lashing out angrily and inappropriately with personalised abuse.

2. In their own eyes, *Streetfighters* are the 'king of the castle', and naturally, everyone else is a 'dirty rascal'. If that seems a childish metaphor, it is singularly appropriate for these charismatic egotists who look to manipulate and dominate through gang politics. Their leadership 'style' (a misnomer for something so innately unstylish) is about rewards and punishments for their gang based on their visceral interpretation of events; it is all about winning at any price. They listen to other gang members as suits them but will not hesitate to put down dissent and crush challengers. They are generous to the loyal and viciously merciless to those they view as disloyal.

3. *Enforcers* are often second-in-command and subservient to street fighters, bullies or absentee leaders, adopting or mirroring their leader's style. They are motivated by money and status but are risk-averse. They are adept at reaching consensus with their leaders while enforcing the same on followers. They typically do not rise to peak leadership positions but assure the success of those to whom they report.

1.2.4 LAISSEZ-FAIRE LEADERSHIP

First described by Lewin et al. (1939), laissez-faire leadership occurs where leaders wholly grant rights and power to make decisions to their followers. Laissez-faire leaders allow followers complete freedom to make decisions about their work. It affords followers self-rule while simultaneously offering guidance and support when requested. Laissez-faire leaders use guided freedom to provide followers with the materials necessary to accomplish their goals. They do not directly participate in decision making unless the followers request their assistance.

Laissez-faire leadership is an effective style when:

- Followers are highly skilled, experienced, and educated.
- Followers take pride in their work and are motivated to do it successfully on their own.
- Followers are experts with more knowledge than their leader.
- Followers are trustworthy and experienced.

These conditions would intuitively mean that the group is already likely to be effective.

This style is not advisable when the leader cannot or will not provide regular feedback to their followers.

Laissez-faire leadership is generally associated with lower productivity than transformational and transactional leadership styles. It has and with lower group member satisfaction than transformational leadership. It is also arguable that laissez-faire leadership be considered non-leadership, leadership avoidance or denial of leadership (Bono & Judge, 2010).

1.2.5 TRANSITIONAL LEADERSHIP

Whicker (1996, pp. 32-33, 59-68, 71-111) identifies transitional leaders with level three of Maslow's (1987) hierarchy: social needs. They lack the capacity or reserves to uplift followers that transactional leaders hold. Transitional leaders are concerned with 'belonging' above all else. They want to be an essential part of the organisation and a member of groups. They seek affection more than respect. Despite seeking organisational status, their personal goals do not align with organisational goals. Instead, their objectives enjoy precedence over those of the organisation. Hence, through grandstanding, controlling the transmission of information, hedonism and poor decision-making, they often lead organisations towards a downward spiral of dysfunction and decline, at best existing in a state of persistent failure (Anheier & Romo 1999).

Whicker (1996, pp. 59-68, 71-111) defines three types of transitional leaders:

1. Controllers are rigid perfectionists often bound by tradition. They are micromanagers, reflecting their need to control and lack charisma. Their primary control tool is the restriction of information, effected through elaborate and selective deployment rules. They desire obedience and attention.

2. Busybodies crave affection and attention. They are energetic, relentlessly dynamic and fear alienation of themselves and others. They have to be the centre of attention and communication through manipulating opinion and rumourmongering. They rarely resolve conflict among their followers (more accurately subordinates in the busybody leader's eyes), ensuring that complaints flow and attention is further assured.

3. Absentee leaders are remote and disengaged, distancing themselves from decision-making. Their focus is on symbolism over substance. Like busybodies, their desire is for affection and approval, and they seek the consensus of followers around these. They are rarely malicious and more mindless, but their disengagement leaves power vacuums that ambitious and often toxic followers seek to fill. Turmoil, chaos, or malaise are symptomatic of absentee leadership.

1.2.6   TRANSACTIONAL LEADERSHIP

Transactional leadership, like transitional leadership, focuses on supervision, organisation, and performance. Transactional leadership is a style of leadership in which leaders promote compliance by followers through both rewards and punishments. Through a rewards and punishments system, transactional leaders can keep followers motivated for the short term. Unlike transformational leaders, those using the transactional approach are not necessarily looking to change the future. Transactional leadership "occurs when one person takes the initiative in making contact with others for the purpose of an exchange of valued things" (Burns, 1978).

1.2.7 TRANSFORMATIONAL LEADERSHIP

Unlike the transactional approach, transformational leadership is not based on a mutually beneficial relationship. Instead, it is based on the leader's personality, traits and ability to make changes through example, articulation of an energising vision and challenging goals. Transforming leaders are idealised in the sense that they are a moral exemplar of working towards the benefit of the team or organisation. Burns (1978) theorised that transforming and transactional leadership were mutually exclusive styles. Bass (1985) expands upon Burns' (1978) original ideas. According to Bass (1985), transformational leadership is defined based on its impact on followers. Transformational leaders, Bass (1985) suggests garner trust, respect, and admiration from their followers.

Bass (1985) extended Burns (1978) by explaining the psychological mechanisms underlying transforming and transactional leadership. Bass (1985) introduced the term "transformational" in place of "transforming". Bass (1985) added to Burns (1978), explaining to measure how transformational leadership and its impacts on follower motivation and performance. The extent to which a leader is transformational is measured first in terms of his influence on the followers. Followers of transformational leaders feel trust, admiration, loyalty and respect for the leader and because of the qualities of the transformational leader are willing to work harder than expected. These outcomes occur because the transformational leader offers followers something more than just working for self-gain; they provide followers with an inspiring mission, vision and identity (Bass, 1985). The leader transforms and motivates followers through their idealised influence (charisma), intellectual stimulation and individual consideration. In addition, transformational leaders encourage followers to initiate new and unique ways to challenge the status quo and alter the environment to support success. Finally, in contrast to Burns (1978), Bass (1985) suggests that leadership can simultaneously display transformational and transactional leadership.

Whicker (1996) defines trustworthy leaders, aligning them to Burns (1978) transformational leaders, which in turn, he defines in terms of Maslow's (1987) hierarchy of needs. Burns (1978), and by adoption Whicker (1996, pp. 32-33), identifies transformational and trustworthy leaders respectively with levels four and five of Maslow's (1987) hierarchy: esteem and self-actualisation needs.

Whicker (1996, pp. 26-31) characterises transformational leaders as having:

1. Knowledge of themselves.
2. Knowledge of the external world.
3. Self-motivation and drive.
4. The ability to motivate others.
5. Integrity.
6. An ability to formulate persuasive, uplifting and unifying messages for followers.
7. Cultivation of talent.
8. Vision.

Whicker (1996, p. 32) contends that transformational leaders have considerable self-respect in operating 'at' level four. Accordingly, they can command the respect of others and work to expand that respect. Their healthy self-image further means that they neither need to put others down nor hold them back to advance their self-image. Trustworthy leaders do not play destructive games or deploy malevolent tactics. As such, they enjoy enhanced esteem from those with whom they work.

Better yet are those leaders who are motivated by self-actualisation (Whicker, 1996, pp. 32-33); driven by learning and as a part of their leadership skills, they actively seek to develop others' talents. They are not above making tough, difficult decisions that command the respect of their followers. Although they are empathic, level five leaders are seldom profoundly concerned about what others think of their behaviours. Leaders such as this contribute at least as much to their organisation and society as they take. They are maximisers operating from an ethic of giving from their talents.

Whicker (1996, pp. 37-48) distinguishes between three types of transformational leaders:

1. Commanders use meetings to communicate information downward to followers, focus on task achievement and distribute rewards based on productivity.
2. Team leaders use meetings to exchange information with followers, emphasise mentoring, developing followers' skills, and distributing rewards based on impartial, external standards.
3. Consensus builders use meetings to gather information, build consensus, emphasise diverse opinions through consultation, and distribute rewards to minimise conflict and differences.

1.2.8 THE EVOLUTION OF TRANSFORMATIONAL LEADERSHIP: POSITIVE LEADERSHIP

The transformational leadership paradigm is well established. However, events across 2016 -2021 and on-demand further evolution. Our take on furthering transformational leadership lies in our interpretation of the positive leadership paradigm (Cameron, 2005, 2012; Pascale et al., 2010), grounded in positive psychology (Diener & Seligman, 2004; Peterson & Seligman, 2004; Seligman, 2012; Seligman et al., 2005) and positive deviance (Cameron et al., 2017; Pascale et al., 2010).

Like so many leadership challenges, it is about negotiating order in complicated socio-technical systems (Baiada-Hireche et al., 2011; Fine, 1984; Maines, 1982; Mnookin, 2004; Schulman, 1993; Strauss, 1978). Establishing order relies on creative problem-solving (Brown, 2009), excellent communication (Carey, 2009; Craig & Muller, 2007), and evidenced-based decision-making (Klein, 1998).

1.2.8.1 Negotiating Order

Positive leadership is the ability to negotiate order by setting the direction and the 'tone' in business and political conversations between people as they interact socially, negotiating an orderly and ideally civil workplace or society (Fine, 1984; Maines, 1982; Strauss, 1978). Conversations resolve multiple and complicated options and tensions in workplace operations and political dialectics. They are how positive leaders manage power asymmetries, differing interests and complex issues. The central factors to assuring effectiveness in all of this are effective communication (chiefly deep listening (Trimboli, 2017)), healthy working or political relationships, based on positive culture (Cameron, 2012), and the establishment of conversations grounded in principles rather than ideological positions or dogma (Fisher & Brown, 1988; Fisher et al., 2011; Scott, 2004; Zeldin, 1998). Ideological and dogmatic positionings are significant barriers to effective negotiations, conversations, civility, and workplace and societal order (Mnookin, 2010).

Negotiations construct social order in workplaces and society. (Mnookin, 2004, 2010) identifies three critical "tensions" (challenges) to resolve in these negotiations. The first is to resolve the tension between opportunities to create value ('expanding the pie' through growth or creating solutions to the negotiation challenge) and the necessity of distributing value (dividing the pie). At the heart of this negotiating challenge is what and how much information can be disclosed to another party? Limiting disclosure limits the opportunities to create value, and overly generous disclosure leads to the risk of exploitation. Here, the tipping point is how to serve underlying interests best; that is, how can the differing principles of the negotiating parties be aligned?

Mnookin's next challenge is the resolution of the tension between empathy and assertiveness. How to effectively express to the other side one's interests, needs and perspectives?

The third challenge is the tension between principals and agents, a tension that stretches far back in time in the form of capital versus labour. Agents negotiate on behalf of individuals and groups; the most typical example is trade unions. Principals are either the manager or owner of some entity to which the individuals or groups represented by the agents contribute something. This standard tension arises because the principals' positional interests and the agents' positional interests do not align.

Mnookin majors on the second challenge because it is foundational to resolving the other two. As he put it in a workshop a few years back: "you have to teach people to negotiate".

1.2.8.2 Creativity

For some artists and others, creativity is a solitary affair. However, in organisations, it is a 'contact sport' (Brown, 2009; Ogilvie & Liedtka, 2011). The process of creating a solution to a challenge or refining an existing solution to a problem that affects an organisation or community requires contact with communities that consume or build the solution. It requires:

1.   Collecting information on what people need by asking good questions,
2.   Developing breakthrough ideas by pushing past incremental or obvious solutions,
3.   Building prototypes to learn how to improve ideas, and
4.   Communicating the story to encourage others to act.

1.2.8.3 Communication

Communication in the second machine age is complex yet vital to effective leadership (Barrett, 2006). Its purpose is to successfully share information through interwoven digital, visual, verbal, and non-verbal channels.

Digital communication refers to communication through social media, texting, messaging and email. Digital technologies have transformed communication (Willis, 2017), creating a sense of urgency and a need to share. Conventional communication is information transmission and feedback. Telephony aside, it was the case that written communication took a little while to compose and send. Social media now balances the opportunity for instant gratification in sending messages while allowing recipients the opportunity to respond. However, enabling and encouraging rapid and accidental transmission has opened a huge window for error. The physical process of writing letters and transmitting them via post, telex or fax, would usually cause pause for thought. The immediacy of digital transmission confers no such discipline. In short, what happens in Facebook, LinkedIn and email are on the Internet for life.

1.2.8.4 Decision-making

There are many models of decision-making, mostly presenting it as a rational process. Frequently, it is irrational. Even decisions based on the most complete information possible rely on someone, somewhere to make a subjective judgment based on expertise or experience, or both.

The naturalistic decision-making paradigm deconstructs decision-making through detailed analyses of discourse, narrative and social action by decision-makers with a strong focus on context (Gore et al., 2006). It has been used extensively in the study of real-world decision-makers, particularly in high-risk work environments (Elliott, 2005; Gore et al., 2006; Gore et al., 2015; Klein, 1998; Lipshitz et al., 2006; Lipshitz et al., 2001; McDaniel, 1993; Shattuck & Miller, 2006; Zsambok & Klein, 1997). It describes what people do under the pressure of time, ambiguous or absent information, ill-defined goals, and an evolving context (Klein, 1997). Further, it describes how people can use their experience (in the form of heuristics) to arrive at sound decisions without the need to compare potential positive and negative outcomes of a course of action. Finally, its tacit acceptance of the discursive mind's role (Edwards & Potter, 1992; Harré & Gillett, 1994; Moore, 2002) in decision-making represents a marked departure from earlier decision-making paradigms (Smallman & Moore, 2010).

In this paradigm, decision-making is not about rational choice. We all develop heuristics through which we make decisions. These heuristics are the product of lived or simulated experiences, including learning and training; indeed, the word's etymology is the Greek εβρικα ("I have found"). We use heuristics to make decisions based on interpreting patterns that we perceive in cues (signals. Or evidence) that we perceive in the context in which we work and live. The human senses (taste, sight, touch, smell and sound) yield the cues we use.

1.2.8.5   Positive Leadership Defined

Like their toxic counterparts, 'positive leaders' have almost certainly existed for as long as homo sapiens. Positive leaders are well-adjusted, contented, benevolent and supportive. They engage in constructive, productive behaviours and exhibit highly functional personality characteristics, both to the extent that they bring lasting and enduring benefit to their followers, organisations, society, or the natural environment.

Positive leaders essentially operate with a growth mindset (Dweck, 2017). They encourage employee engagement, productivity, innovation and self-expression. Their position on Maslow's (1987) hierarchy means they have a transcendent sense of self in which they embrace deep listening (Trimboli, 2017) in pursuit of change.

Positive leaders' success comes through promoting others and their works. Their mission is to uplift followers, vicariously but humbly sharing their accomplishments. They seek to mentor, relishing consensus and openness. In short, they induce flow in individuals (Csíkszentmihályi, 2008, pp. 39-41) and organisations (Marer et al., 2016). They delight in promoting and encouraging the virtues of wisdom, courage, humanity, justice, temperance and transcendence (Jarvis, 2004; Peterson & Seligman, 2004). They provide coherent direction and structure, developing their followers' self-efficacy, promoting the ideal conditions for experiential learning (Bandura, 1977, 1982, 1986, 2005; Kolb, 2015). They support followers and question opponents by offering clear feedback on actions taken at their behest, promoting structured rationality.

Based on one of only two scientifically valid personality tests, a recent university study of 1.5 million people revealed a commonly occurring 'role model' personality type, identified with good leaders who are dependable (a synonym of trustworthy) and open to new ideas. Role models tend to be stable, honest, humble, agreeable and conscientious extraverts (Ashton, 2017; Gerlach et al., 2018).

In corporations, positive leadership ultimately creates improved performance, productivity and output. Positive leaders are strongly associated with strong economic performance, operational excellence and extraordinary efficiency, high quality, ethical behaviour, strong and enduring positive relationships. Organisations so led flourish, and individuals within such organisations commonly enjoy vitality and flow. Such organisations positively impact society more generally (Cameron et al., 2017; Cameron, 2005, 2012; Hsieh, 2014).

1.3 THIS BOOK

This book is designed as a companion to the *Certified Transformational Leader* (CTL) course, originally developed by Lester Massingham, accredited by the Chartered Management Institute and delivered through CMC Consultants and Masters Pro Management. CTL was further developed by Clive Smallman for online delivery through Clive's business in Australia and also through the International Institute for MBA Studies.

The book targets leaders and aspiring leaders who wish to:

- Improve their transformational leadership skills.
- Expand the number of potential job opportunities for which they qualify.
- Differentiate themself as a job candidate.
- Re-energise and accelerate their career.
- Establish or change their own business.

Throughout and after the course we see in our participants:

- Increased readiness for transformational challenges.
- Immediate impact in their workplace or business.
- Heightened confidence and sense of achievement.
- Increased recognition among peers, mentors, managers and leaders.
- Improved communication.
- Expanded (growth) mindset.

Hence the structure and most of the content of the book reflects the structure and content of the six modules that comprise the CTL:

1. *Strategic Thinking for Transformation* – chapters 2, 3 and 4.
2. *Leading Strategy Design* – chapters 5, 6 and 7.
3. *Leading Strategic Change* – chapters 8, 9 and 10.
4. *Enabling Organisational Transformation* – chapters 11, 12 and 13.
5. *Business Model Transformation* – chapter 14.
6. *Strategic Planning* – chapters 15 and 16.

Chapter 2, *Strategic Thinking*, considers what strategic thinking is, its importance, why it is considered by some to be a rare competence, how it might be encouraged, why it is needed, why it is valued, and whether or not leaders can do without it.

The key concepts we explore are systems thinking, intention, time, objective versus subjective and opportunism,

On completing chapter 2, you should be able to:

1. Define strategic thinking.
2. Understand the difference between strategic thinking and strategic planning.
3. Identify the major attributes of strategic thinking in practice

Chapter 3, *Critical Thinking*, considers what is critical thinking, and the traits of critical thinkers.

The key concepts we explore are premonition, foresight, perception and common fallacies.

On completing this chapter, you should be able to:

1. Define critical thinking,
2. Outline the critical thinking process, and
3. Identify the major attributes of critical thinking in practice

Chapter 4 introduces the core principle of *Soft Systems Methodology* (SSM).

The key concepts we explore are systems thinking, action learning, root definitions and modelling.

On completing this chapter, you should be able to:

1. Explain key concepts in SSM,
2. Identify the main stages of SSM, and
3. Describe the principles and purpose of building rich pictures (root definitions).

Chapter 5, *Principles of Strategy*, considers what is strategy, its importance, why it is misunderstood, why it often is not communicated effectively, why we need it as leaders and its necessity in organisational transformation.

The key concepts we explore are problem awareness, problem exploration, decision-making, execution and monitoring impact.

On completing this chapter, you should be able to:

1. Define what strategy is.
2. Explain the meaning of 'death in the drawer' for strategy.
3. Debate the role of strategy in organisational transformation.

Chapter 6, *Designing Strategy*, explores how strategy is determined, evaluated and chosen.

The key concepts we explore are environmental analysis, internal appraisal, generic strategies, strategic evaluation and strategic choice.

On completing this chapter, you should be able to:

1. Determine a strategy for an organisation.
2. Evaluate strategic options.
3. Make strategy proposal.

Chapter 7, Growth and Strategy Frameworks, aims to develop your understanding of growth and explores four competitive strategy frameworks.

The key concepts we explore are growth and conventional competitive strategies.

On completing this chapter, you should be able to:

1. Create growth strategies.
2. Create business strategies aligned to your organisation.

Chapter 8, *Classic Change Models*, considers why strategic change leadership a priority for many organisations, why transformational change is considered to be difficult, and why there is not a template for universal adoption. It also looks at what sources of guidance are available and how theory can help.

The key concepts we cover are gap analysis, change models and theory, action research and execution.

On completing this chapter, you should be able to:

1. Evaluate your personal and organisational performance.
2. Identify performance gaps and plan for how to close them.
3. Execute action research projects.
4. Adapt theoretical perspectives on change to lead change projects.

Chapter 9, *Strategic Interventions*, explores strategic change interventions at the individual, group and organisational levels.

The key concepts we consider are strategic interventions and management styles.

On completing this chapter, you should be able to:

1. Implement appropriate strategic change interventions.
2. Adopt a management style that aligns to the interventions you are implementing.

Chapter 10, *Leading Change*, aims to develop readers' understanding of leading the process of change and leading stakeholder change.

The key concepts we cover are change processes, stakeholder change and forcefield analysis.

On completing this chapter, you should be able to:

1. Plan change.
2. Create a forcefield analysis.
3. Analyse stakeholder systems.
4. Execute a change management strategy involving stakeholders.
5. Identify points of resistance to change.
6. Develop strategies to facilitate stakeholder support.

Chapter 11, *Strategy and Performance*, explores the strategy to performance gap and performance management.

The key concepts we cover are gap analysis, organisational underachievement, performance management and performance assessment.

On completing this chapter, you should be able to:

1. Evaluate gaps between planned strategic and actual performance.
2. Identify factors underlying organisational achievement.
3. Assess and manage organisational performance.

Chapter 12, *Engagement and Culture*, explores employee engagement and culture change.

The key concepts we explore are employee engagement and culture change.

On completing this chapter, you should be able to:

1. Define employee engagement.
2. Explain the major influences on employee engagement.
3. Identify what constitutes a well-engaged employee.

4. Define organisational culture.
5. Explain the formation of organisational culture.
6. Explain the role of culture in organisational life.

Chapter 13, *Structure, Process and Relationships*, chapter aims to develop readers' understanding of organisational structure, processes, business process reengineering and relationship management

The key concepts we cover are organisational structure, processes, business process reengineering (BPR) and relationship management.

On completing this chapter, you should be able to:

1. Demonstrate you understand the concept of organisational structure and its appropriate implementation.
2. Explain what processes are and the contribution they make in organisations.
3. Outline the principles of business process reengineering
4. Demonstrate and understanding of the principles of relationship management.

Chapter 14 introduces *Business Models* and our '5D' approach to their development.

The key concepts we cover are business models, the 5D approach and defining business models.

On completing this chapter, you should be able to:

1. Explain what a business model is.
2. Describe the 5D approach in outline.
3. Define a business model.

Chapter 15, *A Strategy Framework*, considers what is strategic planning, who strategic leaders are, values, culture, power, vision, mission and objectives.

The key concepts we cover are strategic planning, strategic leaders, values, culture, power, vision, mission and objectives.

On completing this chapter, you will be able to:

1. Summarise the strategic planning process.
2. Explain the principles of strategic leadership.
3. Articulate the role of values culture and power in strategy.
4. Evaluate an organisation's vision, mission and objectives.

Chapter 16 aims to develop readers' understanding of *Choosing and Implementing Strategy*.

The key concepts we cover are strategic direction, strategic choice, blue ocean strategy, implementing strategy and the strategic plan.

On completing this chapter, you should be able to:

1. Identify potential strategic directions based on analysis.
2. Choose appropriate directions.
3. Develop a blue ocean strategy based on reviewing the business model.
4. Explain the principles of implementing strategies.
5. Draft a strategic plan.

Chapter 17 offers our concluding thoughts.

On completing this book, you will be better able to:

1. Analyse your business.
2. Analyse your market.
3. Evaluate constraints on and opportunities for value innovation in your business.
4. Plan required change.
5. Create stakeholder value.
6. Lead required change.

We anticipate you will find stimulation and challenge in equal measures.

STRATEGIC THINKING

"Strategic planning is not strategic thinking. Indeed, strategic planning often spoils strategic thinking, causing managers to confuse real vision with the manipulation of numbers."

Henry Mintzberg

2. STRATEGIC THINKING

"Strategic Thinking = Systems Thinking + Creativity + Vision."

Pearl Zhu

2.1 CHAPTER OUTLINE

In this chapter we consider what strategic thinking is, its importance, why it is considered by some to be a rare competence, how it might be encouraged, why it is needed, why it is valued, and whether or not leaders can do without it.

The key concepts we explore are systems thinking, intention, time, objective versus subjective and opportunism,
On completing this chapter, you should be able to:

1. Define strategic thinking.
2. Understand the difference between strategic thinking and strategic planning.
3. Identify the major attributes of strategic thinking in practice.

2.2 STRATEGIC THINKING DEFINED

Strategic thinking is a mental or cognitive process, producing insights on a continual basis that are applied by an individual in the context of achieving an objective or set of objectives yielding competitive advantage or value innovation in any endeavour (Horwath, 2014; Kim & Mauborgne, 2005b; Porter, 1980, 1985).

In strategic management processes (Luffman et al., 1991), especially transformational strategic processes, strategic thinking involves the creation and implementation of value innovations intended to differentiate the organisation or reduce its cost base (Kim & Mauborgne, 1997, 1999, 2005b). Value innovation creates a marked improvement in value for both customers and the organisation itself.

Strategic thinking can be done individually, as well as collaboratively among key stakeholders who have the power to alter an organisation's strategic direction and future. Group strategic thinking may create more value innovation through enabling active and creative strategic conversations. In these conversation individual group members share their perceptions on critical and complex issues in a process of knowledge creation; a significant benefit in highly competitive and fast-changing business landscapes.

2.3 A COMMERCIAL PERSPECTIVE ON STRATEGIC THINKING

Rich Horwath is an author, professor, strategist and speaker who helps managers think strategically to create competitive advantage. He is the president of the Strategic Thinking Institute, a former Chief Strategy Officer and author of four books, on strategy and strategic thinking, including *Deep Dive: The Proven Method for Building Strategy, Focusing Your Resources, and Taking Smart* (Horwath, 2009) and *Elevate: the Three Disciplines of Advanced Strategic Thinking* (Horwath, 2014).

Horwath (2009) identifies three basic disciplines of strategic thinking.

Acumen generates key business insights. One paradox of strategy is that in order to elevate your thinking to see the 'big picture' you need first to dive below the surface of the opportunities and challenges in your organisational context to discover insight. A strategic insight is a new idea that combines two or more pieces of information that has the potential to positively affect the overall success of the business and lead to competitive advantage.

Allocation focuses resources through trade-offs. It is one thing to have a neat strategic plan. The actual or realised strategy of an organisation is another matter entirely: the result of the resource allocation decisions made by managers each day. It is critical to have a deep understanding of resource allocation and how to maximise its potential for your organisation. What trade-offs will you make to focus resources?

Action executes strategy to achieve objectives. It is commonly assumed that once a sound strategy has been formulated, its execution will take care of itself. Research seems to indicate otherwise (Sterling, 2003). The effective action or execution of strategy involves the discipline to focus on the important issues, not the urgent ones.

Building from this base, Horwath (2014) defines a further three disciplines of *advanced* strategic thinking.

When strategic thinkers *coalesce*, they take acumen to the next level. They combine pieces of information to create a new idea that enables them to challenge or possibly change a building block of their current business model (Osterwalder & Pigneur, 2010). Known as value innovation (Kim & Mauborgne, 1997, 1999, 2005b), we will return to this discipline throughout the book.

Creating a strategy system enabled by strategic thinking enables businesses to *compete* and achieve competitive advantage. Most managers think functionally, within their discipline. They do not see beyond their 'silo' (Hodes, 2017; Jacques, 2006). A systems perspective enables leaders to rise above their silo walls, addressing opportunities and challenges across the whole business. Solving functional issues will not necessarily yield a competitive advantage. Addressing whole of business issues from a strategic view, changing the business model will.

Leading others to think and act strategically to execute strategy is the discipline of a *champion*. Functional managers are transactional (Burns, 1978). They work in their business. Leaders working at the whole of business level are transformational (Burns, 1978). They champion business model change drawing followers with them.

2.4 STRATEGIC THINKING FOR TRANSFORMATION

Strategic thinking for transformation involves knowing how to critically assess organisational problem situations arising from environmental challenges and then to design a road map for leading contextually relevant strategic transformations.

Leadership thinking for strategic transformation should:

1. Create prescriptions that define organisational transformation requirements.
2. Demonstrate how change can be achieved through conceptual modelling and strategy road maps.
3. Translate complex problem situations into clearly defined and manageable problem specifications.
4. Apply a systematic methodology that can assist leadership in the future and enable better problem analysis even in social situations that are beyond organisational boundaries.

There is neither a generally accepted definition of strategic thinking nor common agreement on its importance. There are various lists of the key attributes of strategic thinkers. There is also no consensus on whether strategic thinking is an uncommon gift held by a few or a common observable strategic commodity, widely seen in boardrooms and C-suites worldwide. Many writers content that conventional models of strategic planning do not produce high-quality strategy.

2.5 THE DESIGN SHIFT

Strategy has recently moved away from the basic 'strategic planning' to more of 'strategic thinking', notably incorporating design thinking as it moves to focus on value creation more than market share. However, conventional techniques of strategic planning (PEST analysis, value chain analysis, industry competitive analysis and so on) still very much have a role to play in present day strategy design. The introduction of design thinking into strategy has redefined that the real heart of strategy as the 'strategist'. Better strategy execution requires strategic thinkers who discover novel and imaginative strategies that shift strategic focus from market share to value add. Moreover, they set in motion active processes that shape new markets out of value innovation.

2.6 STRATEGIC THINKING AND STRATEGIC PLANNING

2.6.1 'AND' NOT 'OR'

Much of the writing on strategy from the 1990s suggests a false dichotomy wherein strategic thinking and strategic planning are somehow opposite points on a continuum. When we look at the evolution of what strategic academics call 'strategy as practice', we see that strategic thinking and strategic planning complement each other. They may be distinct thought processes, but they are interrelated (Graetz, 2002). Effective strategic management needs strategic thought that is built on the analytical strength conferred by strategic planning.

Strategic thinking should be fundamentally creative in search of value innovation. This creative drive should lead to the creation of new value propositions and markets and the means of delivery at optimised cost. Strategic planning's role is to support that creative effort, ensuring that creative strategic decision-making is based as far as possible on data. At the same time, we need to acknowledge that strategic thought is subjective, because it is based on how we process reasonably objective data through our individually unique mental models of the world.

Mintzberg (1994) writes that strategic thinking is more synthesis (i.e., "connecting the dots") than analysis (i.e., "finding the dots"). He finds that it is about "capturing what the manager learns from all sources (both the soft insights from his or her personal experiences and the experiences of others throughout the organisation and the hard data from market research and the like) and then synthesising that learning into a vision of the direction that the business should pursue."

Mintzberg (1994) further argues that strategic thinking cannot be systematised and is the critical part of strategy formation, as opposed to strategic planning exercises. His view is that strategic planning happens around the strategy formation or strategic thinking activity, providing inputs for strategists to consider and developing plans to attempt control of the implementation of strategy after it is formed. Mintzberg's argument is similar to ones that say you it is teach creativity; he's wrong.

2.7 THE DIFFERENCE BETWEEN STRATEGIC PLANNING AND STRATEGIC THINKING

Simply doing your work does not automatically position you for success. In the past, strategy was considered the domain of strategic planners. Nowadays every person in your organisation, including you your colleagues is expected to think strategically.

Let us explore how strategic thinking differs from strategic planning.

Strategic planning is the process through which leaders set your organisation's forward direction. During strategic planning leaders decide on a course of actions targeting success that guides how people set priorities, allocate resources and plan how to achieve key objectives. It is your organisation's action plan.

As we have seen above, *strategic thinking* is how you and your colleagues, help implement the plan, creating the means to pursue success.

Strategic thinking requires you to put the smallest decisions in the context of the organisation's broader long-term objectives. To think strategically, you will need to keep alert to your organisation's operating environment, including your customers and your competitors, and to frame your decisions based on thinking for the future, rather than simply reacting to the present.

So, how do you start to think more strategically? You start by pushing past your assumptions about the way things work. Keep your eyes open for opportunities to better serve your customers. Use these insights to guide the way you make choices in support of your organisation's overarching objectives. Your decisions make a difference. When you think strategically, you are aligning yourself and your organisation with strategic success.

2.8   ATTRIBUTES OF STRATEGIC THINKERS

Liedtka (1998) reckons that there are five major attributes of strategic thinking in practice.

Having a *systems perspective* (Checkland, 1999; Checkland & Scholes, 1999; Hodes, 2017) refers to being able to understand the implications of strategic actions, wherein strategic thinkers have cognitive representations of their organisations business model, their role in that system, and an understanding of the building blocks it contains.

Being *intent focused*, which means they are probably more determined and less distractible than rivals in the marketplace. This couples two interesting phenomena: implementation intention (Gollwitzer, 1999; Gollwitzer & Brandstaetter, 1997) and a bias for action (Bruch & Ghosal, 2004). Implementation intention is about setting concrete, procedural behaviours to goals. A bias for action means that taking action is your default state.

Thinking in time means being able to hold past, present and future in mind at the same time to create better decision making and speed implementation. Strategy is about closing the gap between today's reality and future intent.

Being *hypothesis driven*, ensures that both creative and critical thinking are built into strategy development and implementation. This broadly builds scientific method into strategic thinking.

Intelligent opportunism is about responding to good opportunities. Using a rigorously designed strategy to guide organisational efforts effectively and efficiently must always be balanced against the risks of missing out on alternative strategies better suited to a changing environment.

2.9   THE SURPRISING HABITS OF ORIGINAL THINKERS

In a much-viewed TEDx talk[2], organisational psychologist Adam Grant relates the story of a student approaching him to invest in the student's company. Working with three friends, the student aimed to disrupt an industry by selling some items online.

Grants asked: "you guys spent the whole summer on this right?" The answer was "No, we all took internships, just in case it does not

---

[2]   https://www.ted.com/talks/adam_grant_the_surprising_habits_of_original_thinkers accessed 17 March 2021

work out." Grant: "All right, but you're gonna go in full time, once you graduate?" Student: "Not exactly we've all lined up backup jobs."

Grant recalls that six months later, the day before the company launched, there was still no functioning website. This is a company focused on Internet sales. Grant declined to invest.

The company is Warby Parker. They sell glasses online. They were recently recognised as the world's most innovative company. In September 2020 they were valued at US$3 billion.

A partial result of his short-sighted decision, Grant (2017) studies people that he calls 'originals'. Originals are non-conformists, people who not only have new ideas, but take action to champion them. They are people who stand out and speak up. Originals drive creativity and change in the world. They are the people you want to bet on.

Grant (2017) identifies three things about recognising originals, enabling other to become a little more like them.

First, Warby Parker was *really* slow getting off the ground. Superficially, it seems they were procrastinating. However, what Grant's research reveals is that it is not that simple. He cites the great screenwriter and producer Adam Sorkin: "You call it procrastinating, I call it thinking." What Grant (2017, pp. 92-113) observes with a lot of great originals, is that they are quick to start, but slow to finish.

This is what Grant believes he missed with Warby Parker. When they were dragging their heels for six months, he judged that a lot of other companies were starting to sell glasses online, and that Warby Parker's 'first mover' advantage was gone. However, Grant then acknowledges that he realised they were spending all that time trying to figure out how to get people to be comfortable ordering glasses online. And it turns out the first mover advantage is mostly a myth.

Golder and Tellis (1993) studied over 50 product categories, comparing the first movers who created the market with the improvers who introduced something different or better. The first movers had a failure rate of 47%, compared with only 8% for the improvers. For example, Facebook, waited build a social network after MySpace and Friendster. Google launched years after Alta Vista and Yahoo. It is easier to improve on someone else's idea than it is to create something new from scratch. The lesson learned is that to be original, you do not have to be first, just have to be different and better (Grant, 2017, pp. 92-113).

In passing on Warby Parker, Grant notes that they were also full of doubts. They had backup plans lined up, and that made Grant doubt that they had the courage to be originals, because Grant expected that originals would look confident and be confident. What (Grant, 2017, pp. 210-243) finds is that behind the scenes originals feel the same fear and doubt that the rest of us do. They just manage it differently.

When feel doubt, they do not let it go. Originals feel fear too. They are afraid of failing, but what sets them apart from the rest of us is that they are even more afraid of failing to try. They know you can fail by starting a business that goes bankrupt, or by failing to start a business at all. They know that in the long run our biggest regrets are not our actions or inactions, the things we wish we could redo if you look at the science or the chances, not taken.

Grant's third point is that like everyone else, originals have bad ideas, lots and lots of bad ideas (Grant, 2017, pp. 29-61). The difference is the volume. The greatest originals are the ones who failed the most, because they are the ones who try the most. The more output you turn out, the more variety you get, and the better your chances of stumbling on something truly original. For example, when they were trying to name their company the Warby Parker founders sought something sophisticated and unique with no negative associations. They tested over 2000 possibilities before they finally put together Warby and Parker.

Grant (2017) puts this all together (and more) and finds that originals are not that different from the rest of humankind. They feel fear and doubt, they procrastinate and have bad ideas. Sometimes they succeed because of these qualities not in spite of them. Know that:

- Being quick to start but slow to finish can boost your creativity,
- You can motivate yourself by doubting your ideas and embracing the fear of failing to try, and
- That you need a lot of bad ideas in order to get a few good ones.

2.10 QUESTIONS

1. Identify three 'takeaways' from Horwath's thinking. Write down your impressions of how these can help you develop your strategy skills?

2. What do you think are the major differences between strategic thinking and strategic planning?

3. CRITICAL THINKING

"You have a brain and mind of your own. Use it and reach your own decisions."

Napoleon Hill

3.1 CHAPTER OUTLINE

This chapter considers what is critical thinking, and the traits of critical thinkers.

The key concepts we explore are premonition, foresight, perception and common fallacies.

On completing this chapter, you should be able to:

1. Define critical thinking,
2. Outline the critical thinking process, and
3. Identify the major attributes of critical thinking in practice.

3.2 CRITICAL THINKING DEFINED

3.2.1 A MODEL OF CRITICAL THINKING

Critical thinking is the capacity to think plainly and reasonably through a systematic process to detect common fallacies, better enabling us to develop premonitions or foresight of what our actions or the actions of others might bring about. One way to adopt critical thinking is to ask questions about something you heard from someone in a position of some authority (Dyer, 2019) (Figure 2).

What are you trying to achieve in questioning this 'authoritative' statement? Who said it, and does that make a difference? Did they communicate a different perspective on realities from your understanding, including their version of the facts? Did they miss anything? Was it said privately, or did others have the opportunity to react? Is the timing of their statement significant? Was their reasoning made clear and what do you think was the purpose of saying it? What was their apparent emotional state when making the statement?

Figure 2: The critical thinking process

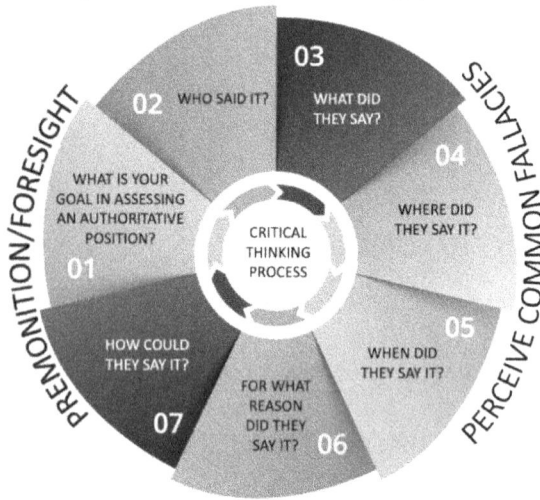

3.2.2 IT IS LIKE THE SIX HONEST SERVANTS

A good metaphor for critical thinking is Rudyard Kipling's 'six honest serving men'. Forgive the dated language, but the first stanza of the poem goes:

> *I keep six honest serving-men, (They taught me all I knew).*
>
> *Their names are What and Why and When*
>
> *And How and Where and Who.*
>
> *I send them over land and sea, I send them east and west.*
>
> *But after they have worked for me, I give them all a rest.*

3.2.3 WHAT'S THE POINT OF CRITICAL THINKING?

Critical thinking is about understanding the consistent association between thoughts. It is the capacity to take part in intelligent and autonomous reasoning. It fundamentally expects you to utilise your capacity to reason. It is about being a functioning student as opposed to a semi-disconnected beneficiary of data. It questions thoughts and presumptions instead of tolerating them without needing any proof. You try to decide if the thoughts, contentions, and discoveries speak to the whole picture and are open to finding and accepting that they do not.

Economic uncertainty, climate change, political upheaval and other risks abound in the modern workforce, and it's an employee's critical thinking skills that will enable a business to assess these hazards and act on them.

For example, risk assessment occurs in any number of different contexts. For example, a chemicals company has to identify all potential hazards on a manufacturing site to assure that its employees are working safely. Without such analysis, there might be injuries or even deaths, causing severe distress in the workplace and negatively impacting the company's reputation; not forgetting legal consequences.

In the finance industry, organisations have to assess the potential impacts of new legislation on the way they advise clients and process business. This requires critical thinking skills such as analysis, creativity (imagining different scenarios arising from the legislation) and problem-solving (finding a way to work with new legislation). If the institutions like this do not utilise critical thinking, they may end up losing profit or even suffering legal consequences from non-compliance.

3.2.4   AN EXAMPLE: DEEP WATER HORIZON

On the night of 20 April 2010, the Deepwater Horizon oil rig, one of many operating in the Gulf of Mexico, exploded. The event killed eleven men and put one of the most rich and diverse coastal regions on Earth in imminent danger of petroleum poisoning. BP had been drilling in waters a mile deep. Over the next two days the rig slowly sank and ripped open the pipe leading to the ocean floor oil well. Over the following three months, two hundred million gallons of crude oil poured into the Gulf, before the undersea well was sealed. It was the worst environmental disaster in American history, and the largest peacetime oil spill ever (National Commission, 2011).

BP's then CEO Tony Hayward seemingly presided over an organisational culture that condoned extreme risk-taking, ignored expert advice, overlooked warnings about safety issues and hid facts. Their failure to respond to the disaster with sufficient speed and attention was a direct consequence of this flawed culture.

BP exacerbated the massive impact of the disaster by, rather than tackling it head-on, aggressively developing a public relations campaign. Hayward should have realised or been advised that there are some situations that cannot or should not be 'spun'. Instead, damaged BP's reputation with gaffes and an apparent inability to understand public reaction to his comments.

This is where non-critical thinking can take you.

3.3 FURTHER THINKING ABOUT CRITICAL THINKING[3]

3.3.1 A FURTHER DEFINITION OF CRITICAL THINKING

Critical thinking is about making sure that you have good reasons for your beliefs. What does that mean?

Suppose that you and your friend are talking about who's going to be at tonight's party. And she says to you quite confidently that "Nikos won't be at the party". You are not sure whether or not to believe her, so it would be natural for you to follow up by asking, "why do you think so?"

There are a lot of different things that she might say in response, but there are at least three possible answers she could give. First, she might say, "I can't stand him, and I want to have a good time". Second, she might say, "well, he's really shy and rarely goes to parties". Third, she might say, "he's in Beijing and it is impossible to get here from Beijing in an afternoon". (Let's assume you are a long way from Beijing.)

The first response that she gives you, does not give you a good reason to believe that Nikos won't be there. The second reason though, is a good reason to believe that if he's really shy and rarely goes to parties, then it is probable that he won't be at tonight's party. Similarly, the third reason also gives you a good reason to believe that if he's in Beijing and it is impossible to get here from Beijing in an afternoon, then it is guaranteed that he won't be.

When you notice things like that. When you distinguish between good and bad reasons for believing something you are exercising your critical thinking skills.

So critical thinking is making sure we have good reasons for our beliefs. Hence, one of the essential skills that you learn when you are studying critical thinking is how to distinguish good reasons for believing something from bad reasons for believing something.

In this context, 'good' is not related to morality or ethics. It is not morally right or morally good to believe something on the basis of

---

[3] Based on Geoff Pynn's *Introduction to Critical Thinking*. https://youtu.be/Cum3k-Wglfw, accessed 24 March 2021

good reasons. Similarly, it is not morally wrong and evil or wicked to believe something on the basis of a bad reason rather hear what it is to say that a reason is good is closely tied to the notion of truth.

In critical thinking, a good reason for belief is one that makes it probable, that is it is one that makes the belief, likely to be true. The very best reasons for a belief, make it certain. They guarantee it.

So why does this matter? The reason that critical thinking is important is because since we are rational (not necessarily objective), we want our beliefs to be true. Rational people want to have true beliefs and not to have false beliefs. The best way to be rational in this way is to form beliefs, only when you find the reasons for them.

3.3.2 WHAT IS AN ARGUMENT?

An argument is a set of statements that together comprise a reason for a further statement.

For example, we can consider one of your friend's responses before as an argument. She's given you two statements: "Nikos is really shy" and "Nikos rarely goes to parties", which together comprise a reason for believing that Nikos won't be at the party. The statements that are the reason we call the arguments premises. "Nikos is really shy" is premise one and "Nikos rarely goes to parties" is premise two. The statement that those premises give you a reason to believe we call the arguments conclusion.

A good argument is one in which the premises give you a good reason for the conclusion; that is the premises make the conclusion likely to be true. In that case we say that the argument supports the conclusion. Good arguments support their conclusions, bad arguments do not support their conclusions. Hence, an essential part of critical thinking is learning to evaluate arguments to determine whether or not they are good or bad, that is whether or not their premises support their conclusions.

Argument 'A' is the first response that she gave to premises, "I can't stand Nikos and I want to have a good time". The conclusion is Nikos won't be there. The third argument, 'C', has two premises: "Nikos is in Beijing, and you can't get from Beijing to the party in time, so he won't be at the party".

As indicated before, argument A is not good, while argument C is good. Why so?

Consider what argument A's premises say (that your friend can't stand Nikos and she wants to have a good time) and think about their relationship to the conclusion of the argument. You'll see that those statements do not make that conclusion any more likely to be true. The fact that your friend can't stand Nikos and wants to have a good time does not do anything to make it more likely that Nikos won't be there. It is unrelated to the conclusion in the peripheral argument, though the premises if they are true, they guarantee that the conclusion is true. So, they make it very probable. The truth of the premises guarantees the truth of the conclusion. In argument C the premises do support the conclusion.

It is worth pointing out that argument A, though it is bad as it stands, could be made a good argument, with the addition of further background premises. For example, if you found out that your friend was the person who decided who was going to be invited to the party, then the fact that she can't stand Nikos and wants to have a good time, would give you a good reason to believe her because it would give you reason to believe that she didn't invite him.

3.3.3   AMPLIATIVE AND DEDUCTIVE ARGUMENTS

Argument B is the second response that your friend gave "Nikos is really shy" and a further premise "Nikos rarely goes to parties". Argument C is, "Nikos is in Beijing" (the first premise), and "you can't get from Beijing to the party in time" (the second premise). Both have the same conclusion ("so he won't be at the party"). Both of these are good arguments. They both give you reason to believe the conclusion, that is both of the premises support the conclusion.

However, there is an important difference between the two arguments. If you consider argument C and think about what its premises say, you'll notice that if those premises are true (if Nikos is in Beijing and can't get from Beijing to the party in time), then it must be true that Nikos won't be here, and the premises *guarantee* the conclusion.

In an argument where the premises guarantee the truth of the conclusion, we call the argument deductive or deductively *valid*. If a valid argument has true premises, then the argument is said also to be *sound*. All arguments are either valid or invalid, and either sound or unsound. There is no middle ground, such as being somewhat valid. Just thinking about the information in the premises and inductive argument gives you all you need to deduce the conclusion.

If you look at argument B though, you'll notice that that's not the case. Even if those premises are true, the conclusion might still be false.

Even given that Nikos is really shy and rarely goes to parties, it is still possible that he'll get over the shyness and unexpectedly show up; it is unlikely, but it is possible.

Hence, the truth of the premises of argument B does not guarantee the truth of the conclusion. We call arguments like this ampliative: conclusions go beyond their premises and *amplify* the scope of our beliefs. Inductive arguments and arguments to the best explanation are not deductively valid but may yield credible conclusions. The truth of the premises makes the conclusion probable, but do not guarantee it.

When you are evaluating an argument, it can be important to know whether or not the argument is supposed to be deductive or merely ampliative. If an argument is supposed to be deductive but careful consideration of the argument reveals that the premises *do not* guarantee the truth of the conclusion (the conclusion could be false, even though the premises are true), that's a good reason to reject the argument as a bad argument. However, in an ampliative argument to notice that the truth of the premises does not guarantee the truth of the conclusion is simply to notice that it is an ampliative argument.

If you were to object to argument B by pointing out that still the conclusion could be false, you'd really be missing the point. In an ampliative argument, it is taken for granted that the conclusion is not guaranteed by the premises. Rather, what an ampliative argument is doing is giving you reasons to think that the conclusion is probable.

3.3.4 SUMMARY

Critical thinking is making sure that we have good reasons for our beliefs, when we understand a good reason is one that makes the belief probable or likely to be true.

An argument is a set of statements which you call premises that together comprise a reason for another statement, which we call the argument's conclusion.

In a good argument, the premises support their conclusions. That is the premises give you a good reason for believing the conclusion. They make a proper deductive argument (one where the conclusion is guaranteed by the premises); if the premises are true then the conclusion must be true.

An ampliative argument is one where the premises do not guarantee the conclusion, but they do make it probable, so they can still provide you with good reason for believing.

3.4 CRITICAL THINKING SKILLS

Critical thinking skills embrace a huge range of human abilities, more some skills, some aptitudes (Dyer, 2019). We combine these to enable us to think critically (Figure 3).

Figure 3: Critical thinking skills

Perception is our ability to process cues we sense from our environment through our mental model of the world. *Investigation* is how we dig deeper by gathering more information about our world, based on our interpretation of cues. *Elucidation* occurs when we generate an explanation of what we have found through investigation, based on perception, which clearly explain to us what is happening. *Reflection* requires us to deconstruct the events we have witnessed and is often another place where the six honest servants arrive). *Assessment* is what we make of our reflections; what value is there is the event we are considering. *Derivation* occurs when we derive fresh thinking based on our assessment, which we then further *clarify, explicitly thinking* through what this all means. *Basic leadership* applies the thinking to the situation (Dyer, 2019).

Critical thinking has three central aptitudes incorporating these 12 skills:

1. *Interest* is craving to adopt more data and look for proofs just as being available to new thoughts

2. *Wariness* includes having a solid interrogating disposition concerning new data that you are presented with and not indiscriminately thinking everything everybody lets you know.
3. *Quietude* is the capacity to concede that your sentiments and thoughts aren't right when looked with new persuading proof that states generally.

3.4.1   THE IMPORTANCE OF CRITICAL THINKING

In the digital age critical thinking has become even more, well, critical. While machines have the ability to collate huge amounts of information and reproduce it in a readable format, the ability to analyse and act on this data is still a skill only humans possess.

Take accountants. Many of their more mundane tasks have passed to technology. Accounting platforms have the ability to produce profit and loss statements, prepare accounts, issue invoices and create balance sheets. But that doesn't mean accountants are out of a job. Instead, they can now focus their efforts on adding real value to their clients by interpreting the data this technology has collated and using it to give recommendations on how to improve. On a wider scale, they can look at historic financial trends and use this data to forecast potential risks or stumbling blocks moving forward.

The core skill in all of these activities is critical thinking – being able to analyse a large amount of information and draw conclusions in order to make better decisions for the future. Without these critical thinkers, an organisation may easily fall behind its competitors, who are able to respond to risks more easily and provide more value to clients.

Here is another example of the importance of critical thinking.

Growing from being the son of a peddler to the richest man in the world, John D. Rockefeller is undoubtedly one the greatest critical thinkers in history.

Rather than the conventional strategy of buying volume as wells were drilled and opened. Rockefeller aimed to control the inefficiencies of the oil market and bring the price of oil under control.

His first move avoided competition almost completely. Instead of fighting for market share on price, Rockefeller used several different approaches. First, he hated the waste of throwing out by-products of refining and developed markets for lubricants; Kerosene, common grease, Vaseline and other useful products generated revenue where other competitors literally threw it away. Second, Rockefeller took control of distribution, buying up all oil barrels, limiting the number of trains, purchasing all equipment and equipment suppliers and refusing to sell replacement parts to competitors. Third, he used scale to increase efficiencies, so lowering prices and squeezing competitors. He bought out owners once they couldn't compete. Rockefeller's critical thinking enabled him to control 90% of the oil market and become one of the richest Americans in history.

Looking at this now, it reads like *Blue Ocean Strategy* was created well before Kim and Mauborgne (2005a) thought of it!

3.4.2 FIVE STEPS TO IMPROVE YOUR CRITICAL THINKING[4]

Every day, a sea of decisions stretches before us, and it is impossible to make a perfect choice every time. But there are many ways to improve our chances; critical thinking is a particularly effective technique.

Critical thinking is a way of approaching a question that allows us to carefully deconstruct a situation, reveal its hidden issues, such as bias and manipulation and make the best decision. If the critical part sounds downbeat, that's because, in a way, it is, rather than choosing an answer because it feels right. Critical thinking subjects all available options to scrutiny and scepticism, using the tools at your disposal. They'll eliminate everything but the most valuable and reliable information.

There are many different ways of approaching critical thinking, but here is one five-step process that may help you solve many problems.

3.4.2.1 Step 1: Formulate your question.

Knowing what you are looking for is not always as straightforward as it sounds. For example, if you are deciding whether to try out the newest diet craze, your reasons for doing so may be obscured by other factors like claims that you'll see results in just two weeks. However, suppose you approach the situation with a clear view of what you are trying to accomplish by dieting, whether that's weight loss, better nutrition, or having more energy. In that case, critical thinking equips you to sift through this information critically. You can find what you are looking for, deciding whether the new fad suits your needs.

---

[4] Based on an animation written by Samantha Agoos, narrated by Addison Anderson and animated by Nick Hilditch: https://youtu.be/dItUGF8GdTw, accessed 23 March 2021

3.4.2.2 Step 2: Information Gathering

There is lots of information out there, so having a clear idea of your question will help you determine what's relevant. If you are trying to decide on a diet to improve your nutrition, you may ask an expert for their advice or seek other people's testimonies. Information gathering helps you weigh different options, moving you closer to a decision that needs your goal.

3.4.2.3 Step 3: Apply the Information

You apply the information by asking critical questions when facing a decision. Ask yourself what concepts are at work? What assumptions exist? Is my interpretation of the information logically sound? For example, in an email that promises you millions, you should consider what is shaping my approach to this situation? Do I assume the sender is telling the truth? Based on the evidence, is it logical to believe I will win any money?

3.4.2.4 Step 4: Consider the Implications.

Imagine it is election time, and you've selected a political candidate based on their promise to make it cheaper for drivers to fill up their cars with fuel. At first glance, that seems great, but what about the long-term environmental effects? If cost less restricts fuel use, this could also cause a massive surge in air pollution, and it is essential to think about unintended consequences.

3.4.2.5 Step 5: Explore Other Points of View

Ask yourself why so many people are drawn to the opposing political candidate's policies, even if you disagree with everything that candidate says. Exploring the full spectrum of viewpoints might explain why some policies that do not seem valid to you appeal to others.

3.5 QUESTIONS

1. Think about the BP Deepwater Horizon case, take a look at its Wikipedia entry. Then ask yourself:

   - What questions would need to be asked to establish a clear set of perspectives about Tony Hayward and BP's management of the incident?
   - What evidence will you need to confirm these perspectives?

- What types of argument or statements could you propose based upon the quality of evidence provided?
- What role does truth or validity play in establishing an argument?
- Why do we make inferences?
- Why do we become sceptical?
- What are the implications of the potential risk which may arise?

2. You are conducting a tour for aliens (yes extra-terrestrials) who are visiting Earth and observing humans. You are all in their spaceship when you fly over a cricket stadium. One of the aliens is confused, and turns to you for help, asking a series of questions:

- What is a game, and why do humans play them?
- What are "teams" and why are they so important for humans to be part of?
- Why is it these games seem to get more attention than other matters on your planet, like disease and poverty?
- Why do humans get so emotional and even violent when watching games?
- What would happen if no human could ever play these games again?
- How might you respond?

4. SOFT SYSTEMS METHODOLOGY

"Systems Thinking is a mixed bag of holistic, balanced and often abstract thinking to understand things profoundly and solve problems systematically."

Pearl Zhu

4.1 CHAPTER OUTLINE

This chapter introduces the core principle of Soft Systems Methodology (SSM).

The key concepts we explore are systems thinking, action learning, root definitions and modelling.

On completing this chapter, you should be able to:

1. Explain key concepts in SSM,
2. Identify the main stages of SSM, and
3. Describe the principles and purpose of building rich pictures (root definitions).

4.2 INTRODUCING SOFT SYSTEMS METHODOLOGY

4.2.1 SSM VALUE PROPOSITION

Today, business and managerial complexities become increasingly challenging at senior and top management levels; the demands on the individual are more diverse and the pressure for performance escalates year on year. The ability to achieve a balanced view in decision for the benefit of the organisation as a whole and also to give a targeted return to shareholders becomes of paramount importance. Achieving an understanding of the 'big picture' is not easy, it requires holistic thinking so that issues can be viewed and treated in context and with the priorities needed. These demands on management at a strategic level are not often supported with the best tools with which to assess problems or even opportunities. Yet rational, balanced decisions must be taken which appear equitable to all stakeholder groups.

4.2.2 STRATEGIC ANALYSIS BRINGS STRATEGIC PERSPECTIVE

A management tool is required that:

1. Enables the 'big picture' to be viewed as a whole.

2. Allows an understanding of how the parts of the organisation work together as a whole and where change is needed.
3. Effectively summarises problem themes, issues and challenges in relevant contexts.
4. Achieves a concise, comprehensive, yet complete consensus of what needs to be done to address prevailing challenges,
5. Delivers a road map to manage through strategic challenges to achieve tangible outcomes.
6. Achieves clarity and commitment for future strategic moves and for an overall image to be conveyed to stakeholders.

One management tool that enables leaders to achieve this is SSM. SSM is a creative yet powerful tool for strategic analysis that allows the user to conduct a complete enquiry to understand the 'big picture' and then to deal with the challenges faced from a systemic viewpoint.

Through the process of SSM, problems and challenges can be viewed in relation to each other by those involved and in a complete context. This overcomes taking a piecemeal approach to future development needs. Through the application of this management tool, a more rational, sequential process can be achieved for more effective planning, strategy determination and decision making.

4.2.3   THE ORIGINS OF SSM

The methodology developed from earlier systems engineering approaches, primarily by Peter Checkland (1999; Checkland & Scholes, 1999) and colleagues, including Brian Wilson (2001; Wilson & Haperen, 2015). The primary use of SSM is the analysis of complicated situations where there are divergent views about problem definition. These situations are 'soft' problems, for example:

- How to improve rail services?
- How to manage crisis management?
- When should psychologically disordered offenders be diverted from custody?
- What to do about the climate crisis?

In such situations, the actual problem to be addressed is commonly not agreed upon readily. In such cases, the soft systems approach uses the notion of a "system" as an interrogative device that will enable debate amongst concerned parties (Checkland, 1999; Checkland & Scholes, 1999). In its 'classic' form, the methodology consists of seven steps, with an initial appreciation of the problem situation leading to the modelling of several human activity systems that might be thought relevant to the problem situation (Checkland, 1999; Checkland & Scholes, 1999). By discussions and exploration of these, the decision-makers will arrive at accommodations (or, exceptionally, at consensus) over what kind of changes may be systemically desirable and feasible in the situation. Later explanations of the ideas give a more sophisticated view of this systemic method, focusing on locating it in its philosophical underpinnings (Mingers, 2014). The earlier classical approach (Checkland, 1999; Checkland & Scholes, 1999) is the most widely used practice.

SSM remains the most widely used and practical application of systems thinking (Augustsson et al., 2020; Kish et al., 2016; Temesgen Kitaw & Chris, 2017). Other systems approaches such as critical systems thinking (Jackson, 2019) have incorporated many of its ideas. Several hundred documented examples of the successful use of SSM in many different fields (ranging from ecology to business and military logistics) exist. It has been adopted by many organisations and incorporated into other approaches (Holwell, 2000).

4.2.4   SSM'S EVOLUTION

SSM evolved considerably between 1972 and 1990. This period saw four different representations of SSM. Each was progressively more sophisticated yet, at the same time, less structured and broader in scope (Checkland & Scholes, 1999).

In the first studies of what became SSM, the methodology follows a sequence of stages with iteration back to previous stages (Checkland & Scholes, 1999). The sequence was: analysis, root definition of relevant systems, conceptualisation, comparison and definition of changes, selection of change to implement, design of change and implementation, and appraisal.

Systems Thinking, Systems Practice (the first book written about SSM in 1981 (Checkland, 1999), presented the methodology as seven activities in a learning process:

1. Enter situation considered problematical
2. Express the problem situation
3. Formulate root definitions of relevant systems of purposeful activity

4. Build conceptual models of the systems named in the root definitions
5. Compare models with real-world situations
6. Define possible changes which are both possible and feasible
7. Take action to improve the problem situation

The *two-stream model* of SSM recognised the crucially important role of history in human affairs. This expression of SSM presents an approach embodying both a logic-based stream of analysis (via activity models) and a cultural and political stream, enabling judgements about the accommodations between conflicting interests that might be attainable by the people concerned, encouraging action (Checkland & Scholes, 1999).

The four-activities model subsumes the cultural stream of analysis in the four activities (Checkland & Scholes, 1999):

1. Finding out about a problem situation (including culturally and politically)
2. Formulating some relevant purposeful activity models
3. Debating the situation, using the models, seeking both:
    - Changes, regarded as both desirable and (culturally), feasible that would improve the case, and
    - Accommodations between conflicting interests enabling action
4. Taking action in the situation to bring about improvement.

4.2.5 THE SSM APPROACH

SSM, as a consulting tool can be applied individually or facilitated in teams through focused workshops to deliver to users:

1. A powerful system for conducting an enquiry or situation analysis into the current position.
2. A way through complex even messy problem situations.
3. A logical set of proposals from which key decisions can be taken.
4. A strategy road map for the future.

SSM opens the eyes to new horizons and thereby can lead to more rational, methodological productive planning and decision-making for transformational strategy.

4.2.6   SYSTEMIC AND SYSTEMATIC STRATEGIC THINKING

Two terms, derived from the noun system produce two different interpretations:

1. *Systematic* implies a step-by-step procedure.
2. *Systemic* relates to the 'body' as a whole.

From the idea of systemic, we need to consider the term system as something that has emergent properties (outputs) and resources (inputs). To be purposeful, the system must 'do something' and achieves this through a transformation process, usually with a sense of hierarchy.

A system, which is dynamic in nature, therefore brings about change. A relevant system will be relevant to the problem situation discovered in the real world (i.e., to bring about the needed change). A relevant system would have inherent properties of communication and control in order to relate to and adapt to the changes in the environment.

As leaders, we typically do not think about systems as such. Our world is perceived through ideas and maybe concepts. For this reason, a more powerful and creative approach may be needed to understand real world problems, issues and challenges.

4.3   THE SSM PROCESS

4.3.1   CHECKLAND'S CLASSICAL SSM MODEL

Checkland's (1999) process starts with identifying and 'entering' a problematic situation (Figure 4).

We then move around the process anti-clockwise in this picture, next expressing the problem situation. We then formulate what is termed a root definition, which is a synopsis of the 'world' in which the problem sits. From there conceptual models of the systems named in the root definitions are built, which are then compared with the real world. This enables us to define feasible and possible changes in the systems the encompass the problem, which then enable us to take action.

Figure 4: Seven steps of SSM

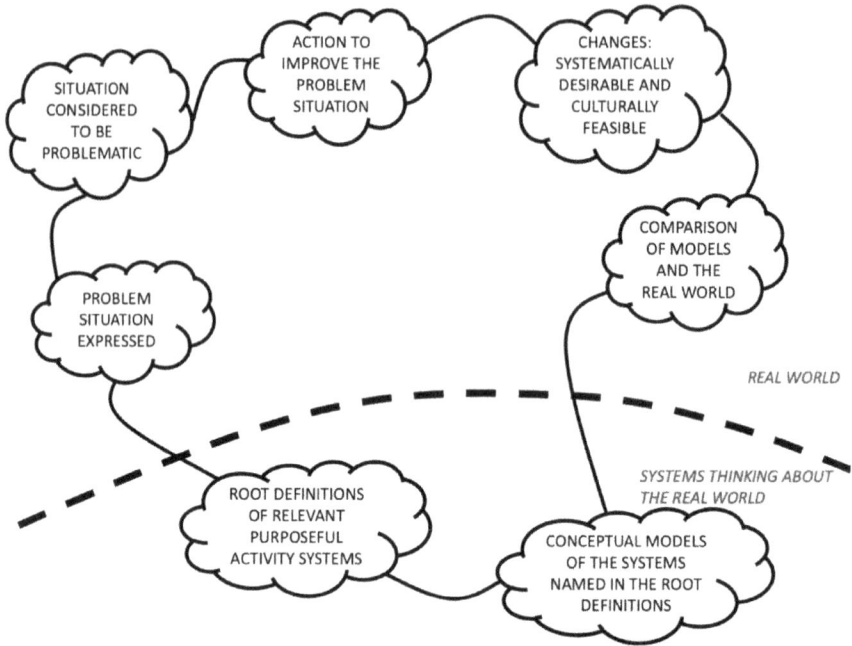

It is like putting planet Earth in your hands, thinking about a singular problem (there are so many), building models of the different systems that affect the problem and then looking for real world data from which to develop your analysis. This enables you to work through solutions that are realistic in the complicated political, economic, social, technological and ecological systems that operate in the world. Realistic solutions enable realistic action.

4.3.2 PROBLEM IDENTIFICATION

4.3.2.1 Identifying Common Business Challenges

There are common, well-known business challenges:

- Poor defined market segments.
- Difficult customer acquisition or retention.
- Badly defined value propositions.
- Poor performing communication, distribution or sales channels.

- Difficult customer acquisition or retention through mismanaged customer relationships.
- Poor or variable revenue streams.
- A shortage of good staff or other key resources.
- Ineffective or inefficient business processes.
- Underperforming partnerships or a lack of partners
- Poor cost control.

These are all clear challenges, but they are also symptomatic of deeper causes, which is what approaches like SSM are designed to get at.

4.3.2.2 Deeper Causes of Challenges

Poor Purpose

If your business feels adrift or if you change your mission statement constantly, you are probably experiencing one of the most common sources business challenges: a lack of purpose.

Positive leadership (Cameron, 2012) is synonymous with having a sense of purpose. When an organisation's leader truly believes they will be successful, a thriving business usually follows. A well-defined purpose gives a leader and their team passion, drive and certainty. It confers on them you the ability to overcome severe and lesser challenges.

Purpose is defined by a business's values, vision and mission. Values are the things that define our businesses: the non-negotiables in the way that we aim to do business. They set the scene for our vision: where the organisation wants to be in the future. This is enacted through our mission, which describes what the organisation needs to do now to achieve the vision.

Weak Brand Identity

One of the biggest challenges faced by businesses, especially during growth is having a weak brand identity; this is key to marketing and sales success. Your identity defines what your company stands for, reflecting your purpose. It should be integrated with your company culture, which in turn determines whether you can hire and retain top staff.

Brand identity drives the emotional connection with your consumer and ultimately should create customer loyalty. A weak or absent brand identity means you do not know who you are or what direction you should working towards. If you do not know, you won't have an audience, and if you do not have an audience, you won't have customers, let alone loyal customers.

Not Providing Value

Shrinking margins is among the commonest of business issues. Disregard this and bankruptcy follows, slowly at first and then very quickly. It is easy to blame the market when this happens, market shift for a reason. Customers go where they find the most value. When you do not provide what they want you are not providing them with value.

To be successful in business, you must practice strategic value innovation. In each element of your business model what can you raise, reduce or eliminate to improve value to the customer, as well as your business? Is there anything you can create? How do you bring more value to your customers? What's your distinctive difference? If you do not know the answers, it is time to sit down and think about them.

Failing to Plan is Planning to Fail

Purpose and identity are crucial to the success of any business, but then so is a plan. There is a saying that plans survive until you begin their implementation, but if you do not write your plan down it is never going to happen.

Do not get too detailed. Broad plans are the best, because plans change. Break down your goals, work out the best way to track through them and then build a work breakdown. Once you've got that prioritise.

4.3.3 EXPRESSING THE PROBLEM: BUILDING RICH PICTURES

4.3.3.1 What is Rich Picturing?

Analysts and managers in organisations tend to talk or write about situations. You probably write many emails and attend many meetings every day! It is the accepted way of doing things.

The problem is that there are limitations to the spoken and written word. Neither helps us to view situations holistically, or express dynamic relationships well. It can limit our understanding. If a situation is not well understood, it is difficult to take purposeful action, which leads to stagnation, or failure. There are plenty of recent examples of failed strategic initiatives to support this idea.

In the 21st century, markets can be transformed, redefined, or made irrelevant very quickly. Our business environment has changed but we generally use the conventional media to understand it. We need alternative ways to process this new, complex environment, and to appreciate the opportunities and threats it presents. We question whether the conventional approach is always fit-for-purpose! What are the alternatives?

Rich picturing is a richer and more challenging medium that presents new possibilities for analysts and managers. It refers to the practice of representing a problem situation visually. You could say that it is drawing out your situation on paper. It can be done individually, or in groups.

4.3.3.2   The Process of Building a Rich Picture

Step 1: Structure
1. Identify and list the elements of structure.
2. Identify visual icons to represent each element of the structure.
3. Draw these in a way that makes sense to you (or your group).

Step 2: Processes
1. Identify processes that connect the elements of structure, using lines and annotations.
2. Capture problem and opportunity themes that emerge at this stage.
3. Consider the nature of the general environment (context) and reflect this in your rich picture.

Step 3: Interpretation
1. Extract obvious challenges and general problem themes from the picture.
2. Look at the processes again. Are there are missing, that could be added to the list defined in step 2.
3. Are there structural elements absent which might be added to the list defined in step 1.

4.3.4   WRITING ROOT DEFINITIONS: THE *CATWOE* CRITERIA

Root definitions describe what needs to be done to embrace, contain and potentially resolve the identified problem. It is common to name the problematic system that describes its purpose and to develop a series of root definitions that describe it. Best practice is to refine, test, retest and finally select an idealised root definition, as in the following process.

Step 1: Identify the CATWOE Elements of the System

C = Customers affected by the outcome of the system proposed.

A = Actors involved in resolving the general problems and challenges.

T = Transformations considered essential.

W = World view (or image) to be created in the minds of stakeholder groups.

O = Owners holding resourcing and control power.

E = Environment within which the system has to function, internally and externally.

Step 2: The Ideal Sequence for Using CATWOE

T W C A O E

This is not a rule. Find what works best for you.

Step 3: Writing and Testing Root Definitions

1. Prepare notes against all elements of CATWOE.
2. Try to assemble a root definition.
3. Remember this is the very essence of what needs to be done

Step 4: Testing the Root Definition

1. Have all elements of CATWOE been expressed?

   C ☐ A ☐ T ☐ W ☐ O ☐ E ☐

2. Does the proposed transformation process meet the five 'E' tests? Is it potentially *efficacious* - can it work? Is its potential use of resources *efficient*? Is it potentially *effective* in meeting its owners' *expectations*? Is it potentially morally *ethical*? Is it *elegant*, that is potentially pleasing when *executed*?
3. Does the proposed transformation fit with context specific criteria (e.g., alignment with future vision & mission, respect for core values, fulfilment of unmet needs, sustainability, organisational gap analysis, human capital competencies)?
4. This cautionary step should help to prevent rejection of your proposals by owners of the system.

4.3.5 FINDING SOLUTIONS: IMPLEMENTING CONCEPTUAL MODELS OF CHANGE IN THE REAL WORLD

4.3.5.1 Building Conceptual Models

Conceptual models are used to build a road map of strategic initiatives for change by deciding 'how' and 'when'.

Models are built out of root definitions by first identifying all actionable elements. Then for each element you use brainstorming to build a mind map of how each element will be achieved. The change initiatives should be specified as actions to be taken. Hence, they should start with a verb.

Figure 5 is an example that deals with the challenge of attracting new doctors to a hospital.

The element of the problematic system is at the centre: 'attract new doctors'. A series of actions surround it. You might also choose to sequence the actions in more complicated models.

Figure 5: Conceptual model of the challenge of attracting new doctors to a hospital

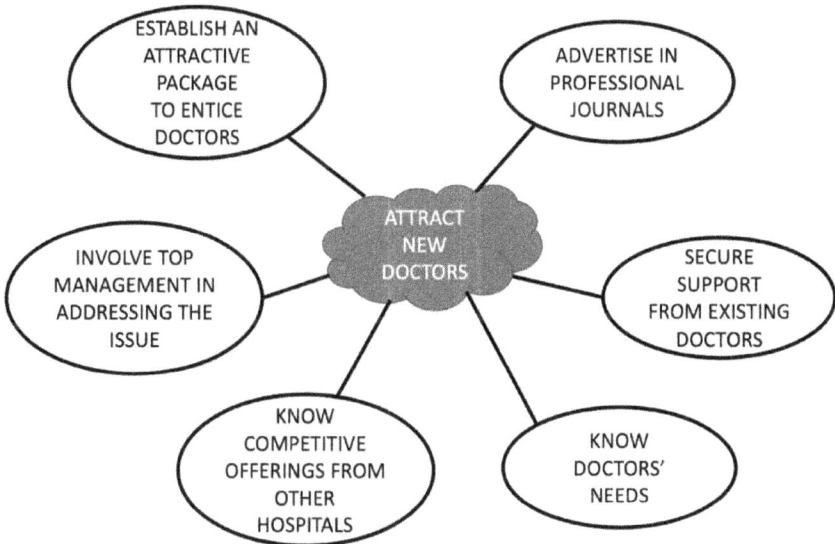

4.4 BACK TO THE REAL WORLD

The proposals achieved using a Systems Thinking approach now need to be reflected back into the real-world where clients, owners, customers and actors reside.

The proposed actions now need to be compared with the real-world position in the rich picture to consider, reaction, constraints, tensions and resistance, defining the future challenges in managing proposed changes.

For each action proposed, in discussion and consultation with 'owners', 'actors' and 'customers' the desirability and feasibility should be determined for acceptance and adoption into an actionable change agenda.

An action plan will be agreed for prioritised steps to be taken to face the challenges and resolve problems and issues identified in SSM stage 1 (problem definition) and visualised in stage 2 (rich picture). This is a plan for change that will become the confirmed road map for the future.

It is essential that the adopted change programme be effectively managed to ensure sustained support, motivation, progress and achievement.

This is the end of our brief introduction to SSM. To master this entire methodology requires greater practice to exploit its the full value. SSM is a useful methodology that can even become a mindset for introducing managing and achieving transformational change.

4.5 QUESTIONS

1. Take a look at your own business or company. What do you think are the major challenges?
2. Have a go at building a rich picture of a problem you are familiar with. What do you think of the process? What are your thoughts on your experience of drawing your picture?
3. Try writing a root definition based on the rich picture you developed for activity 2. What do you think?
4. Build a conceptual model out of the root definition you built in activity 3. Reflect on your experience.

LEADING STRATEGY DESIGN

"Design is intelligence made visible."

Alina Wheeler

5. PRINCIPLES OF STRATEGY

"Strategy without tactics is the slowest route to victory. Tactics without strategy is the noise before defeat."

Sun Tzu

5.1 CHAPTER OVERVIEW

This chapter considers what is strategy, its importance, why it is misunderstood, why it often is not communicated effectively, why we need it as leaders and its necessity in organisational transformation.

The key concepts we explore are problem awareness, problem exploration, decision-making, execution and monitoring impact.

On completing this chapter, you should be able to:

1. Define what strategy is.
2. Explain the meaning of 'death in the drawer' for strategy.
3. Debate the role of strategy in organisational transformation.

5.2 STRATEGY DEFINED

5.2.1 A VOLATILE, UNCERTAIN, COMPLEX AND AMBIGUOUS (VUCA) WORLD

5.2.1.1 Globalisation: Driving Change of Society, Work and Business

Globalisation means that businesses and organisations are developing increasing international influence and often on an increased scale (Dobbs et al., 2015). Hence, borders are not what they used to be (Rodrik, 2012); the world's economic profile is changing (Gray, 1998). The global economic locus, intensity and dynamics are shifting to the Brazilian, Russian, Indian and Chinese (BRIC) emerging economies and cities within them. Urbanisation in the form of smart cities is on the rise (Townsend, 2013). Healthcare technology and improved diet is leading to longer lives for many, but sadly not all. So much so that in the west and parts of the BRIC economies, the 100-year life is upon us; it brings with it longer work lives, challenges our present understanding of retirement, and simultaneously presents issues for younger people seeking work (Gratton & Scott, 2016). Underpinning and enabling each of the preceding three forces is technological change, which is accelerating at an unprecedented rate (Brynjolfsson & McAfee, 2016).

Individually, the effects of these changes are remarkable, but the multiplier effect of their interactions is more remarkable still. Information and communications technologies (ICT) enable globalisation and urbanisation. Moreover, urbanisation and globalisation drive demand for ever more sophisticated ICT solutions. Manufacturing technology is similarly enabling and enabled. Medical and bioscience innovation increases our longevity, and as we live longer our expectations and demands of these technologies drives yet more creative solutions to ageing and its implications.

The economic impacts of globalisation on an ageing population are not well understood but it is apparent that conventional ways of thinking about ageing are weakening. The economic effects of globalisation have clear implications for health and healthcare, work and financial circumstances, culture and identity, and politics and policies (Hyde & Higgs, 2016). Further, as wealthier people age, they will grow in economic and commercial influence, driving further change in the internationalisation of business and commerce.

As noted previously, globalisation is driving urbanisation, and multinational corporations switch their manufacturing operations in search of optimised production costs. In turn urbanisations acts as a magnet for skilled workers, as well as markedly improving the technological infrastructure of previously under-developed cities, offering attractive locations for multinationals.

5.2.1.2 Advancing Technology: Changing Work Lives and Business

At the heart of this activity are our private and work lives, which are intimately intertwined, and which are hugely impacted by these substantial forces. That noted, without question the most challenging issue for us all is the way in which information technology, notably artificial intelligence (and specifically machine learning) is changing the world of work (Brynjolfsson & McAfee, 2016; Gratton, 2011; Gratton & Scott, 2016; Susskind & Susskind, 2015). Technology invades and occasionally dominates just about every aspect of our social and working lives. Its advance is unprecedented. As foreshadowed by many polemicists this is driving change in our social and work lives.

To put this in perspective, one forecast predicts that by 2025 there will be more than 100 billion connected devices across the Internet of Things (IoT). That will be 14 devices for every person on the planet.

The revenue associated with these products is US$10 trillion (Research and Markets, 2017).

The future of many present jobs is bleak, with automation forecast to take job tasks that are routinely analytical or manual. Retail sales remains the most common job, but as the pilot of Amazon's checkout-free supermarket indicates, such jobs have a 90+% chance of becoming automated. Nurses and teachers are likely to soon become the most common jobs. It is mostly low-income jobs that risk being automated. Jobs that require creativity, decision-making and communication skills, as well as certain types of higher education are less likely to be reduced. With automation and fewer low-skilled jobs, the days of the managerial classes and professions too look numbered (Frey & Osbourne, 2013; Susskind & Susskind, 2015).

The world is complex and increasingly interconnected. The isolation sought by some countries will not last. The democratising power of technologies has or will shortly doom that drive to fail. The world is indeed complex, and the centralisation of power and its concentration in the hands of a few, whilst still predominant, is slowly being brought to its knees by the forces outlined above. Yes, new power brokers are emerging (notably the tech giants), but the forces unleashed and now driving change may well yet overwhelm their progenitors.

5.2.2   IS THE WORLD GETTING BETTER OR WORSE?

Pinker (2019) argues that for over 200 years, the *Age of Enlightenment* has been a wellspring of steady human progress, especially in life quality (Harari, 2011). The Enlightenment, "placed in the last two-thirds of the 18th century, though it [flowed] out of the Scientific Revolution and the Age of Reason in the 17th century", follows a set of foundational principles and ideals: "reason, science, humanism and progress".

The primacy of reason is a path for understanding the world and humanity and rejecting religious faith and dogma. Science moved away from the Enlightenment's devotion to reason, offering people a means to understand natural world processes and human nature. Humanism depends on reason and science. It concerns ethical life and polity (how people organise themselves into societies). Humanism grounds ethics in reason, instead of religion, prioritising individuals over their community, nation or race. The Declaration of Independence and the US Constitution are products of the Enlightenment.

Pinker (2019) contends the Enlightenment ideals fuelled humanities progress from human health and human rights to efforts to combat poverty, crime and war.

5.2.2.1   Entropy is important in grasping the human condition

Following the second law of thermodynamics, entropy describes how the elements in a "closed system" gradually disperse over time, becoming less used. For example, when a fire dims, and its heat dissipates, it can no longer boil water or cook food.

This law is essential in understanding human life. Like that of any organism, human biological structures allow people to absorb the energy they need to remain alive, survive, and counteract entropy. How could such an improbable being come into existence?

Religious thinkers assert that only God could design such a complex creature (Dawkins, 1976, 2006a, 2006b). To the extent that Enlightenment thinkers were religious, some were deists, theists or pantheists (Cobb Jr. & Griffin, 1976). Moreover, some were atheists, not religious at all. Deists believed that only a deity could explain the origins of complex organisms like human beings and that "God set the universe in motion and then stepped back, allowing it to unfold according to the laws of nature".

Pinker (2019) holds that Charles Darwin's theory of evolution (Darwin, 1859/2015) rendered God unnecessary. Evolution explains how improbable creatures like people come into existence and persist despite entropy's pressure (Dawkins, 2006a; Harari, 2011). Entropy applies to closed systems that cannot add more energy. People and all other life forms live in open ecosystems: they renew their dissipated energy with energy from food, water and the sun (Costanza & Daly, 1992). Humans have larger, more complex brains than other species (Harari, 2011). Hence, people can work with more information, reason, articulate their desires, formulate goals and develop plans to pursue them (Pinker, 2019).

5.2.2.2   The human brain makes progress possible

20th-century theoretical neuroscience discovered that neurons retain information and manipulate it in 'intelligent' ways. Hence, the brain performs enormously complex tasks (Purves et al., 2018). Hence, evolving highly complex brains changed human destiny. We learned to raise animals and cultivate plants (Harari, 2011). We invented writing, articulated ideas, transmitting them across space and time (Zerubavel,

2003). We moved away from archaic, magical belief systems and created religions, philosophies, art and works of literature (Harari, 2011; Pinker, 2019).

With the energy provided by broader, more reliable food access, human beings built larger cities and more elaborate civilisations. This process continued for millennia, through the Scientific Revolution (Harari, 2011), the Enlightenment and the Industrial Revolution. The Enlightenment brought about political systems that value freedom of speech, human rights and cooperation (Harari, 2011; Pinker, 2019; Zeldin, 1994).

5.2.2.3   Some thinkers are suspicious of the Enlightenment

Opposition to the Enlightenment (the "counter-Enlightenment") appeared in the generation following the Enlightenment. The first who objected were Romantics, such as Jean-Jacques Rousseau, Johann Herder and Friedrich Schelling, who believed rationality and feelings were inseparable. Since the Enlightenment devalues religion's primacy, anyone insisting faith matters more than reason resists Enlightenment thinking (Pinker, 2019).

The Enlightenment focuses on individuals' integrity. Those valuing nations or races more highly than individuals object to the Enlightenment. It embraces science, especially concerning the pursuit of knowledge. The Enlightenment is problematics for thinkers uneasy about science and its methods. Pinker (2019) dismisses counter-Enlightenment views (from whenever) as ignorant, finding that rejecting reason is irrational since science is humanity's most outstanding achievement in history and because humanism brought democracy and defeated fascism.

Caution is needed here. In this contention, Pinker (2019) is arguably too readily dismissive. His professed expertise is in psychology and science. However, whilst apparently well read, he is arguably less expert in philosophy and literature. Further, as an acknowledged atheist, he rather too easily casts aside religion as backward and irrational. Science is complex, far-reaching and incommensurate (there is always more than one answer to explain a set of data); being suspicious of its centrality in all aspects of life is not the same as wholly rejecting it. Moreover, as Robinson (2011), Brynjolfsson and McAfee (2016), (Gratton, 2011) and Flanagan and Gregory (2019) argue creativity is an essential human skill, which is not the sole preserve of science..

5.2.2.4 The idea of progress frightens some people

Pinker (2019) finds that many who believe in Enlightenment principles agree that knowledge makes humanity better but still doubt progress's reality. The media often view claims of health or crime prevention progress sceptically. Polemicists have forecast the 'decline of Western Civilisation' since the 19th century. Recently, many intellectuals have rejected the idea of progress, surveying a declining world (Bauman, 1998a, 1998b, 1999, 2000, 2001; Beck, 1992, 1998, 1999, 2000; Gray, 1998).

However, psychologists observe that most individuals look at their lives positively (Kahneman, 2000; Lyubomirsky, 2007, 2013; Seligman, 2012; Seligman et al., 2005). They think they are unlikely to be victims of everyday misfortunes: loss of a job, disease, robbery or divorce. While functioning within this personal "optimism gap", the same people regard society as being in disastrous shape (Bauman, 1998a, 2001; Beck, 1992, 1998, 1999, 2000; Giddens, 1984, 1990, 1998; Hutton, 1995, 2002). The nature of news coverage provides a partial explanation. Magazines, newspapers, and broadcast and online news focus on adverse events like wars, terrorist attacks, epidemics and political scandals (Smallman, 1997). People estimate an event's likelihood based on how quickly they can bring an example to mind (Tversky & Kahneman, 1974). If news bombards you with violence, you are likelier to regard violence as typical, even when it is not.

5.2.2.5 To counteract pessimism, adopt a 'quantitative' mind-set

Pinker (2019) argues that we should adopt a quantitative mind-set that looks beyond the immediate horizon towards the world's future as a whole to refute pessimism. He wants us to get past the headlines and explore widely available data. He argues that 'real' information when examined carefully should restore our faith in progress and help solve problems that plague humanity. Pinker (2019) overestimates the capacity of most people to apply quantitative reasoning and evaluate data. He also seems not to account for the qualitative interactive effects of context and behaviour on cognition (Bandura, 1986, 2005).

However, in a global culture, this approach is surely worth suggesting and trying. Pinker (2019) cites positive trending data on health, wealth, inequality, terrorism, and much else. However, there remains a long journey ahead on the United Nations' sustainable development goals (UNDP & UNIRSD, 2017; United Nations, 2006).

5.2.2.6 The future of the Enlightenment and human progress depends on politics

Pinker (2019), claims that hard data proves the Enlightenment's accomplishments. Indeed, the world on average is more affluent than it was 200 years ago; fewer people live in poverty or encounter murder or even war. People are healthier, living in freer societies. However, humanity's advancement varies hugely between nations and especially between the developed and developing worlds.

Overall, our progress against the United Nations sustainable development goals has been strong. This is especially the case for income poverty, access to education and health services, and improved sources of clean water. Unfortunately, progress has been steady but less marked in other areas, including on gender equality, nutrition and access to sanitation facilities (UNDP & UNIRSD, 2017).

Furthermore, anti-Enlightenment forces are powerful, as represented by the rise of authoritarian populism and associated toxic leadership (Smallman, 2021). Exemplified in ex-President Trump's posturing in withdrawing from the World Health Organisation and the Paris Climate Agreement, these forces threaten humankind's achievements in medicine, economics, politics, ethics, science and social science. In 2020, the American public threw Trump out. However, the anti-Enlightenment forces Trump and other populists harness continue to coalesce around these extreme and toxic 'leaders', threatening political stability (however faulty it is) and undermining the fundamentals of the Enlightenment (Pinker, 2019).

5.2.3 STRATEGY IS A MEANS TO BRING CERTAINTY TO A VUCA WORLD

Strategy is an idea, a conceptualisation. It is a unique positioning in a market that others cannot match. You may have different strategies for different value propositions or markets, but too many (probably more than nine (Miller, 1956)) will confuse the organisation; in fact, one is best.

The 'Godfather' of strategy Porter (1980, p. 34) describes

> *"competitive strategy as taking offensive or defensive actions to create a defendable position in an industry, to cope successfully with … competitive forces and … yield a superior return on investment for the firm."*

A more modern take (Kim & Mauborgne, 2005a) is

> *"to create uncontested market space and make the competition irrelevant."*

Either way, identifying your organisation's strategy and positioning in a VUCA world gives a sense of purpose and certainty to your organisation.

5.2.4   WHY STRATEGY MATTERS

There are some people who argue that the VUCA world in which we live is too fast moving for a deliberately designed strategy to be effective or worthwhile. There are three counterpoints to this:

1. Failure to match your value proposition to the market can have devastating consequences.
2. If you do not write down your strategic intent, it is difficult to communicate to your stakeholders (e.g., employees, customers, shareholders).
3. If you do not write down your strategic intent, it is highly unlikely it won't happen (from a proven psychological concept call implementation intention).

Whatever framework for strategy is adopted the essence of strategy is better matching value propositions to a current or existing market or creating new value propositions for an existing or current market.

Organisational transformation is all about improving the production, sales and delivery of your value propositions; that's why we need strategy as leaders and why it is a necessity in organisation transformation.

5.2.5   FAILURE TO COMMUNICATE

The communication of strategy commonly fails where:

1. It is not written down or it is written down badly.
2. It is not developed through a strategic conversation with involved stakeholder.
3. It is not communicated early and often.

Hence the key elements of leading strategy design are that

1. If you do not write it down, it is not going to happen.
2. The best strategic plans are designed and revised through collaborative engagement with the stakeholder communities that are affected.

3. Once the plans are developed and as they are revised, they are communicated to stakeholder relentlessly and consistently.
4. As plans are implemented you have an easy-to-understand scorecard in place that communicates performance against lead and lag measures.

5.3   WHY STRATEGIES FAIL

5.3.1   WHY DO MOST TRANSFORMATIONS FAIL?

Harry Robinson, a global leader of McKinsey's Transformation Practice,[5] reckons that the academic research is unequivocal that transformation is a word that gets used quite a lot. Still, when corporations launch transformations, something like 70% fail.

Robinson finds that the root causes of those failures are readily identifiable. As McKinsey built their transformation practice, they studied the causes of transformation project failures. There are several commonly occurring factors.

The CEO not setting a sufficiently high aspiration is one of the significant failure drivers. They fail to build conviction in their team during the early stages of the transformation. They do not stress the importance of the work or fail to build commitment around a change narrative explaining why the transformation is needed. People throughout the organisation do not commit, so leaders do not account for people's willpower, not getting them to the point where they want to invest extra energy to try to make change happen.

Another challenge is where the CEO or the leadership team do not address the skill issues in the organisation. They simply do not have the capabilities in place to drive the transformation. Alternatively, people with the essential capabilities aren't freed from their regular commitments to work on the transformation.

Then there are all sorts of procedural elements around making a transformation genuinely transformative that are sometimes missed:

- Appropriate change management infrastructure
- Building a cadence of leadership
- Oversight meetings

---

[5] Adapted from 'Why do most transformations fail? A conversation with Harry Robinson, a global leader of McKinsey's Transformation Practice' available from https://www.youtube.com/watch?v=F0idgdkMgfY accessed 7 April 2021

- Performance management discussions to track where things stand.

These are just some of the elements that lead to failure in transformation projects.

5.3.2 MAKING STUFF THAT PEOPLE WANT

Germany has a highly stable and successful economy. The backbone of its success is the *Mittelstand*, medium-sized (usually privately held) manufacturing firms that account for the largest share of the country's economic output. They employ about 60 per cent of all workers, provide crucial training and make significant contributions to Germany's corporate tax revenue. They are not 'flashy' although the manufacturing processes they use may be 'hi-tech'. They focus on employing high quality employees to produce high quality goods that are marketed well to international markets and once purchased are supported sensibly (although it is rare that they fail).

What's their secret?

They make stuff that people want.

5.3.3 STRATEGY IS NOT GOALS

Vermulen (2017) writes, many strategy execution processes fail because the firm does not have something worth executing. Unlike the Mittelstand, they do not make stuff that people want or at least that's how it appears to the market.

The issue is that more often than not firms do not do enough research, developing value propositions and the strategies that support their production, marketing, sales and support. What they present to the market as a result is a strategy that does not represent a set of clear choices. If you think back to Porter (1980), what many people present as strategies are goals rather than coherent strategies.

A former colleague of Clive, in a financial services consulting firm, loudly announced in the office one day that he was going to be "number one in Singapore" (he sold computer-based testing of financial advisory skills), Clive asked the deadly question "why?" His response was "I've got a grant". Clive asked two other questions "what" and "how?" Again, the answer was the same: "I've got a grant". No sign of a strategy, just a means to a hopeful outcome. He had no idea of how he was going to become 'number one' and no strategy. For the record, he had a lovely time in Singapore, but sold no business.

Vermulen (2017) identifies another form of strategy, representing two or more of an organisation's priorities and choices, for example "we want to increase operational efficiency; we will target Europe, the Middle East, and Africa; and we will divest business X". These may be laudable priorities and decisions, but they are certainly not a strategy.

5.3.4 STRATEGY IS ABOUT CLEAR CHOICES

LEGO began manufacturing interlocking toy bricks in Billund, Denmark in 1949. LEGO grew over decades by creating infinite possibilities of imaginary worlds for generations of kids. Yet, LEGO almost faced bankruptcy in 2005.

Lego failed to assess its core competencies and concentrate on core products, which resulted in substantial financial losses, placing the firm on the edge of survival. In 2003, Lego sales dropped by 26% or $228 million (Ashcroft, 2014; Robertson & Breen, 2014). The US market experienced a drop of 35%, while Asian markets declined by 28%. In large part, the fall is attributable to shortfalls in the sale of movie tie-in products (e.g., *Harry Potter, Star Wars*). In the 2000s, the entire toy industry experienced significant challenges. However, Lego's failure derived from a loss of strategic focus (Ashcroft, 2014; Robertson & Breen, 2014).

The company failed to develop a well-defined strategy, clearly articulated core competencies, and a focus on core products that should have provided it with a sustained competitive advantage. Worst of all, Lego management appeared to be out of touch with their customers. Lack of communication between buyers and end-users (i.e., children) on the one hand, and R&D teams, marketers, and executives, on the other, saw the company at risk of bankruptcy and breaking up. Further, ignoring stock turn and margin compromised logistics. Retailers overstocked with unsold products saw diminished margins resulting from clearance sales.

According to (Robertson & Breen, 2014, p. 63), the unsold inventory level at some outlets of giant retailers, like Target and Walmart, sky-rocketed by 40% in 2003. Sales decreases tracked failed projections of movie tie-in products' sales (particularly from *Star Wars* and *Harry Potter*) in 2003 when new movies were not released. At the same time, Lego's, *Bionicles* brand appeared to be in great demand, leading to its inclusion in the Top 10 'most wanted' presents for Christmas (Ashcroft, 2014). Unfortunately, Bionicles' sales also declined by 20%.

Even Lego's own retail stores and Legoland theme parks frustrated management. First, they were capital intensive, often failing to generate adequate returns on investments. Second, Lego stores compromised key retailers' revenues, like Walmart, Kmart, Target and Toys R Us.

Lego pulled off a spectacular business turnaround, quadrupled its revenues in less than a decade and brought Lego bricks back to households around the world. Today, they occupy the top spot in the toy manufacturing business.

Why was Lego so successful? It made two clear choices, which fitted together to form a clear strategic direction.

First, *they reengineered their operations.* Lego first streamlined its operations and decreased the complexity of its manufacturing processes. In particular, they reduced the number of different Lego bricks by eliminating those that were difficult and costly to source. Lego focused on a standard design of their bricks, which made their operations more efficient, allowing them to react quickly to market trends. LEGO also decided to get rid of Lego branded products that were tangential to their business and weren't profitable.

Second, once their operations were more robust, *they expanded their value proposition.* Inspired by the success of PlayStation, Xbox and the like, Lego management believed that the future would be digital, collaborating with the Miramax Film Company. Within their diversification strategy, Lego also embarked on developing lifestyle products (Lego childrenswear), learning concepts (e.g., Lego Mindstorms include smart bricks with both software and hardware to build customised robots), girl toys (Lego Friends), publishing, television and cinema (Ashcroft, 2014; Robertson & Breen, 2014). Lego also expanded to emerging countries where their growth was soaring.

5.3.5 COMMUNICATE YOUR THINKING

You have to communicate your thinking behind the choices you make. A set of limited choices that fit together - such as Lego's reengineering its operations and expanding their value proposition - is easy to communicate. Science tells us that while you might communicate 20 choices, employees and other stakeholders it is remember more than nine at best. The fewer the better. It is highly likely that Lego's engineers can tell people their company's new choices and take a stab at relaying the underlying strategic logic. Creating clarity like this more often than not establishes a genuinely shared purpose that employees buy into and which influences their commitment to their daily work.

5.3.6   THE IMPORTANCE OF STRATEGIC CONVERSATIONS

Vermulen (2017) notes that, like economics, successful strategy execution processes rarely work where they are a one-way 'trickle-down' cascade of decisions. He takes this further in citing Burgelman (1994, 2002), finding that while a clear, 'top-down' strategic direction is vital, but that will only be successful if, simultaneously, your employees are enabled to contribute to strategic intent through developing 'bottom-up' initiatives.

Burgelman's (1994, 2002) major work centred around a multi-year project tracking the strategic management of Andy Grove, the President of Intel. When it was still a company focused on producing memory chips, Intel's top-down strategy was clear: (1) to be on the forefront of (2) semiconductor technology and (3) to be aimed at the memory business (not coincidentally a set of three clear choices). Intel implemented this strategy by providing autonomy and decentralised budgets to its employees to experiment with initiatives that would bring this strategic intent to fruition.

Many of the experiments failed but others became successes. One of them formed the basis of the Pentium microprocessor, which turned Intel into one of most successful technology companies in world ever. It was the combination of a broad yet clear top-down strategic direction and ample bottom-up initiatives that enabled this.

Ertel and Solomon (2014) find that meetings and brainstorming sessions are conventional planning and strategy settings. However, they argue that meetings put people to sleep, and brainstorming is often ineffective. Strategic conversations ('interactive strategic problem-solving sessions') are an innovative means enabling:

- Leaders to better engage in complicated decision-making
- Entrepreneurs to work effectively with boards and investors
- Agents to facilitate social change, and
- Business-school faculty to engage effectively with their students.

It is a variant of the Socratic method (Tsoukas & Chia, 2002).

5.3.6.1   Messy, Open-Ended and Ill-Defined

Ertel and Solomon (2014) use the example of the fact-based film *Moneyball*. It stars Brad Pitt as Billy Beane, the major league Oakland

Athletics baseball team's general manager. His team is deeply troubled because its top three stars have moved to wealthier clubs. Frustrated, Beane sits in a conference room with his talent scouts, all old-school practitioners and conventional thinkers. They rehash traditional ideas about how to find new talent.

In a volatile, uncertain, complicated, ambiguous (VUCA) world, many leaders today are wary of conventional strategy tools built for tackling challenges occurring in more stable times.

Beane didn't want to have a conventional meeting. He tried to engage in an energetic, strategic conversation. Beane and his scouts seemed to focus on the same issue on the surface: figuring out how to put together a talented team. However, in reality, they did not. Beane recognised they faced an 'adaptive challenge', a messy, open-ended and ill-defined situation calling for creative, original problem-solving. He understood that to win, the team needed a new tactical course. Most conventional meetings fail to deliver the total engagement required to wrangle challenging issues. Instead, participants play out their established roles, multitasking on the side. What is needed is to accelerate leadership teams' abilities to generate new solutions and move them forward.

5.3.6.2   VUCA World

Adaptive challenges like Beane's are increasingly common in a VUCA environment. Such problems prove infinitely more difficult to solve than 'technical challenges', which experts can resolve a lot more efficiently by applying well-honed skills to well-defined problems. Adaptive challenges are ill-structured (Simon, 1973) and often 'wicked' (Rittel & Webber, 1973). In the VUCA world, resolving such challenges in organisations and society is a top priority for leaders.

The Athletics' baseball-talent scouts thought they were dealing with a conventional technical challenge. Beane knew they were not. He had the vision and clarity to see that the team faced, literally, a game-changing adaptive challenge. These messy, ambiguous and open-ended problems involve baffling circumstances in which it is difficult to ask the right question, let alone find a good answer.

5.3.6.3   Strategic Conversations

Ertel and Solomon (2014) find that conventional meetings or brainstorming sessions it is effectively address adaptive challenges. They contend that these gatherings are suitable for dealing with clear-cut technical challenges, but their format almost guarantees failure if they turn to more opaque, fluid or novel situations. For Ertel and Solomon (2014), strategic conversations (creative and collaborative problem-solving sessions) are the best way to find solutions to complex problems.

When you get the small stuff right, people notice it, often subconsciously, in a way that increases their engagement and confidence.

Strategic conversations with diverse participants nourish and inspire imaginative insights. Adequately framed and conducted, strategic conversations draw on participants' analytical skills, creativity and emotions. The goal of a strategic conversation is to arrive at "a true moment of impact...some deep alignment on important insights" (Ertel & Solomon, 2014). These moments lead to positive change (Heath & Heath, 2017).

5.3.6.4 Designing a Strategic Conversation

To plan strategic conversations, we need to think like a designer, not a mechanic. People who design and implement strategic conversations are "black belts … skilled masters" of an important craft (Ertel & Solomon, 2014). Ogilvie and Liedtka (2011) explain, "successful designers...are great conjurors". They have a "capacity for creative visualisation". Black belts can "conjure" a vision of the future that contains a solution to the problem at hand.

The best way to help people embrace any new idea is to give them a visceral experience of a future possibility. That's what creates a moment of impact (Ertel & Solomon, 2014; Heath & Heath, 2017).

As they design strategic conversations, black belts develop an understanding of "users and their needs" (Ertel & Solomon, 2014). They segue through different ideas, investigate inspirational sources, quickly make prototypes of possible solutions, adapt these solutions by incorporating feedback from the marketplace, test the solutions with small user groups, and scale up the best ideas (Brown, 2009; Ogilvie & Liedtka, 2011).

Dealing with adaptive challenges requires a high tolerance for ambiguity. But many leaders and managers...are impatient with ambiguity. Design strategic conversations using five core principles, each of which is based on three key practices (Ertel & Solomon, 2014).

Principle 1: Define the Purpose

Strategic conversations require total clarity about the desired change. Organise and lead multiple sessions to define your purpose, using these practices:

- Seize your moment. Step out of your comfort zone and aim for creative problem solving along "an arc of divergence and convergence" (Ertel & Solomon, 2014). Adopt a wide perspective and narrow it down to a few viable solutions. Repeat this process through "several diverge-converge cycles" (Ertel & Solomon, 2014). Your team's moments of impact will move the process forward productively through each step.

- Pick one purpose. Focus individual sessions on one of three different objectives: First, work on "building understanding" (Ertel & Solomon, 2014). You may not know what your organisation faces, or everyone may have a different opinion. Then start "shaping choices" (Ertel & Solomon, 2014). Begin with a number of likely ideas and slowly hone them down. "Making decisions" (Ertel & Solomon, 2014) can be the most difficult step or the simplest. Trust where the process takes you.

- Go slow to go fast. When organisations face an adaptive challenge, they tend to reach for solutions too quickly. Your team needs time to sift through an issue's complexity. Never rush this process. Black-belt practitioners advise creating "a container for the uncertainty" (Ertel & Solomon, 2014). Give your team time and space to achieve "deep alignment on important insights" (Ertel & Solomon, 2014). Then act quickly.

Principle 2: Engage Multiple Perspectives

Find value from a combination of different perspectives. Strive to understand and clarify the opinions and views of all the participants in your strategic conversation and all relevant stakeholders, using these practices:

- Assemble a dream team. Find people with different areas of expertise who have some familiarity with each other. Do not be afraid to include outsiders.

- Create a common platform. Look for shared objectives, group identity, agreement on the nature of the challenge and its defining terms, a feeling of urgency, a combined information base, willingness to confront tough problems and "common frames" (Ertel & Solomon, 2014) through which to view the issues.
- Ignite a controlled burn. Writing on "technical and adaptive challenges, Heifetz and Laurie (2012) call this step "orchestrating the conflict". Your dream-team members have diverse opinions, so focus on "assumptions, not conclusions" and be willing to suggest and honour difficult trade-offs.

Principle 3: Frame the Issues

The frameworks you use to conceptualise your adaptive challenges will shape your discussion and affect your success or failure. "Having a strategic conversation without a strong frame or two is like trying to do a jigsaw puzzle without the picture on the box" (Ertel & Solomon, 2014) but the right framing enables your group to develop insights that "stick". To succeed, follow these practices:

- Stretch (do not break) mind-sets. Understand and adjust your conversational style, pace and rhythm to fit your participants' current mental models.
- Think inside different boxes. 'Thinking outside the box' is a cliché. Instead, help your strategic-conversation participants view solutions through different lenses (boxes).
- Choose a few key frames. Having too many frames (e.g., questions, catchphrases and metaphors, visual frameworks and stories) confuses the issue. Set up three or fewer.

Principle 4: Set the Scene

Consider every aspect of the venue where your strategic conversation group will meet. This includes the physical space and items in the room (artefacts) and how the design and feel of the room (aesthetics) might affect what goes on in it. Follow these practices:

- Make your space. Most meeting rooms are "mediocre or terrible" (Ertel & Solomon, 2014). Look for rooms that are light, open and comfortable. Avoid cramped or cavernous spaces. Ask, "where and how can we create the best environment for creative collaboration?" (Ertel & Solomon, 2014) Make any necessary changes to your room to suit your group.

- Get visual. Medina (2014) explains, "text and oral presentations are not just less efficient than pictures for retaining certain types of information – they are way less efficient."

- Do sweat the small stuff. Steve Jobs understood that "Details matter, it is worth waiting to get it right". What is the temperature? Are the chairs comfortable? Can everyone in the room hear everyone else? Is the necessary technology on hand? Review your space and solve every likely problem before your group meets.

Principle 5: Make It an Experience

Do not be a party to run-of-the-mill meetings. Organise your sessions to be "exhilarating and memorable" (Ertel & Solomon, 2014). Be sure to:

- Discover, do not tell. Too many meetings involve "sages on...stage". Experts' lectures are terrible learning experiences. Offer a "bit of guidance" that enables your strategic-conversation participants to "discover key insights...for themselves."

- Engage the whole person. Intellectual analysis and gut instinct can work together.

- Create a narrative arc. When you plan a strategic conversation, think like a screenwriter and develop an emotionally engaging story line for your sessions.

5.3.6.5 Confronting the 'Yabbuts'

Larry Keeley developed the term "yabbuts" for those who say, "Yeah, sure this all sounds good – but here is why this would never work in my organisation" (Keeley et al., 2013). Yabbuts can quickly undermine the good work of strategic-conversation sessions, resulting in inglorious "moments of nonimpact." Keep the yabbuts out and hold their undermining negativity to a minimum.

Yabbuts take one of three forms:

- Politics. Shakespeare, Greek drama and Machiavelli all make it clear that certain people will always strive for political control of any group. Politics are inevitable. Steer towards good politics, not destructive ones.

- Near-termism. Naysayers focus on the immediate and do not consider the long-term.
- The karaoke curse. Executives who are proficient at "presenting, group facilitation" and "collaboration skills" are not necessarily sound strategic thinkers.

5.3.6.6 Make Your Moment.

To plan, organise and implement the best strategic conversation sessions, follow these tips:

- Start with a 'ripe' issue. Deal with urgent situations calmly. Hold off discussing situations that are "too distant or too immediate."
- Fight for the time to do it right. Never rush a thoughtful, necessary conversation. Set no deadlines and let the process itself take the reins.
- Lead with empathy. Gather the "points of view" of all participants prior to any meeting or discussion. Stay open and empathetic to everyone's thoughts and opinions.
- Put all the core principles to work. Utilise all five core principles; this method won't work if you try shortcuts.
- Simplify, simplify, simplify. Do not bring in additional people or extra topics. Stick to your core groups and only the most important points.
- Start small, then build. Since you will be learning as you go, start with the least confusing, least important situations and build to those that are more complex.
- Prep like hell – and then let go. Black belts prepare with care and in depth. This helps them deal with unforeseen events.
- No kamikaze missions. Avoid strategic conversations in which the yabbuts call the shots. You won't accomplish anything, and you will discredit the process.

5.3.7 LET THE PEOPLE SPEAK

It is common for executive managers to select from initiatives proposed by employees, picking the ones they like best. This is not 'bottom-up' execution. Better to design a process that does the selection for you, through some form of objective formula.

Many years ago, at a British life assurance company, Clive's colleagues were supposedly empowered to put forward changes to systems to improve efficiency. Executive management 'swooped' in and 'picked the winners'. All of the projects failed.

5.4 STRATEGY AND ORGANISATIONAL TRANSFORMATION

5.4.1 WHY YOU NEED AN ORGANISATIONAL TRANSFORMATION STRATEGY

Developing an organisational transformation strategy identifies purpose and specifies direction and for all other change management activities. Outlining the characteristics of the change, and identifying its risks and potential resistance, transformational leaders set themselves and their project team up for success.

'One-size-fits-all' generally does not work for organisational transformation. Consider the following projects:

- Executive leadership changes.
- Leasing or building new office accommodation and relocating to it.
- Restructuring a business unit.
- Responding to regulatory action.
- Migrating legacy information systems to new information systems.

These should all be familiar transformational projects; we have usually seen or experienced one or more of them if we have any experience in business life. The only commonalities are that they are all transformational, require effective leadership to be successful, impact people and how they work. Each has risks associated with people not engaging in the required transformation activities or resisting change, and each might be struck by low utilisation and slow adoption.

Each requires transformational leadership, but the approach and amount will differ in each case. Transformational strategies build on the unique properties of a given project to define the approach needed to lead the transformation.

5.4.2 THE SECRET OF TRANSFORMATIONS: THE ELEMENTS OF EXCELLENCE

First published in 1982, *In Search of Excellence* (Peters & Waterman, 2004) reports the results of research conducted between 1979 to 1980. The project investigated the qualities common to the best-run companies in the USA. The study closely examined the practices of 43 companies from six major industries. Nearly 40 years, some of the exemplars no longer exist, but the results provide a model of eight core principles for excellence that still hold for companies today. The secret of transformations is to seek excellence in each of the eight principles. These eight principles may seem like common sense, but this research was the first to identify these qualities systematically.

5.4.2.1 McKinsey's 7-S Framework

The study began when American business was under tremendous competitive pressure due to growing global competition, mainly from Japan. Peters and Waterman (2004) wanted to find out what made excellent American companies so very good, to provide guidance other companies could utilise. They began the project by examining seven key variables. They turned these into a matrix with shared values at the centre and the other principles around it. Hence, they created McKinsey's '7-S Framework', translated into a series of terms beginning with the letter S (Figure 6).

Using this model, Peters and Waterman (2004) selected their corporate models of excellence, starting with 75 companies, eventually winnowed down to 43. They began with a list of companies that businesspeople, consultants, business journalists and academics in the business field considered to be innovative and excellent in six key industries. Then, they established specific minimum criteria of excellence:

- The company showed growth over 20 years.
- The company was currently in good economic health.
- The company had a record of innovation in bringing out new products and services.
- The company was able to respond rapidly and effectively to changing markets and environmental conditions.

Figure 6: McKinsey 7S framework

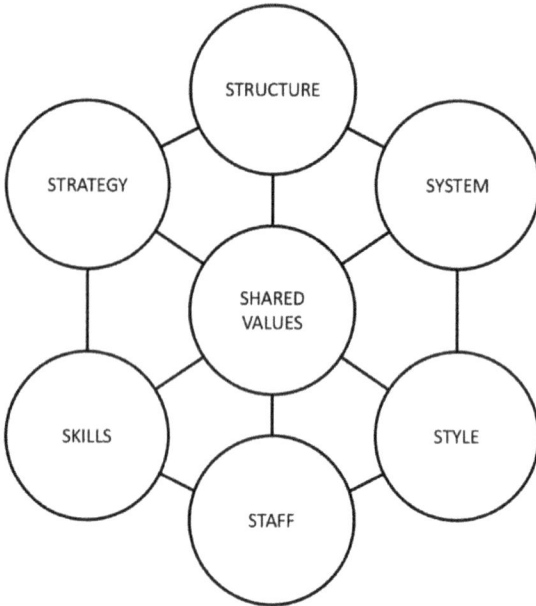

Ultimately, they ended up with the 43 companies. Some of them are still well-known 20 years later: Hewlett-Packard, Intel, Procter & Gamble, Johnson & Johnson, Caterpillar, 3M, Marriott, McDonald's, Disney, Boeing, Bechtel, Exxon and Du Pont.

5.4.2.2 Emphasise the "Messy Human Stuff"

The excellent companies demonstrated one fundamental discovery: good management does not conform to the traditional principle of "hard-headed rationality". Such principles dominate the teaching of business in business schools. They prioritise finding "detached, analytical justification for all decisions". However, while excellent companies are good at getting the numbers, analysing them and using them to solve problems, they also emphasise the importance of "soft" qualities. These include devotion to customers and making employees feel like winners. They make a place for commonly derided "messy human stuff". These companies understand that people aren't always rational and that feelings motivate employees and customers. In fact, the eight principles of good management in excellent companies are all about people.

Of people working in 'normal' companies, Peters and Waterman (2004) observe: "We all think we're tops. We are exuberantly, wildly irrational about ourselves. And that has sweeping implications for organising. Yet most organisations, we find, take a negative view of their people".

Some fundamental realisations about using rationality and intuition underlie these principles. Rationality may "drive the engine of business", but it has some shortcomings if you rely on it too much. These potential pitfalls include:

- An overly negative and judgmental mindset
- Resistance to experimentation and making mistakes
- Support for complexity and inflexibility
- Discouragement of informality
- Denigration of the importance of values.

By contrast, the underlying motivators that inspire managers, employees and customers arise from nonrational, right-brain qualities. For instance, people like to think of themselves as winners, even if they aren't as good as they think. Many companies celebrate winning with awards, hoopla and other methods.

People find it easier to learn with simple systems and procedures. Hence, you should have only a few objectives or guidelines instead of an extensive list. Positive reinforcement works better to encourage people than negative reinforcement. The eight principles that characterise excellent companies are optimistic, people-oriented reinforcers that come from a more right-brain, intuitive approach to business management.

First Principle: "A Bias for Action"

Excellent companies have a bias for action. They are ready to respond quickly, efficiently and effectively. They use short-term task forces composed of small groups of people who take action after a few days, sharply contrasted with a large group labouring for several months to produce a report recommending action. Such small task groups often cut across traditional structural barriers in the company. They assemble in response to a particular project and draw on their members' essential skills.

The most discouraging fact of big corporate life is the loss of what got them big in the first place: innovation.

Some companies, such as Walt Disney, encourage communication by having a "first name" policy. Others, such as IBM and Delta Airlines, have an "open door" policy. The technique called "chunking" also promotes this action orientation. "Chunking" involves "breaking things up" to make the organisation more fluid and encourage action. Chunking can take various forms: creating teams or task forces, organising quality circles, establishing project centres and setting up "skunk works" secret innovating areas (Rich, 1996). It involves using the small action group as a building block within the organisation. These groups usually organise and follow up quickly and do not have to supply much documentation. "The small group is the most visible of the chunking devices. Small groups are, quite simply, the basic organisational building blocks of excellent companies" (Peters & Waterman, 2004).

Excellent companies' willingness to experiment also promotes action. They are willing to take chances on new projects and make mistakes. A kind of playfulness is associated with this experimentation. For example, at Hewlett-Packard, product-design engineers leave prototypes of the new products they are developing out on their desks so anyone can try them. If these experiments do not work, the companies are quick to end the development. The process works a little like playing good poker: You know when to "hold 'em and when to fold 'em". Companies further develop working innovations, as happened with many GE breakthroughs in new plastics and aircraft engines. Simplifying systems creates clarity and encourage this bias to action. Such simplification includes reducing action plans to only a few objectives or milestones and keeping memos short (one or two pages, at most).

Second Principle: "Close to the Customer"

> *"Despite all the lip service given to the market orientation these days, the customer is either ignored or considered a bloody nuisance."*

Peters and Waterman (2004)

Excellent companies follow a second central principle: They are "close to the customer". They are obsessed with giving the customer quality, reliability and service. They are "more driven by their direct orientation to their customers than by technology or by a desire to be the low-cost producer" (Peters & Waterman, 2004). For example, IBM became the market leader in its field because of its commitment to service, not just because of its technology.

Sometimes a commitment to service means taking actions that do not seem to make economic sense in the short run. However, in the long run, this service pays off in customer loyalty. For example, Frito sometimes spent several hundred dollars to send a truck to restock a store that needed just a few cartons of potato chips. Sometimes its salespeople helped clean up a store after an accident or hurricane. Their acts of going the extra mile for the customer contributed to the company's success.

These organisations also impress upon all their employees the importance of putting the customer's interests first. They train their employees to develop this orientation. Such customer focus means that the companies are concerned about providing quality and reliability. Some examples of customer focus include McDonald's fanaticism about cleanliness, HP's concern with meeting "quality objectives" in its "Management by Objectives" program, and Digital's emphasis on providing reliability, even if this meant lagging behind the 'state of the art'.

Nothing is wrong with financial measures, mind you. Can't live without them. But they are far from the whole picture.

For many companies, this emphasis on serving the customer has also meant finding a niche where the firm can be the best at something, such as "astute technology manipulation, pricing skill, better segmenting, a problem-solving orientation and a willingness to spend in order to discriminate" (Peters & Waterman, 2004). Cost and technology generally do not drive excellent companies. Instead, these companies are quality-driven, impelled by service, reliability or high-value-added "nichemanship" (Peters & Waterman, 2004). Being close to the customer means having deep listening skills (Trimboli, 2017) and hearing what the users of their products or services want. In this way, input from customers leads to innovation and future developments, so that "most of their real innovation comes from the market" (Peters & Waterman, 2004).

Third Principle: Autonomy and Entrepreneurship

To build autonomy and entrepreneurship, excellent companies encourage employees to become champions of innovation. They actively encourage researchers to explore. They want their brand managers to promote the development of new and promising ideas. These companies recognise and reward champions at different levels. For instance, a company might acknowledge a product champion who is often a loner but believes in a specific product. Excellent companies recognise that these champions are pioneers; therefore, they provide a support system to help champions flourish, such as a skunkworks or team of innovators.

Additionally, these companies tolerate failure. They recognise that experiments do not always work and that "champions have to make a lot of tries and consequently suffer some failures" (Peters & Waterman, 2004). For example, 3M used this approach to develop more than 50,000 products and bring out more than 100 significant new product offerings each year.

Fourth Principle: Productivity Through People

Excellent companies respect the individual, including

- Providing good training
- Setting reasonable and clear expectations
- Giving the individual "practical autonomy" to take the initiative and contribute to their job (Peters & Waterman, 2004).

Different companies express this people orientation in various ways. Delta promotes a "family feeling." HP believes in "managing by wandering around" (Peters & Waterman, 2004). They both create a suitable environment in which employees can flourish. This approach may sometimes lead to celebration and hoopla, but this kind of corporate 'razzle-dazzle' works. It keeps people feeling good and motivated (Walsh, 2009).

Fifth Principle: Hands-On, Value-Driven

> *"We wonder whether it is possible to be an excellent company without clarity on values and without having the right sort of values."*

> Peters and Waterman (2004)

Excellent companies are hands-on, and value driven. They are clear about what they stand for, and they take the process of shaping values seriously. They have a "well-defined set of guiding beliefs", and they want their employees to embrace these values. These companies weave assorted stories, legends, and myths that support their values into their organisational culture (Deal & Kennedy, 1982). However, they limit the specific content of these prevailing beliefs to just a few fundamental values.

Sixth Principle: Stick to the Knitting

Excellent companies stick to the knitting, which means they focus on a core business in which they excel. For example, 3M focuses on products that employ its coating and bonding technology and aligns itself with companies that branch out in related fields. By contrast, companies that diversify into a wide variety of fields tend to be less successful. Research confirms that organisations that stick close to their primary skill perform better than others (Prahalad & Hamel, 1990; Rumelt, 1974).

Seventh Principle: Simple Form, Lean Staff

Along with size comes complexity, unfortunately. And most big companies respond to complexity in kind by designing complex systems and structures.

Excellent companies follow the principle of "simple form, lean staff" (Peters & Waterman, 2004). They try to keep their rules and procedures simple. They have as few layers of management as possible. This simplicity gives them the ability to be more flexible in reacting to rapidly changing conditions.

Eighth Principle: Simultaneous Loose-Tight Properties

Initially, excellent companies embrace a combination of central direction with individual freedom. They have rigid controls in place, but they are flexible and open to change. The essence of this principle is that the company permits the "coexistence of firm central direction and maximum individual autonomy" (Peters & Waterman, 2004).

5.5 QUESTIONS

1. Think about what Pinker (2019) says. Bear in mind it was written in 2019. Think about recent and current events. Is the world getting better or worse?
2. Can you think of an example is your business or another where strategy has failed due to communication? What do you think were the main causes of communication failure?

6. DESIGNING STRATEGY

"Perception is strong and sight weak. In strategy it is important to see distant things as if they were close and to take a distanced view of close things."

Miyamoto Musashi

6.1 CHAPTER OUTLINE

This chapter explores how strategy is determined, evaluated and chosen.

The key concepts we explore are environmental analysis, internal appraisal, generic strategies, strategic evaluation and strategic choice.

On completing this chapter, you should be able to:

1. Determine a strategy for an organisation.
2. Evaluate strategic options.
3. Make strategy proposal.

6.2 DETERMINING STRATEGY

The route to Strategy Determination can be envisaged as a 7-Step Process (Figure 7).

Figure 7: Strategy determination

6.2.1   STAGE 1: STRATEGIC REVIEW FRAMEWORK

There are three steps in strategic review (Figure 8).

Figure 8: Strategic review

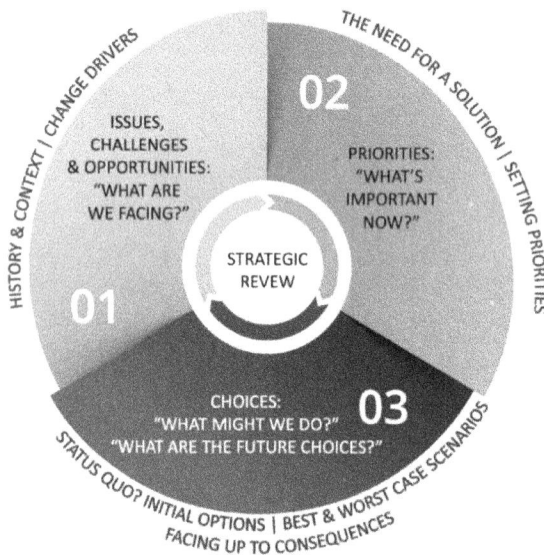

6.2.1.1   Issues, Challenges and Opportunities

Issues challenges and opportunities come from external and internal sources. They may be identified through regular strategic review processes, quality assurance initiatives. They might emerge when you identify a new market opportunity or as one such presents itself. Not uncommonly issues and challenges emerge as the result of production or service failures, accidents, public health incidents or natural disasters. In other words, there is a rich range of reasons why we might review strategy.

In this lesson, we are going to take the perspective of conventional 'Design School' strategy (Figure 9), which we identified in Chapter 1 as the dominant model for strategic thinking (Christensen et al., 1978; Luffman et al., 1991). We'll come back to how this is handled in the Blue Ocean Strategy (Kim & Mauborgne, 2005a) paradigm later in this chapter, and again later in this book.

We are going to take look at five pieces of analysis that form the foundation for strategy design: PEST analysis; industry and market analysis; internal appraisal; financial appraisal; and SWOT analysis (Luffman et al., 1991).

Figure 9: Design School strategy process

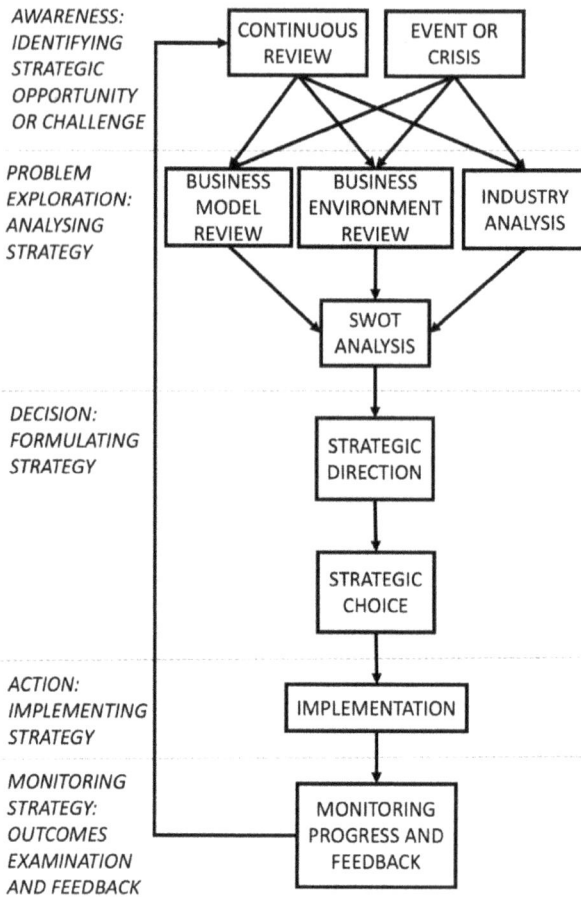

AWARENESS: IDENTIFYING STRATEGIC OPPORTUNITY OR CHALLENGE

CONTINUOUS REVIEW

EVENT OR CRISIS

PROBLEM EXPLORATION: ANALYSING STRATEGY

BUSINESS MODEL REVIEW

BUSINESS ENVIRONMENT REVIEW

INDUSTRY ANALYSIS

SWOT ANALYSIS

DECISION: FORMULATING STRATEGY

STRATEGIC DIRECTION

STRATEGIC CHOICE

ACTION: IMPLEMENTING STRATEGY

IMPLEMENTATION

MONITORING STRATEGY: OUTCOMES EXAMINATION AND FEEDBACK

MONITORING PROGRESS AND FEEDBACK

What are We Facing? Business Environment Analysis

Let's first deal with understanding change drivers from the external context, before turning to internal factors.

For some companies, the environment is more turbulent than for others. And some, such as coal mining or gas fracking companies may find themselves in a situation where everything appears hostile. For example, tobacco is a product in long term decline due to health factors, government action on cigarette packaging, taxation advertising, and increasing social disapproval.

So, it is essential to have means of screening the context surrounding a company that changes while you are operating in it, and the consequential opportunities and threats posed to the company. Where these risks are in the future, then it is a form of forecasting. However, it is often the case that it is sufficient to gather together and analyse the trends already apparent within the environment. We can use this framework to prepare an overview of the factors influencing the company at the time, the changes currently underway (trends), and the potential implications of these. Figure 10 distinguishes between those environments in which a company has some discretion and where it has little. The symbolism of the yin and yang is deliberately chosen. It describes the dualism inherent in the business environment. It captures how seemingly opposite or contrary forces may actually be complementary, interconnected, and interdependent in the world, and how they may give rise to each other as they interrelate to one another.

Political, Economic, Science and Technological (PEST) Environment Analysis

We analyse the given environment through what is commonly called PEST analysis, which is essentially a series of questions about the given environment that we are operating in:

- What impacts are development in the *political environment* going to have on the organisation?
    - What trading policies impact business?
    - What regulations must you follow, and have they changed in the last 5, 10, 20 years?
    - What environmental or public health issues, if any, should be addressed (i.e., eco-friendly resources/products, natural disasters, etc)?
- What is the impact of globalisation, taxes, and the current state of the *economy*?
    - How much does globalisation affect your market share?
    - What taxes must you follow, and how does it affect your service offerings (if at all)?
    - Is the economy stable, unstable, or growing for your industry?

Figure 10: Organisational environment

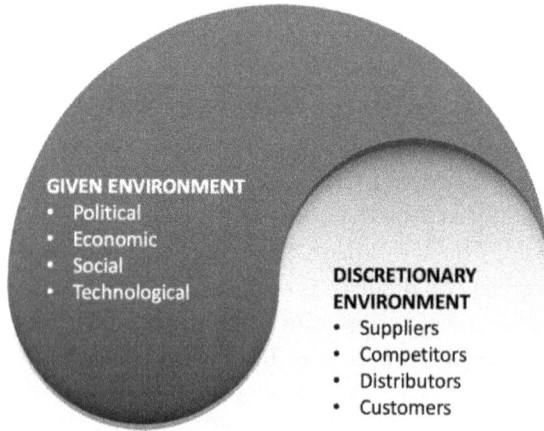

- *Social factors* are determined by people. You should consider how your customers, target market, and buying habits affect profits and purchases.
    - ○ Who is your target market?
    - ○ How are consumer opinions changing regarding your product or service?
    - ○ Is the population demographic growing or slowing down and if so, how is it affecting your business?
    - ○ Have you documented changes in how and when your customers purchase your products?
- *Technological* questions focus on technology related to your business, such as the technology you use daily, and how advancements provide a competitive edge. You also need to think about how technology is disrupting or might disrupt your business.
    - ○ What technology is critical for your day-to-day operations?
    - ○ What new technology is available that could streamline decision-making and product development?
    - ○ Do you depend on 3rd parties for any tech support or solutions?

o Are you using technology to stay ahead of the competition and if so, how?

This is the classical form of PEST analysis. It has become common to extend these questions to include response on factors in the natural environment. These will vary considerably on the type of business you are analysing. In this analysis these issues are covered by questions about the economic environment.

Industry and Competition Analysis

The second phase of environment analysis is industry and competition analysis, looking at the forces that drive industry and competition. This based on Porter's (1980) classic text, *Competitive Strategy: Techniques for Analysing Industries and Competitors*. Porter identifies 'five forces' the influence competition (Figure 11).

Figure 11: Five forces affecting industry competition

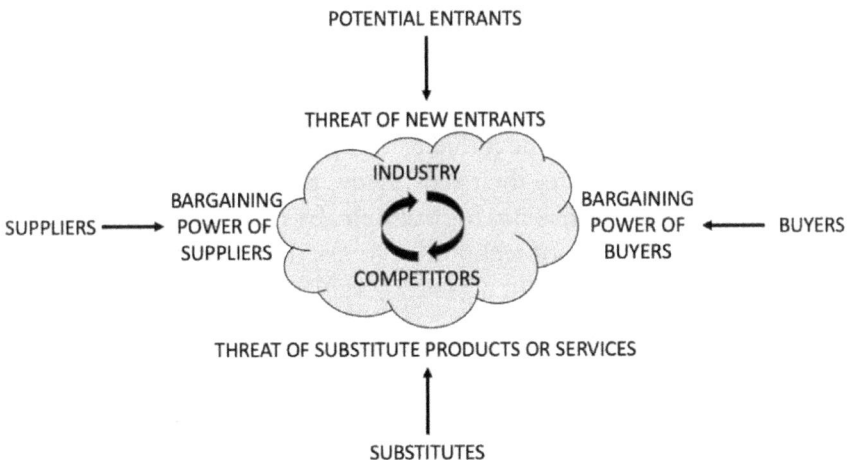

Again, it is a matter of asking questions:

1. Industry competitors
   a. How many competitors are there?
   b. What's their approx. market share?
   c. What size are they? Are they part of a larger group?
   d. Where are we and our competitors on the learning curve?
   e. Where is the product or service on the life cycle?

      f.   What changes are taking place in the competitive environment and what are the implications of these changes?

2. Suppliers
    a.   Is entry to the market likely to come from our suppliers?
    b.   How much power do they have over our supply chain?
    c.   Buyers:
    d.   Is entry to the market likely to come from our buyers?
    e.   What is the loyalty of our buyers like?

3. Potential entrants
    a.   Are there any entry barriers?
    b.   Are companies currently not making the product or supplying the service likely to enter the market?

4. Potential substitutes
    a.   How closely substitutable are competitors' products or services?
    b.   Are technological or other changes likely to generate a substitute product?

Outside of the detailed analysis, it is important to recognise that the given environment cannot be influenced directly through planning. Still, organisations can alter their sensitivities to their context through their strategic decision making, for example, by choice of country to manufacturing and types of technology to use. However, once we make choices, the new environment acts as a given in the planning process for the organisation.

Prioritising Issues

The task of environmental scanning is twofold. First is to isolate those contextual variables to which the organisation is sensitive. And second, to collect data to understand the trends in the selected variables. There is not, unfortunately, an effortless way of accomplishing the first task. It is mostly a matter of learning by examining the effects of the environment on objectives over time.

Mostly it is a process of prioritising environmental variables in terms of the likelihood of certain things happening, and their consequent effect upon organisation. Figure 12 shows how you might go about making that sort of assessment: an issues priority matrix (or risk management matrix). You can see that you consider the likelihood of an occurrence and its probable impact. And this gives you some idea of where your priorities might lie.

Figure 12: Issues priority matrix

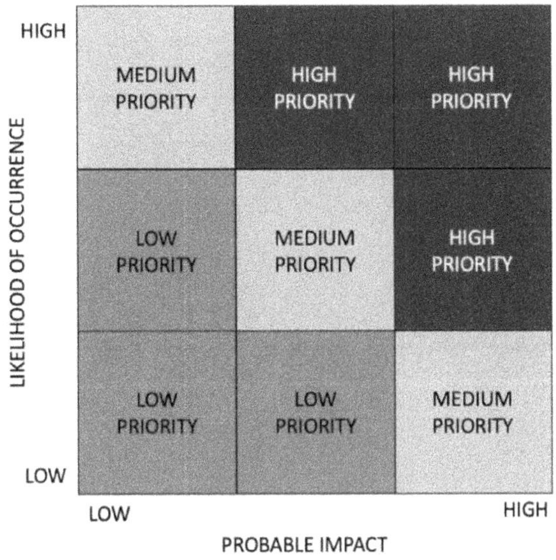

6.2.1.2 Internal Appraisal

The next step in understand the issues, challenges and opportunities facing your organisation is to look at what's going on inside the business itself. This is sometimes called value chain analysis, based on Porter's (1985, pp. 33-61) model from *Competitive Advantage: Creating and Sustaining Superior Performance* (Figure 13).

Based around this model, once again, analysis consists of answering a series of questions:

1. Strategic objectives
    a. Are the objectives specific, measurable, achievable, realistic and time bound, and capable of communication easily within the organisation?
    b. Are there operational objectives that are consistent with overall strategi objectives?
    c. Will the objectives satisfy owners and leaders?

Figure 13: The generic value chain

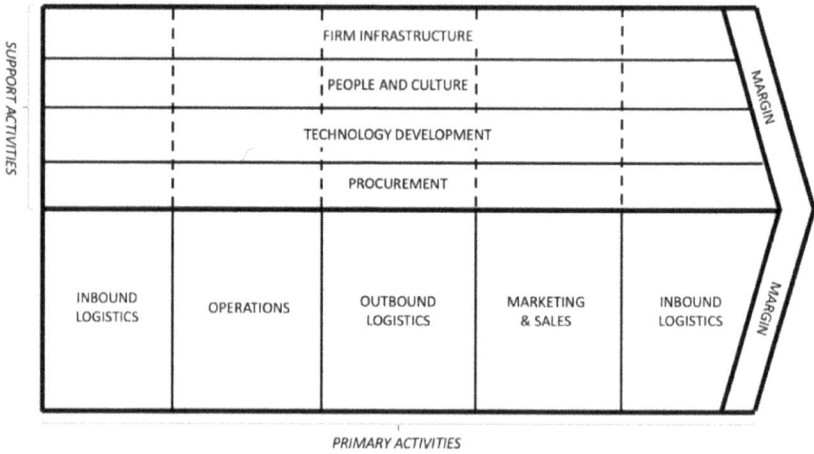

2. Strategy
   a. Is the strategy consistent with objectives and the resource capabilities of the organisation?
   b. Does it build directly on strengths?
   c. Does the strategy realise synergy within the organisation?
   d. Is the strategy appropriate for the organisation's environment?
3. Structure, systems and procedures
   a. Is the organisational structure consistent with the declared strategy?
   b. Are the systems and procedures providing the means by which strategy can be implemented?
4. Finance
   a. Has the company sufficient financial resources to fund its strategy?
   b. Is the mix of funding flexible?
   c. How low, is the cost of capital?
   d. Can the company raise new capital?
   e. How effective is financial planning and control?
5. Marketing
   a. How efficient and effective are the component parts of the marketing mix (product, price, place, promotion)?

b. How strong in terms of market share, is the company in the market served?
c. How effective is product development?
d. How good is the company at market research and identifying trends and gaps in the market?
e. What is the relationship between turnover and profits?
f. What is the relationship between profits, and the customer base?

6. Operations[6]
a. How does the company compare in terms of product production cost?
b. How does the company compare in terms of production quality?
c. How up to date is the production technology?
d. How effective are the production systems for maintenance quality control production scheduling and stock control?
e. How easily can new products be assimilated into production?
f. How near to full capacity utilisation is the company
g. How flexible is the plant?
h. Are we producing in the right location is purchasing taking advantage of bulk discounts?
i. Is there a major sourcing problem with scarce raw materials?

7. Research and development
a. How technologically competent, are the staff?
b. How good are the laboratories and equipment?
c. How market orientated is R&D?
d. How much is spent on R&D?

8. People and culture
a. Is the recruitment policy developing the number and quality of people required to implement strategy?
b. Is the training policy developing the necessary new skills and improving existing competence?

---

[6] Remember to substitute equal questions for service organisations over production organisations.

c. Are the leadership and management development programmes, providing the quality of leadership and management necessary to implement the corporate strategy?

6.2.1.3 Pulling the Review Together: Strengths, Weaknesses, Opportunities and Threats (SWOT) Analysis

Once the three pieces of analysis are complete, we summarise the organisations strengths, weaknesses, opportunities and threats in a SWOT analysis framework.

There are four questions to ask:

1. Looking at your internal analysis, what stand out to you as strengths of your organisation?
2. Looking at your internal analysis, what stand out to you as weaknesses of your organisation?
3. Looking at your PEST analysis and Industry Competition analysis, what stand out to you as opportunities to your organisation?
4. Looking at your PEST analysis and Industry Competition analysis, what stand out to you as threats to your organisation?

6.2.1.4 Linking with Strategic Intent: Strategic Alignment

Once we have candidate strategies, we need to think about how they link with our overall strategic intent.

We need to think about whether their strategically logical, i.e., do they 'fit'. There is also the question of whether or not they fit with the resources available to us and with the economics of the business sector we are in. What constraints are we operating under? Can we ease them?

We also need to think about the scope of the proposed strategies and the value chain activities involved.

Do they fit with our core values, our vision and our mission, as well as our exiting strategies?

What we are focusing on here is termed strategic alignment, which ensures an organisation's structure, use of resources, and culture support its strategy (Miles & Snow, 1978, 1994). Awareness of the wider environment, regulation and technological change further promote successful outcomes (Miles & Snow, 1994).

Strategic alignment contributes to improved performance by optimising operations and the activities of teams and departments (Miles & Snow, 1994). Clear, measurable operational objectives linked to superordinate goals help ensure effective resource utilisation (Locke & Latham, 1990; Stajkovic et al., 2006).

The concept is also significant in coordinating activities across regions and time zones in the global business environment. Strategic alignment encompasses technical and functional routines and issues relating to human resource management and how best to develop people's motivation and capability. The process may extend across organisations that share complementary objectives, e.g., business partners.

Creating operational alignment involves translating an organisation's superordinate goals and overall strategy into the more immediate objectives of a team or department (Peters & Waterman, 2004; Waterman et al., 1980). As well as reviewing processes and systems, leaders must develop the skills, competencies and motivation of people in the organisation.

The following questions prompt reflection on strategic alignment (Trevor & Varcoe, 2016):

- How well does your business strategy support the fulfilment of your company's purpose?
- How well does your organisation support the achievement of your business strategy?

6.2.2 STRATEGIC POSSIBILITIES

Lafley et al. (2012) find that the ultimate creative act in business is constructing strategic possibilities, especially ones that are genuinely unique. You need a clear idea of what constitutes a possibility to generate wildly creative options. A grounded, imaginative team is a further requirement as is robust process for managing debate. Let's follow Lafley et al's (2012) thinking.

6.2.2.1 Possibilities

In essence, a possibility is an uplifting story describing how a firm might achieve success. Each story lays out the company's value proposition in its market and how it wins. It should feel internally consistent but strong evidence is not required yet. As long as it is plausible, it makes the cut. Characterising possibilities as stories without an evidentiary base helps people discuss viable options that do not yet exist. It is easier to tell a story about why a possibility could make sense than to provide data on the probability of its success (Lafley et al., 2012).

It is tempting is to outline high level caricatures of possibilities only. However, advertising straplines ("Go global") or a goal ("Be number one") do not constitute strategic possibilities. Teams should be pushed for detailed specifications of the competitive advantage they aim to target or leverage, the market scope of the possibility and the business model elements that would deliver value innovation across the target scope. Otherwise, it is impossible to unpack the possibility's underlying logic and subject it market testing (Lafley et al., 2012).

"How many possibilities should we generate?" is a common and understandable question; the context determines the answer varies. In industries where there are few good alternatives, concomitantly there are few uplifting stories. Others have many potential directions, notably those whose context is volatile, uncertain, complex or ambiguous, or who enjoy multiple customer segments (Lafley et al., 2012).

In practise it is best to develop between three and five in-depth possibilities. For sure it has to be more than one! Otherwise, the strategy-making process will not start, because the team does not see the company facing a choice. Further, analysing a single possibility is unlikely to encourage a bias for action or, for that matter, any action at all (Lafley et al., 2012).

It is important that the *status quo* or current trajectory is among the possibilities examined. In the later stages of the process, this requires the team to identify what must be true for a viable *status quo*; this eliminates the common implicit assumption that "in the worst case, we can just keep doing what we're already doing." On occasion, the *status quo* is a route to decline. Considering it among the set of possibilities renders it subject to investigation and question (Lafley et al., 2012).

6.2.2.2 The People

Any group required to create strategic possibilities should demonstrate diverse specialties, backgrounds and experience. Otherwise, generating creative possibilities and developing each one in sufficient detail is difficult. It pragmatic to include people who did not create the *status quo*, without emotional ties to it. This encourages the participation of emerging leaders. It is also true that individuals from outside the firm, or better yet the industry, often offer up the most original ideas. It is essential to include operations managers in the process. This deepens practical wisdom and builds early commitment to and knowledge of the future strategy. Companies where the strategic planners are different from those who execute strategy, rarely follow what was planned (Lafley et al., 2012).

Optimal group size varies by organisation and culture. Inclusive companies should assemble a large group. In such cases it is essential to use breakout groups to discuss the specific possibilities; a group of more than eight or 10 tends to be self-censoring (Lafley et al., 2012).

It is rarely a good idea to have the organisation's CEO or similar serve as the leader; they are unlikely to be able to convince others that they are not playing their usual role. It is better to choose a respected lower-level insider not perceived as having a strong point of view on future direction. Better yet is to engage an outside facilitator who has some experience with the firm or industry (Lafley et al., 2012).

6.2.2.3 The Rules

Once selected, the team must commit to separating their first step, the creation of possibilities, from the subsequent steps of testing and selecting. It is natural for some managers to be cynical, discounting each new idea by a long list of reasons why it will not work. The leader must constantly remind the group that for now, it must suspend judgment. Creation should be free-form and generous. Anyone persisting with negative critique, should be required to reframe it as a condition, tabled for discussion in the next step. It is essential that possibilities are not dismissed too early. If that happens, this encourages the easy dismissal to too many possibilities. Further pre-emptively removing an option to which a particular team member is strongly attached will discourage their commitment to the process (Lafley et al., 2012).

It is common for teams to attempt to generate strategic possibilities in a single off-site brainstorming session. Such sessions are useful, especially if they are held in an offsite location that breaks people's accustomed routines and habits. However, equally, teams can benefit from spreading the possibility-generation process over time. An elongated approach enables individuals to reflect, think creatively, and build ideas. An effective technique is to ask each team member to take 30 to 45 minutes, sketching out three to five, or more, stories. The stories should truly be sketches, without detail. After this the group (or breakout groups) fleshes out the initial possibilities (Lafley et al., 2012).

Possibility generation focuses on creativity, potentially supported by many techniques. For example, three kinds of probing questions are especially useful:

> *"Inside-out questions start with the company's assets and capabilities and then reason outward: What does this company do especially well that parts of the market might value and that might produce a superior wedge between buyer value and costs? Outside-in questions look for openings in the market: What are the underserved needs, what are the needs that customers find hard to express, and what gaps have competitors left? Far-outside-in questions use analogical reasoning: What would it take to be the Google, the Apple, or the Walmart of this market?"*

(Lafley et al., 2012)

A good set of possibilities for further work is established when (Lafley et al., 2012):

1. The *status quo* does not look brilliant. At least one other possibility intrigues the group enough to make it strongly question the existing position.
2. At least one possibility makes most of the team uneasy. It is sufficiently far from the *status quo* that the team questions whether it is executable or safe. If one or both of these is not true, it is probably time for another cycle of possibility generation.

6.2.3 TESTING THROUGH PEOPLE

Once we have established strategic possibilities and are sure that the align to our overall intent, the next step is to look at how are choices might become a reality. That means we need to look at people.

It may be that we are following convention or indeed breaking it. What we need is independent input based on different types of experience (known as 'requisite variety'). Inclusion of differing viewpoints is crucial to successful strategy. Exclusion leads to 'groupthink' and strategy that is not embraced by the people charged with implementing it.

We need to think about operationalisation, which requires commitment from those work in operations. What we put forward has to be justified.

Getting stakeholder buy-in is crucial. Both hierarchy and culture can get in the way here. The way to break through such barriers is to focus on facilitating teams' involvement in strategy determination.

6.2.4 ESSENTIAL CONDITIONS FOR SUCCESS

We next need to ascertain the essential conditions for success for each identified strategic possibility (Figure 14).

The two key questions are: what must be in place to succeed and what would I have to know and believe as a leader?

Most of the things we need to understand are orientated around marketing:

- Brand values, identity and positioning.
- Are we targeting a distinct segmentation or niche?
- What's the end-use customer value? What problem are we solving? What need are we satisfying?
- What channels do we need to operate through?
- How might the competition react?
- What does the potential market look like?

Figure 14: Essential conditions for success

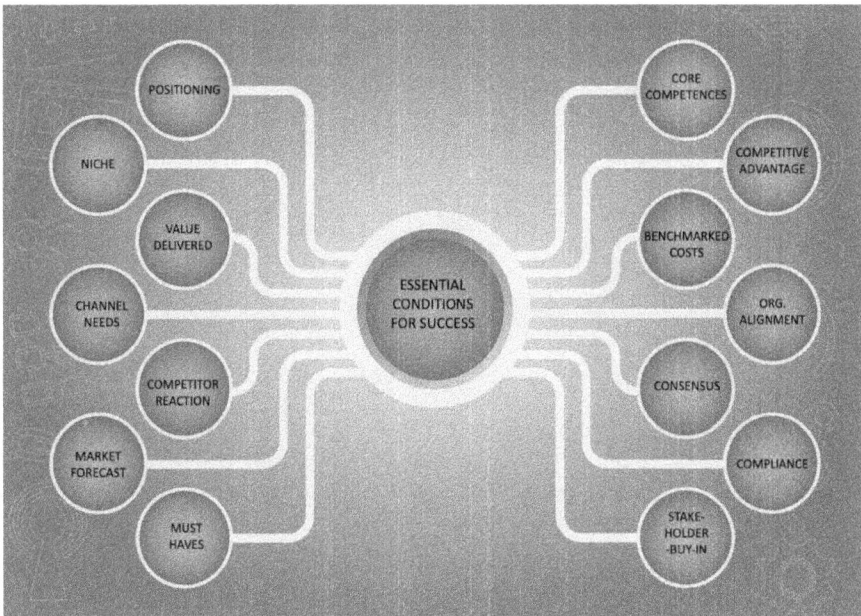

Then there are other competences we need to consider:

- What must exist internally, externally and interactively?
- What core capabilities must we have
- What is our competitive advantage?
- How do our costs compare with our competitors?
- Just how well is our organisation aligned?
- Is there consensus among stakeholder that this is the right thing?
- Are we meeting legal obligations?
- Do we have stakeholder buy-in?

6.3   QUESTIONS

1. This chapter outlines a rigorous series of steps to achieve Strategy Determination. In time as a leader this road map will become part of your leadership mindset
   a. What are your key observations of this process?
   b. Where do you see the major challenges?
   c. How might your behaviour change as a result of this new knowledge?
   d. How would you advise others who may face the task of transformational change strategies in the future?

7. GROWTH AND STRATEGY FRAMEWORKS

"Growth is never by mere chance; it is the result of forces working together."

James Cash Penney

7.1 CHAPTER OUTLINE

This chapter aims to develop your understanding of growth and explores four competitive strategy frameworks.

The key concepts we explore are growth and conventional competitive strategies.

On completing this chapter, you should be able to:

1. Create growth strategies.
2. Create business strategies aligned to your organisation.

7.2 UNDERSTANDING GROWTH

7.2.1 GROWTH AMBITION

Growth is a perennial objective, it is an obsession with most organisations, the ambition is always to grow bigger in the belief that growth will deliver improved returns. It is for this reason that this lesson is devoted to the subject of growth, so it can be defined, determined, discussed and detailed for the leader to make rational growth decisions.

At the most basic level, the growth ambition is part of most business organisations, simply because shareholder value is expected to grow, year on year and also in the belief that growth is achievable. This notion assumes there are no limits to growth, but from a rationale perspective, can this be so?

Sound principles behind strategic planning is that it should focus upon controlled growth, whereby planned growth is forecasted into a future time horizon. This is the normal convention as would be expected, but a more creative way to approach growth is to accept that it has already happened and then ask the question: "what must we have done to get here?"

Then by logical deduction, a growth plan will emerge, in fact more easily than following the conventional approach.

7.2.2   A FOUNDING PRINCIPLE FOR GROWTH

Once the route to growth has been formulated, by whichever approach works best, the founding principle to achieve growth is

> **Concentration, Concentration AND Commitment to Concentration for Growth**

This becomes the prevailing top management mindset.

Growth has a lifecycle effect. This notion in fact is already well-understood, but lifecycles today are really getting shorter and therefore the time boundaries for growth and for profits to be realised are reducing, all as a result of the intensity competition, incremental globalisation and the need for innovation.

Every growth curve has a genetic code for decline, it is just a matter of time. In planning for growth, one therefore must factor into the growth equation a rate of decline so that the returns from a growth strategy can be optimised, as far as this is possible.

What therefore are the ideal conditions for business growth?

This is a common question, and of all the answers were known, then all business would flourish. Nevertheless, it may be useful to simply explore some ideal conditions for growth in order to realise the challenges attached to them, namely

1. Effective empowerment of managerial talent as a reality
2. A 'blue ocean' where business is located in 'uncharted waters', i.e., where nobody else has ventured yet. Moreover, the search for blue oceans will be continuous (we return to that shortly).
3. A high volume of customer enquiries and repeat orders to ensure targeted customer acquisition and effective customer retention. The need to win business and then retain it is of paramount importance.
4. Invention and innovation.
5. Where net profit is a high percentage of sales.
6. A commanding position in the 'mind of the market', so that this unique place will claim dominant 'mind share'.

The list of conditions of course is unachievable ideal, but for most leadership thinking about such requirements does help to create a future vision. Of critical importance is that there must be a belief that growth can be achieved. Therefore, the culture of the business must value growth, live, breathe and digest growth and celebrate it.

Growth has to be driven, engineered and then have growth strategies aligned to maximising asset utilisation, achieving new market opportunities consistently and with a commitment to emergent growth technologies. This is a substantial undertaking where growth energy is the pre-requisite to success.

From a leadership perspective could growth become an obsession or is it an organisational reality? Well to start with, it is a paradox.

Scaling a company is exhilarating, but it is also hard, and the truth is only one out of nine companies manages to sustain even a minimum level of profitability growth in 10 years. So, what was the difference that allowed some companies to scale, while others caved under the weight of their own growth?

7.2.3 ROCKEFELLER HABITS: INCREASING THE VALUE OF THE FIRM

Harnish (2002) interprets a set of managerial best practices he calls the "Rockefeller habits". The habits refer to Standard Oil co-founder John D. Rockefeller (1839–1937), who had three bedrock management precepts: "priorities, data and rhythm". Harnish (2002) details why companies need firm plans, established priorities, big goals, effective delegation and strong values integrated into its performance. Harnish (2002) clarifies how CEOs and senior managers can apply these ideas to nourish their companies' growth.

7.2.3.1 The Fundamentals of Business Management

There are three fundamentals basic guidelines of business (Harnish, 2002):

1. Establish a limited number of rules.
2. Repeatedly stress your real priorities to your colleagues and employees.
3. Always behave according to the rules you set.

Chernow's (2004) Titan, a biography of Standard Oil co-founder John D. Rockefeller (1839-1937), sets out the industrialist's three bedrock management fundamentals: "priorities, data and rhythm".

1. *Priorities*

Every business needs five primary annual and quarterly objectives (plus monthly goals if your firm expands at an annual 100% growth rate). Include one primary target for the periods you measure. These objectives are your "Top 5 and Top 1-of-5 priority list". Do not exceed this number of priorities because an "organisation with too many priorities has no priorities". Every employee should have their work objectives, aligned with your firm's goals. Establish short- and long-term priorities for your company. Make one long-range priority a "big, hairy, audacious goal" (or BHAG). Communicate your priorities to your employees. To engage your workforce, create a compelling theme to go with your objectives.

2. *Data*

Your company must keep daily and weekly records of all operations, including sales, costs and market activity. Each employee should track at least one significant metric daily or weekly. Pay attention to your firm's "smart numbers," the primary metrics measuring your degree of success over the long term. Adapting a method from another industry, retailer Joe McKinney of McKinney Lumber in Muscle Shoals, Alabama, "established and popularised an internally understood Critical Number - a proprietary measurement of plant productivity." At McKinney, the critical number indicates day-to-day profitability trends. Aim for this level of timeliness in your operational and financial reporting.

3. *Rhythm*

The more internal meetings companies conduct, the more successful they will be. Plan to run daily, weekly, monthly, quarterly and annual meetings. Keep your "daily huddles" short - five to fifteen minutes each, tops, but realise that "your execs need regular, face-to-face huddles to discuss new opportunities, strategic concerns and bottlenecks as they arise".

Run your meetings efficiently. Set an organised agenda for every meeting. These meetings fulfil the crucial objective of establishing a rhythm and keeping everyone in your organisation "informed, aligned and accountable." Do not be concerned that this schedule might seem to feature too many meetings with too much emphasis on your primary messages to your employees. "Until your people are 'mocking' you," you haven't gone over the message sufficiently.

Every company must discover and develop its "X factor" - the one unique strategy that delivers sustainable value and, over time, favourable valuations. Rockefeller applied this concept to his oil business. During his era, oil firms found gushers everywhere. Their concern was transporting the oil. Rockefeller involved his company heavily in railroads and produced his barrels to hold his oil, thus cutting his transport expenses in half.

7.2.3.2 Mid-sized Firms

Steve Kerr, who was in charge of GE's well-regarded Crotonville leadership training facility, offers three pieces of advice to the CEOs of mid-sized firms:

1. Plan your tasks for the next 90 days and also plan 10 to 25 years ahead. Focus on what counts to your customers and the factors that differentiate you from your competitors.
2. "Keep everything stupidly simple". If a strategy or procedure seems complicated, it is "probably wrong".
3. Operate as much as possible with "first-hand data". This is the Crotonville way. GE's senior executives visit Crotonville each month to teach the company's managers and to learn from its most important customers." GE benefits from hearing directly from its customer about what they want.

7.2.3.3 Efficiency

Besides setting clear priorities, securing necessary analytical data and utilising regular meetings, CEOs and senior executives must ensure their companies and people operate as efficiently as possible. Conflict among employees or disagreements with customers cost employees 40% of their work time. To reduce this productivity loss, develop a system for employees to communicate to managers about disputes that require solutions quickly. Managers must secure the proper data to quickly, correctly resolve these disputes.

Corporate CEOs must secure the necessary funding to expand their operations in a way that fuels growth. Their ability to raise money depends on how bankers and other financial lenders regard their company's stability and its prospects. The more positively a CEO and a company's representatives shape bankers' perceptions, the more likely the firm is to secure suitable financing with "better terms, less-restrictive covenants, lower interest rates" and "waived fees."

7.2.3.4   Building Your Business

Only 4% of small US firms make a successful transition to becoming large firms. You want to make your company a "gazelle," the name Cognetics founder David Birch applies to enterprises that "grow at least 20% a year for four years in a row."

For example, consider Seattle-based Mostly Muffins. The company started in 1987 as a caterer serving downtown businesses. It is now on schedule to earn $10 million in revenues. Co-founder Molly Bolanos says that an organisation's "stages of growth and the issues you face in a company and as a CEO are very predictable … It is positively textbook".

Companies must meet three requirements to grow from small to large:

1. Leaders must learn to "delegate and predict"; both skills build executive judgment and competence.
2. The firm must develop "systems and structures" to manage rapid growth.
3. The company must be able to operate in a bigger 'sandbox' - that is, an expanded future marketplace.

7.2.3.5   Delegation, Anticipation and Alignment

Most business leaders do not like to delegate; this explains why 96% of all firms have ten employees or less and why most have fewer than three employees. CEOs it is expand their companies without adding people. Adding people means learning to delegate. Successful delegation depends upon hiring the "right people." Remember, "one great person can replace three good people."

Leaders must foresee what is going to happen in their marketplace. Sound leaders accurately forecast revenues and earnings, as Wall Street expects and demands. Generally, though, CEOs do not predict weeks or months ahead. Even being a few minutes ahead of your competitors and colleagues gives you an edge. And, for long-term growth, your firm must be an engine of predictable profitability.

As your company grows, you need a solid organisational framework. Align your systems with your management structure. Organisational charts can help. Every company needs three types of schematics:

1. The standard hierarchical organisational chart.
2. A set of charts that map your "work progress or workflow".

3. The "almost matrix", which tracks the relationships between and among "organisational functions" and "various business units".

Once you have more people, you will need to introduce appropriate systems to enable efficient teamwork. For example, when you reach 50 employees or between $10 million and $50 million in revenue, you should upgrade your information technology systems. At $50 million, upgrade them again.

As more people come on board, and as you secure and implement the systems to support them, predictability becomes increasingly essential. Leaders must be able to chart a proper growth path. Without it, long-term corporate survival can become uncertain.

7.2.3.6 Three Questions for Business Leaders

Executives should ask:

1. "Do we have the right people?" In 2000 and 2001, Fortune magazine put The Container Store atop its list of Best Companies to Work For. The Container Store hires the right people, pays 50% to 100% more than its competitors and provides more than 200 hours of training during a new employee's first year.
2. "Are we doing the right things?" The right things include leading your people, managing all of your firm's activities, keeping accurate records and staying accountable.
3. "Are we doing those things right?" When your revenue or market share, or both, grow at "twice the market," you are doing things right.

7.2.3.7 The "One-Page Strategic Plan"

Keep things simple by creating a one-page strategic plan that outlines how and where you plan to lead your company. Include the name of your organisation, your name, the date, your firm's core values and beliefs, its purpose, the actions it must take to achieve its goals, and who will be accountable for each step. And do not forget your brave BHAG.

Your one-page plan should cite:

1. Your three-to-five-year targets for revenues, profits and market cap.

2. Your 'sandbox', where your firm plans to operate as first or second in its field in the future.
3. The initiatives and capabilities that will enable you to achieve your goals; your "brand promise" that keeps your customers coming back.
4. Your primary goals.
5. Five or six initiatives for the year.
6. One or two critical numbers, for example, a balance-sheet tally and an income statement.
7. Your quarterly actions steps.
8. A quarterly or annual theme.
9. A scorecard tracking your progress.
10. The rewards that will accrue when you achieve your goals.
11. Your "quarterly priorities".

7.2.3.8 Core Values

Establish only a few rules. Focus on them and repeat them often. Base all of your actions on these rules. Create a strong cultural foundation because a solid corporate culture translates to robust performance. That's why core values are so important.

Implement these strategies to strengthen your core values:

- "Create legends". Tell stories to communicate and promote your core values to your employees. Tie relevant stories about your company to specific core values.
- "Recruitment and selection". Refer to your core values throughout your hiring process. Include them in recruitment materials and mention them during job interviews.
- "Orientation". Repeatedly cite your core values when you train new employees.
- "Appraisal process". Connect your core values to your employee performance ratings.
- "Recognition and reward". When you publicly honour employees' outstanding work at quarterly or annual meetings, always refer to your core values.
- "Internal newsletter". Run stories in your in-house publications that describe employees who exemplify your core values.
- "Themes" Build your corporate motifs and patterns around your core values.

- "Everyday management". Link all "decisions, reprimands, praise, customer issues and employee concerns back to the core values".

7.2.4   SOME TRUISMS ABOUT GROWTH

The following statements are worthy of reflection. There may be inherent wisdom embedded in these statements from which new managerial perspectives can be inspired:

1. To grow, find a customer to grow with.
2. Good market share may give too much confidence about future competitive positioning.
3. As a business matures, progressive competitive advantage may face erosion.
4. A pre-occupation with return on investment diminishes the return from growth.
5. 'Business as Usual' is safer.
6. As an industry approaches commodity status, new business growth will be suppressed.

7.2.5   GROWTH AND ENTREPRENEURSHIP

Growth and Entrepreneurship go hand in hand together. It is useful therefore to reflect on the qualities of the entrepreneur which make them different:

- Entrepreneurs are generally more open, adaptable, inspired, energised and committed than employed business leaders
- They are faster in making decisions and in their implementation
- They are ready to do new things and
- They put business opportunities first

This is the character of the entrepreneur, because growth to entrepreneurs is a quantum leap in revenue and profit, potentially. To the entrepreneur, growth must be accelerated. Those with an entrepreneurial drive will know that growth comes from customers, therefore the dedication to customer growth is the number 1 priority.

7.2.6   GROWTH MARKETS

Before customers are found, a market has to be identified, defined, profiled and estimates are needed for its value, volumes and lifecycle.

The challenge facing business today as well as entrepreneurs is "how can we locate a growth market?" Markets are made up of customers with money to spend and as inclination to buy. Therefore, to achieve growth, businesses must be attached to growth markets. To grow, we must attract and hold customers who will grow with us. The message is clear, we have to grow the customer base to grow the business.

For example, in business-to-business markets, if we help customers to reduce cost, improve margin and generate increased revenue, they achieve growth and so we grow with them. Thus a 'partnership model' with customers can be one route to sustainable growth, using a simple 'win-win' approach. To succeed in this partnership approach, our customers must therefore see us as

- Solution Providers -not just supplying products
- Business Growers - not just vendors
- Profit Suppliers - not just selling goods & services
- Growth Experts -not just manufacturing experts

This in turn means that we *must know our customers well*, in fact better than they know us! This is in itself an interesting notion!

To make this approach to growth work, it is important that we have

1. Customers who really want to grow
2. Customers who want us to grow with them
3. Customers who will allow us to grow through them
4. Customers who will value this type of partnership in growth

Market segmentation becomes vital in this process, but if that we can really participate in customer sales growth, the potential to dominate selected segments can become a reality.

7.2.7 GROWTH VALUES

As a business growth strategist, our values must be to

1. Support customer growth
2. Bring incremental profits to customers
3. Quantify results
4. Drive partnerships
5. Know the business growth of our customers
6. Add tangible value to customer operations
7. Enhance market profitability

From an operational leadership perspective as business needs three clear imperatives for growth:

1. How much?
2. How soon?
3. How sure?

Is this known, understood, communicated and regularly reviewed?

7.2.8   GROWTH MISSION

The dedication and purpose of most business is a commitment to growth, in the belief that growth will deliver sustainability.

A well-conceived growth mission combines growth values into an organisational growth culture which is designed to align with growth markets through the resources to deliver growth. A mission for growth, therefore it has to be:

- Customer oriented
- Customer centric
- Customer driven
- Customer derived

7.2.9   THE GROWTH PROCESS

Growth has so far been defined in terms of a functional ambition, but a further perspective of growth is to treat growth as 'a process'.

This means that we must know what is driving growth, the engines which support the momentum for growth and to realise that there are ethical rules from which to discover more about the process of achieving growth within a regulated environment.

7.2.9.1   Growth Drivers

The only genuine growth drivers are people with entrepreneurial mindsets.

To drive growth, you need to develop entrepreneurs to build new business futures. This means that talent management programmes are needed for entrepreneurial managers who in turn will need to build teams to build markets, with a strong profit motive as the prevailing mindset. In fact, the growth drivers will be corporate entrepreneurs.

Corporate Entrepreneurs, require knowledge and application for

- Growth leadership strategies
- Management leadership strategies

7.2.9.2 Growth Leadership Strategies

Good corporate entrepreneurs lead from a customer platform. They lead customers through sustainable, incremental pathways and so lead their business by leading customer-based growth strategies.

7.2.9.3 Management Leadership Strategies

The reality of business is that the recognition of successful leaders will is directly related to the profit that their business generates. Achieving such profit is usually through an attachment to 'an identity' which is acknowledged and accepted in the marketplace. Brand building is therefore an essential management leadership strategy. Leveraging brand values is a certain way to secure market recognition and then in time, market dominance together with the profit which is associated with market share gain.

7.2.9.4 Engines for Growth

Growth drivers must have Growth Engines to be able to participate in the growth race or even the competitive growth marathon. So, how can growth engines accelerate?

Here are some potential strategic moves:
1. Change cost centres to profit centres to modify mindset towards profit generation.
2. Leverage the company's asset base to increase efficiency.
3. Start Development Programmes for in-house entrepreneurial talent to groom people into a team to grow the business.
4. Set up a holding company structure with right-sized subsidiaries to improve decision taking and market timing.
5. New joint-ventures and strategic alliances to create new partnerships for growth.
6. Invest in partnerships for shared risk and reward.
7. Establish a business development division or company dedicated to new business only with main board or top management access.
8. Extend the business through adequate, relevant resourcing.

7.2.9.5 The 80:20 Rule

The work of Pareto is classical, even cliched. His 80/20 rule has been proven time and time and time again. 80% of the customers deliver 20% of profit, but 20% of customers produce 80% of profit. So, if we are driving future growth ambitions, where does growth opportunity reside? However, profit will come from high unit margins and premium prices, whereas business volume is the multiplier for growth, so entrepreneurial business will need both.

It may be worth segmenting the 80% customer base to search for business growth through the customer!

Almost certainly the search will be for the 20% of customers who will deliver 80% of future profits.

It is necessary to realise that secure profits will come from high unit margins and premium prices, but business sales are the multiplier for growth.

Almost certainly the search initially will be for the 20% of customers who will deliver 80% of future profits, which is the normal use of the 80:20 rule. Inverting this rule may also yield profitable growth opportunities. If the 80:20 rule is applied well, this can also add momentum to growth.

7.2.10 THE RATE AND PACE OF GROWTH

The rate and pace of growth must be factored into any growth strategy to avoid the unintended consequences of financial risk, especially in relation to liquidity. From a financial perspective, it is possible to be exposed to the risks of overtrading or even to high operational gearing. Any growth plan must be supported with a financial plan for venture capital, working capital and the risks arising from the pace of growth.

The growth strategist is single-minded, focused and purposeful with the route to profit as the mission that must be achieved. This simple-minded purpose must be coordinated with financial risk analysis, mitigation and management.

One sure formula for long term success is to control growth.

7.3 CONVENTIONAL COMPETITIVE STRATEGY FRAMEWORKS

7.3.1 CORPORATE OBJECTIVES

Statements of strategic intent, supported with embedded with core values and acknowledged competitive positioning provide an essential and sound foundation for strategy development.

The set of corporate objectives that specify *what* is to be accomplished and *by when*, in well-defined terms must be known and understood by all concerned. Corporate objectives will normally be specified as *quantitative* and *qualitative objectives*, whereby the former will relate to financial performance, the 'hard' aspects of business and the latter relating to the paradoxically termed 'soft' part of the business.

Both types of objectives are interdependent and must be capable of being delivered within time and other resource constraints.

These objectives are the basis for assessing performance, provide a sense of focus upon what is to be achieved and in turn pull the organisation together into a cohesive force.

Corporate objectives therefore must be SMART Objectives, i.e.,

- *Specific*, not ambiguous
- *Measurable*, not woolly
- *Attainable*, not vague
- *Realistic*, not wishful thinking
- *Time-bounded*, infinite terms by month, quarter of years

7.3.2   CLASSICAL STRATEGY MODELS

The conventional approach to Strategic Management is to consider options and then from these options, a choice is made upon the best way forward.

These classical essentials apply to the agenda for organisational transformation. We'll return to this in the later section on Strategic Planning, but we summarise some important frameworks for now.

7.3.2.1   The Ansoff Matrix

The Ansoff Matrix (Ansoff, 1970) is a conventional four box model (Figure 15), which outlines four potential strategies for business development and growth to secure a sustainable future.

A market penetration strategy ① is used to capture more market share from an existing product portfolio within existing markets served. In simple terms, this is designed to get more buyers to purchase more and/or more frequently. The intention is to grow customer value within existing market territory.

A product or service development strategy ② is an innovation strategy to widen or deepen the existing product portfolio and sell this new product provision to the existing customer base, thereby building customer loyalty.

Figure 15: Ansoff matrix

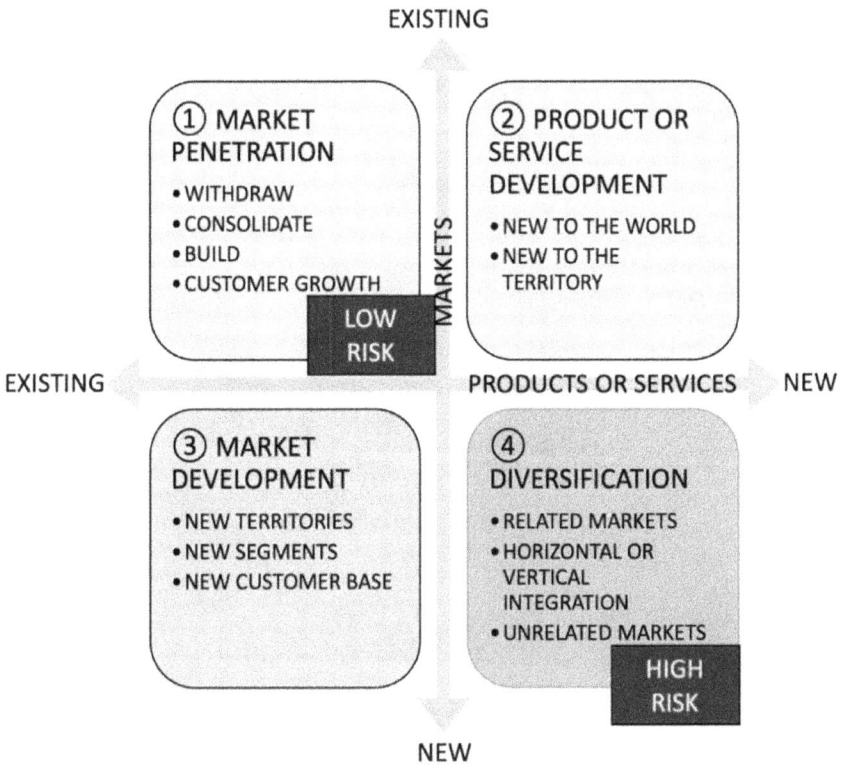

EXISTING

① MARKET PENETRATION
- WITHDRAW
- CONSOLIDATE
- BUILD
- CUSTOMER GROWTH

LOW RISK

② PRODUCT OR SERVICE DEVELOPMENT
- NEW TO THE WORLD
- NEW TO THE TERRITORY

MARKETS

EXISTING ← → PRODUCTS OR SERVICES → NEW

③ MARKET DEVELOPMENT
- NEW TERRITORIES
- NEW SEGMENTS
- NEW CUSTOMER BASE

④ DIVERSIFICATION
- RELATED MARKETS
- HORIZONTAL OR VERTICAL INTEGRATION
- UNRELATED MARKETS

HIGH RISK

NEW

Diversification ④ is achieved both within and also beyond the existing experience and technology base to provide the highest risk strategy.

A market development strategy ③ uses the existing product portfolio, but now the business is focused on new markets. In fact, this strategy is designed to create market segments and in so doing, broaden out the market base. This will gain more market coverage.

The Ansoff Matrix has been used in this format for many years, since the 1950's. In practice, but the reality companies combine Ansoff strategies to produce hybrid strategies. For example, product development and market penetration could be working at the same time. Market penetration and market development could also be the same case.

If the Ansoff Matrix is viewed as a combination of strategies for business growth, rather than independent options, then a more sophisticated approach can be actioned. Moreover, it presents a powerful, easily understood formula for business development strategy.

The Ansoff approach is classical, well-known, commonly accepted and useful particularly to those in search of market extension and growth strategies.

7.3.2.2 Porter's Generic Strategies[7]

"Generic strategies" (Figure 16) are applied to products or services in all industries, and to organisations of all sizes. They were first set out by Porter (1980) in *Competitive Strategy: Techniques for Analysing Industries and Competitors.*

Figure 16: Generic strategies

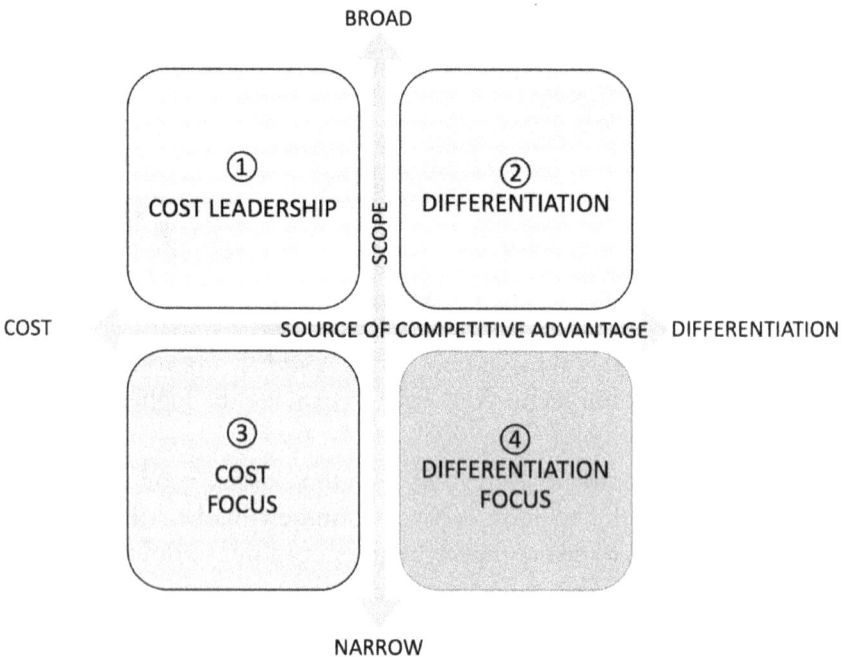

BROAD

① **COST LEADERSHIP**	② **DIFFERENTIATION**

COST   SOURCE OF COMPETITIVE ADVANTAGE   DIFFERENTIATION

SCOPE

③ **COST FOCUS**	④ **DIFFERENTIATION FOCUS**

NARROW

Porter (1980) called the generic strategies ① *cost leadership* (no frills), ② *differentiation* (creating uniquely desirable products and services) and *focus* (offering a specialised service in a niche market). He divides the

---

[7] Adapted from https://www.mindtools.com/pages/article/newSTR_82.htm, accessed 22 April 2021

focus strategy into two parts: ③ *cost focus* (emphasising cost-minimisation within a focused market) and ④ *differentiation focus* (pursuing strategic differentiation within a focused market).

Porter's (1980) generic strategies are ways of gaining competitive advantage. In other words, they are concerned with developing an 'edge' that gets you the sale, taking it away from your competitors.

Cost Leadership

There are two main ways of achieving this within a cost leadership strategy:

1. Increasing profits by reducing costs, while charging industry-average prices.
2. Increasing market share by charging lower prices, while still making a reasonable profit on each sale because you've reduced costs.

Cost leadership is about minimising the cost to the organisation of delivering products and services. The cost or price paid by the customer is a separate issue.

The cost leadership strategy literally involves being the leader in terms of cost in your industry or market. Simply being amongst the lowest-cost producers is not good enough. You leave yourself wide open to attack by other low-cost producers who may undercut your prices and block your attempts to increase market share.

You need to be confident that you can achieve and maintain the number one position before taking the cost leadership route. Companies that are successful in achieving cost leadership usually have:

- Access to the capital needed to invest in technology that will bring costs down.
- Very efficient logistics.
- A low-cost base (labour, materials, facilities), and a way of sustainably cutting costs below those of other competitors.

The greatest risk in pursuing a cost leadership strategy is that sources of cost reduction are not unique to you, and that other competitors either have similar cost reduction strategies or can copy yours. This is why it is important to continuously find ways of reducing every cost.

Differentiation

Differentiation involves making your products or services different from and more attractive than those of your competitors. How you do this depends on the exact nature of your industry and of the products and services themselves, but will typically involve features, functionality, durability, support, and also brand image that your customers value.

To make a success of a differentiation strategy, organisations need:

- Good research, development and innovation.
- The ability to deliver high-quality products or services.
- Effective sales and marketing, so that the market understands the benefits offered by the differentiated offerings.

Large organisations pursuing a differentiation strategy need to stay agile with their new product development processes. Otherwise, they risk attack on several fronts by competitors pursuing focus differentiation strategies in different market segments.

Focus

Companies that use focus strategies concentrate on specific niche markets. Through understanding the dynamics of that market and the unique needs of customers within it, they develop uniquely low-cost or well-specified products for that market. Because they serve customers in their market uniquely well, they tend to build strong customer brand loyalty. This renders their particular market segment less attractive to competitors.

As with broad market strategies, it is still essential to decide whether you will pursue cost leadership or differentiation once you have selected a focus strategy as your main approach. Focus is not normally enough on its own.

Whether you adopt a cost focus or a differentiation focus, the key to success is to ensure that you add something extra in serving only that market niche. It is not enough to focus on only one market segment because your organisation is too small to serve a broader market. If you do, you risk competing against better-resourced broad market companies' offerings.

The 'something extra' that you add should contribute to reducing costs (perhaps through your knowledge of specialist suppliers) or to increasing differentiation (though your deep understanding of customers' needs).

Stuck in the Middle?

According to Porter (1980), for companies not able to make a choice between his generic strategies, they will be 'stuck in the middle' and be going nowhere possible because they are not aware of how to make the next move.

Of course. this will really depend upon the nature of the competitive rivalry within the defined industry. It is the intensity of competition which drives the need for using Porter's (1980) model. In commodity-based markets, such an approach may be more challenging to use.

7.3.2.3   Combining Porter, Ansoff and SWOT

By combining Porter (1980), Ansoff (1970) and SWOT (see Chapter 5), the following derived strategies can be identified:

- An *aggressive* strategy - cost leadership + market penetration, leveraging on strengths to pursue opportunities.
- A *competitive* strategy - differentiation + market / product / service development with more leverageable strengths than major competitions.
- A *conservative* strategy - segment focus + niche market penetration to consolidate strengths into a superior position in the market where few threats are present or anticipated.
- An *exit* strategy - diversification into new markets because little potential exists for current business and where weakness and threats far exceed actionable strengths or current market opportunities.

7.3.2.4   Mintzberg's Approach

Henry Mintzberg is an iconoclastic and contrarian thinker on leadership and management (especially on the subject of MBAs).

Mintzberg's (1987) approach is distinctly different and is more focused upon core business by prescribing how core business strategies can be represented in the belief that core competencies should support core business and provide core income:

Plan

Locating the core business will depend upon the exposure, history and heritage related to the lifecycle stage that the company is in within the defined industry. Core business maybe located upstream, mainstream or downstream depending upon where the main business volume is based (and probably has been originated from).

Pattern

Distinguishing the Core Business will include ensuring that the business can define, acknowledge and retain superior competitive advantage by using viable sources of competitive advantage that are associated with business functions which deliver value to the customer. One way to achieve this is to search for competitive differentiation within the structure of the company's value chain. It is also appropriate to look for other ways of distinguishing the core business by using strategies for differentiation. This can be achieved in at least six basic ways:

1. Price differentiation - this is the most basic way to achieve product differentiation, but price alone may not provide depth in the longer term
2. Image differentiation - this is achieved through branding where brand values attract customer affinity
3. Support differentiation - this is achieved by using value added support services which usually are perceived as being substantial in comparison to other competitors
4. Quality differentiation - this is achieved through, for example product features or raw materials used, packaging and functionality
5. Design differentiation - this is achieved through distinctive design and uniqueness
6. No differentiation -- this is simply a 'do nothing' approach which can work if the market is large enough

Mintzberg has made a substantial contribution to strategic management thinking in the use of core business as a source of differentiation. You may recall, time and time again that under conditions of recession, market decline, intense competition and market uncertainty that one of the first thoughts of top management is to 'return to our core business'.

The question to ask is "why?" What is in the core business which may provide the recipe for survival? The answer is attributable to differentiation, but this cannot be treated as assumption. It must be a known, substantiated fact that the core business will still remain core to its customer group.

Yet further ways of achieving competitive distinction is to have strategies for scope which is also often known as market reach. Approaches to scope would be for example:

- Universal, where 'one size fits all'. This is difficult to achieve but Henry Ford's Model T did.
- Segmentation, where the possibilities are diverse, but it is normal business practice to use segmentation strategies.
- Niche strategies, where the focus is upon one defined segment and have the intention to dominate it.
- Customisation, where each customer represents a unique segment and has a product tailored to meet special needs or be customised from scratch, in which case the strategy is for pure customisation.

Position

Elaborating the Core Business can be achieved in a number of ways. The most useful framework here is to apply some of the ideas which are in the Ansoff Matrix, namely: penetration strategies; market development strategies; and product or service development strategies.

Perspective

Extending the Core Business is intended to take organisations beyond their core business in order to achieve development and growth. This can be achieved in a number of ways:

- *Vertical integration* by moving the business upstream, known as backward integration or downstream known as forward integration. These forms of core business extension are designed to be applied within the current operating value chain of the business.
- *Horizontal integration* is achieved by extending the core business to parallel operations, but not in the same value chain of operations. It is a form of diversification.
- *Diversification* refers to business extension, beyond the current operations, but may be related to some distinctive competence or asset of the organisation. Where diversification is related in

some way to the core business, it is termed concentric diversification.

- *Internal development, acquisition and strategic alliances* - Horizontal, vertical integration and diversification can be achieved either by internal development or by acquisition. The strategy decision will depend upon policies for ownership, control and level of acceptable risks. Forms of Partnerships, Joint Ventures, Licensing, Franchising as well as Purchase of Equity via acquisition represent some of the viable options.

- *Organic growth* is one form of internal development which uses the core competencies as an existing resource base. This also creates a culture to pursue the 'strategic intent of the business'. Organic growth may be supported by: Customer Relationship Management (CRM) systems and Supply Chain Management (SCM) systems; sustained investment is in core competencies; following or influencing quality standards to drive quality excellence; creating a learning organisation culture; building strategic alliances; Human Capital Development and Talent Management for internal company deployment.

Ploy

Re-conceiving the Core Business arises when the combination of the above strategies fails to produce strategic focus for the business as a whole. Where this is the case, there is usually a need to reconfigure the business, redefine it and essentially re-conceive it. The basic approaches are:

- A business redefinition strategy around product, service or customer need. Sometimes a creative redefinition is used to inspire and re-motivate management, for example when a government corporation becomes privatised and the need for a change management programme may in fact require business redefinition, so that the concept of the business is realigned to achieve marketplace relevance.

- A core relocation strategy relocates the 'centre of gravity' of the core business simply because there has been a 'strategic drift' in the market, in which case the core business may have to move upstream or downstream or even look for geographic relocation. It is also possible that the core business has seen a forthcoming sunset on the horizon and there is a need to look for a new core business location. Thereby ultimately there will be 'new rules' of the strategy game to learn.

7.4 QUESTIONS

1. Which of Harnish's Rockefeller habits look useful to you? Do you think they apply to your organisation? How controllable are they?
2. How do you think customer growth can be stimulated?
3. Reflect upon what customers value which keeps them coming back. What are they really buying?
4. As an organisation, what is needed to become more customer-centric, whereby the needs, wants, values and expectations of customers are at the 'epicentre' of business thinking and business deliverables?
5. Within your employing organisation, can you identify the corporate entrepreneurs? Where are they located in the organisation structure? What insights does this reveal?
6. In your employing organisation, what else can be contributed to accelerate the growth engine?
7. Based on your experience:
   a. Can you recall any examples when the owner or executive explained the reason for needing business growth?
   b. Was the adequately explained and given full support by all concerned?
   c. Draft an agenda of what would be needed to be discussed with all staff involved to support an ambitious growth strategy.
   d. Can you imagine a situation where the pace of growth is beyond that projected and the reflect upon the level and nature of stress this could place on the organisation?
   e. How can growth ambitions be effectively led?
8. In your employing organisation, where is the emphasis now? What are the priorities within the framework of the Ansoff Matrix?
9. Where is your organisation's strategic focus now? Where should it be in the future? Is Porter generic strategies framework helpful?
10. Think about how Mintzberg's approach can be applied to transformation strategy design. What insights are there for transformational leadership?

LEADING STRATEGIC CHANGE

"The greatest danger in times of turbulence is not the turbulence – it is to act with yesterday's logic."

Peter Drucker

8. CLASSIC CHANGE MODELS

"If you do not change direction, you may end up where you are heading."

Lao Tzu

8.1 CHAPTER OUTLINE

This chapter considers why strategic change leadership a priority for many organisations, why transformational change is considered to be difficult, and why there is not a template for universal adoption. It also looks at what sources of guidance are available and how theory can help.

The key concepts we cover are gap analysis, change models and theory, action research and execution.

On completing this chapter, you should be able to:

1. Evaluate your personal and organisational performance.
2. Identify performance gaps and plan for how to close them.
3. Execute action research projects.
4. Adapt theoretical perspectives on change to lead change projects.

8.2 CLASSIC CHANGE MODELS

Figure 17 summarises a selection of key models and frameworks for effecting change. This section outlines and explains each of these in turn. It is for you to extract the essence of these models and then to use the concepts contained on a selective basis, as appropriate.

It is fair to say that no one model will be sufficient but probably a combination, or a 'hybrid' of selected models will offer insight for potential application.

Each of the models are demanding from a conceptual standpoint, the real value can only be understood if you can grasp the subject of change, the need for change and the challenges to be faced in achieving change.

With this array of models to explore, there is one starting point, one concept which offers a useful perspective to all organisational change planning, this is *gap analysis*.

Figure 17: Change theory

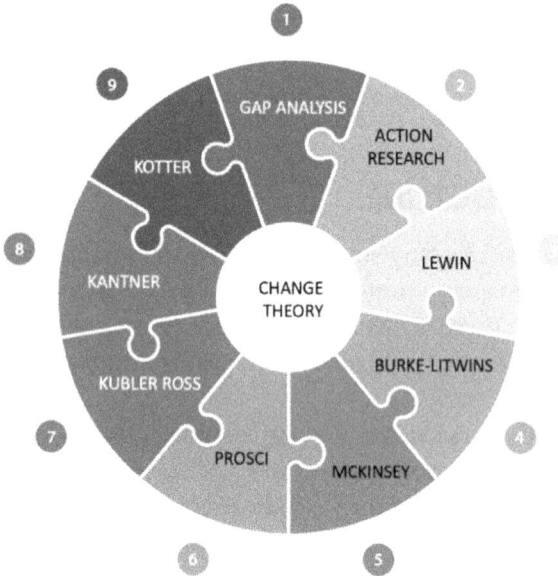

8.2.1 GAP ANALYSIS

The concept of a 'gap' is useful because it helps to convey the difference between an existing position and the position desired. It is 'the gap' between the existing & desired position where changes must be made to reduce or 'bridge the gap'. The gap could originate from a multitude of sources. Strategy is then usually required to achieve realignment to thereby put the organisation on the right track to move ahead by reducing 'the gap'.

Typical Sources of 'gaps' include:

- A mission gap in achieving the organisation's purpose.
- A financial stakeholder value gap which would require strategic intervention.
- A performance gap (or gaps).
- A gap in achieving targets or stretched targets.
- A competency gap.
- A transformation gap.

Indeed, there are many such gaps that have occurred as a result of changes in the internal organisational environment as well as the competitive market landscape.

The core issue to resolve when using gap analysis is to establish:

1. Why there is a gap
2. The conditions which have contributed to the gap
3. The history in the organisation which may have contributed to the gap
4. The realities of reducing the gap and/or bridging it
5. The resultant Strategies for Change which must be implemented

In most cases, the gaps are 'negative' which means there is an under-achievement gap. In more rare cases, the gap is 'positive', which in turn means over-performance has occurred and once again a change strategy for realignment will be needed to achieve a balanced organisation.

Conceptually the Figure 18 displays the notion of a Strategic Gap.

Figure 18: Strategic gap

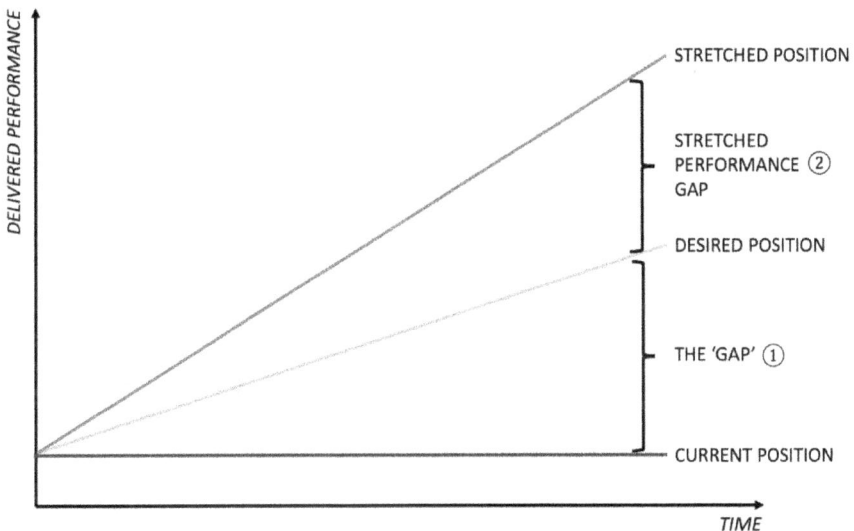

Gap Analysis is a searching process which has two functions:

1. To know the 'size' of the gap; and
2. To understand the 'root cause' of the gap.

From there we plan for change, which may be either: incremental, taking small steps overtime; or transformational, taking much longer steps to take substantial corrective action as needed.

The process of analysis will attempt to examine resource deployment, people, processes, technology and management control systems to reveal key areas where improvements may be needed. It may be discovered that changes may be needed at both the strategic and operational levels of the organisation in order for the enterprise to realist its total potential.

To determine the gap, a measurement of performance is needed against which to benchmark actual achievement, so thereby to use gap analysis as a driver for change the following sequence may be helpful:

1. Determine the levels and areas of performance throughout the organisation to achieve a hierarchy of performance measurements. These are known as Key Result Areas (KRAs).
2. Know the key tasks to be undertaken within each of the KRAs.
3. Assess the performance gap by knowing the projected potential and comparing this against actual achievement.
4. Determine the reason(s) for the gap(s).
5. Then the residual gap(s) becomes a strategy agenda of items for change.

This tool or model for change is also a performance management mindset in reality there will always be gaps, these are perennial.

Within each planning cycle organisation gaps will be revealed for which change will be required to make needed adjustments in order to keep the organisation as a whole internally, externally and interactively aligned with customers and key stakeholders.

8.2.2 ACTION RESEARCH

To reduce an identified 'gap' or even to bridge it will require action. An action plan would normally be drawn up for implementation, monitoring and periodic review. The process of periodic reviews could be conceived as a form of action research (Reason & Bradbury, 2001; Stringer, 1999) simply because

- Action has been implemented; and
- The effectiveness of the action is subject to review to increase the pace of organisational learning.

Even though action research sounds rather grand, the essence of it is simple at operational level: if change is to be implemented, it requires action to be taken.

Action cannot be open-ended or be an open system, it needs feedback and review in accordance with what was originally intended in the change programme.

The process is conventionally known as 'closed loop' control and therein is the underlying model for action research. However, recent research in change management challenges the view of change as a 'loop' or cycle. A better metaphor is the idea of a spiral moving forward through time. The action research process moves in parallel with the process of change to affect its inputs and outputs.

At the heart of much action research is the need for reflection to discover what has worked well and what has not.

An action research project would actually require team participation in the change programme, and therefore be included in the transition programme to achieve change. Through this learning processes, strategies and policies for change and the knowledge acquired can be most useful for future organisational performance improvements.

Hence, action research can be divided into two dimensions:

1. Research into actions to be taken; and
2. Research into actions already being undertaken and the associated reflection upon achievement.

The tension between these dimensions needs to be understood. Clearly both dimensions may be involved in any change programme. Action research actually imposes a form of control on change initiatives because it causes the organisation to check progress and outcomes. Even at the individual manager level, the value of self-assessment and self-reflection in relation to the change process is a form of action research.

So, what are the basic steps to be taken to adopt action research in a programme of change?

1. Review the Current Practices to answer the question 'where are we now?'
2. Focus upon areas which need further investigation based upon the findings from step 1
3. Forecast the Desired Future Position and make necessary projections about the future
4. Intervene to make changes, maybe small scale changes and take a step-by-step approach
5. Review what is happening and what occurred in producing an outcome
6. Make Modifications as required where 'gaps' exist
7. Monitor the modification
8. Evaluate and learn for the next cycle of change

Through action research, organisations learn and evolve.

In summary, there cannot be a programme for change or the adoption of change models without the use of action research and a combined understanding of gap analysis.

8.2.3 LEWIN'S CHANGE MANAGEMENT MODEL

Kurt Lewin's (1947) change management model is a classical piece of work. It has remained as one of the anchor models to manage the process of change. While some may not subscribe to this form of change management, it has been widely acknowledged and used by managers. What Lewin (1947)accomplished was to capture essential processes he felt were needed to bring about change effectively.

Lewin (1947) suggested three essential phases were required which he referred to as:

1. Unfreezing.
2. Change.
3. Freezing (often misquoted as "re-freezing").

To understand Lewin's thinking, the characteristics of each phase should be understood.

8.2.3.1 Unfreezing

Lewin's (1947) belief is that to bring about change, it is necessary to destabilise the surrounding environment to create uncertainty, dissatisfaction and even stress. This process moves the mind out of the comfort zone because the future is then uncertain, unclear and ambiguous.

Destabilisation typically comes from things like:

*   Rumours.
*   Introducing tighter work schedules.
*   Increased and stretch performance targets.
*   Changed patterns of communication.
*   Increased workload and shorter deadlines.
*   Introducing new staff into key positions.

This 'pressure' is all intended to 'heat up' the environment though tension and in so doing 'un-freeze' the mindset of people involved and affected by the changes which are planned. When the organisational system is less secure and the 'psychological contract' between employees and their employing organisation appears fragile, conditions are right to move to the next phase: change.

8.2.3.2 Change

Change can now be introduced, and those employees destabilised in the unfreezing phase welcome the change to restabilise themselves. As a result of the uncertainty, they will be more prone to accept or even welcome the change to reduce the stress which has been created. (This could be explained as psychological manipulation.) The introduced change has to be institutionalised through new reporting systems, new processes and even new systems of recognition & reward to motivate the 'buy-in' to the mandated change.

It is conceivable that management styles may also be modified at this time so that the new rules of the organisational game can be introduced.

From the perspective of leadership, the timing for this period of change has a window of opportunity to be assessed. It cannot be too long otherwise the impact of the unfreezing stage will be lost.

Once changes are known, communicated and understood it is time to move to the third phase.

8.2.3.3 Freezing

From the organisational tensions created during un-freezing and change where higher levels of performance have been set, it is time to refreeze the organisational paradigm.

This is accomplished by:

- Symbolic changes to what are known as visible artefacts, e.g., new office layout, décor, new teams established, training & staff development to introduce the new way of working; and
- Reinforcement of monitoring, control and performance management, together with a system of organisational support through standard operating procedures, new policies & protocols.

This, once institutionalised and in operation, achieves the freezing phase.

As the reader will appreciate, where large scale changes are involved, referred to as transformational change, then to go through all these phases can be painful for those involved. Morale may be low, but the underlying principle of Lewin's (1947) work is to establish a felt need for change. This he does by creating insecurity at the unfreezing stage as described above.

The impact upon organisational psychologies can be substantial and therefore Lewin's (1947) methodologies must be planned with care and must have effective leadership & control, with supportive counselling as required.

8.2.4 BURKE-LITWIN MODEL

The approach taken in this model is very different from Lewin. This model is much more functional in nature and takes an approach of looking at the drivers for change, which are mostly derived from the external environment.

The Burke-Litwin (1992) model appears to be aligned with the field of strategic management (Figure 19). It is procedural in nature in attempting to produce a more descriptive or even definitive model to show the causal nature of change through the organisation.

The key elements for change and change implementation are shown and indeed this is a powerful model at a strategic level to show what is required as it cascades down to individual level.

Readers who have studied strategic management will understand the 'boxes' in the model. At first glance, there is a core sequence which connects the external environment to individual and organisational performance. This runs through the centre of the model. However, this causal process is influenced and enabled by mission, strategy and structure as well as the competency levels of staff.

The 'glue' which holds the core sequence together is the organisational culture which requires functionality through systems, policies and procedures to provide a framework for performance.

The essence of this model is causality, but the model also demonstrates multi-causality in a top-down sequence to help the student to have a framework to understand organisational performance drivers and hence how change is driven.

8.2.5 MCKINSEY'S 7 'S' FRAMEWORK

We have previously discussed the use of McKinsey's 7S framework in the in context of Peters and Waterman (2004) in Chapter 4.

Figure 19: Burke-Litwin change model

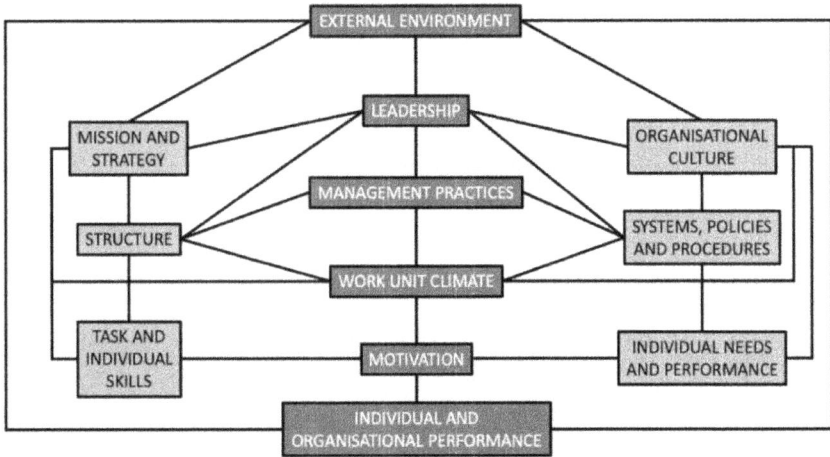

8.2.6   PROSCI'S FIVE BUILDING BLOCKS

The Prosci methodology is also known as the ADKAR model of change (Hiatt, 2006). This model produces a set of five building blocks which require action. Up until Prosci's work, most models dealt with organisational change, whereas the ADKAR Model emphasises individual change. The model was developed in 2003 by the Prosci Change Management Company.

The mnemonic ADKAR stands for:

Awareness

Desire

Knowledge

Ability

Reinforcement

Prosci's ideas are similar to models linked to a process known as the 'hierarchy of effects' often used in marketing, marketing communications and sales training.

The steps in this model are sequential and it assumes that this is the case. Of course, it can also be argued that this may not be the actual sequence in all cases, as with all models suggesting a 'hierarchy of effect'. Nonetheless the elements have value:

- *Awareness* is to understand why change is needed and this must be through planned communication.
- *Desire* is related to the achievement of 'buy-in' by the individual exposed to the needed change. Then the individual will have a desire to support the change.
- *Knowledge* is actually about providing the knowledge required to achieve the change through appropriate methods such as training, counselling, coaching, mentoring and so on to make a 'knowledge transfer'. Essential Knowledge is based upon the need to know how to change and how to sustain changed performance after full implementation has been achieved.
- *Ability* is related to providing the needed support to change behaviour and thereby achieve planned outcomes. Practice, learning from mistakes and providing guidance may be necessary.
- *Reinforcement* is needed so that the changes made stay in place. The need to separate out from the past is vital to prevent individuals returning to working in the old ways before the change was made. Usually this can be achieved by setting new performance targets and reusing them.

It is the need for reinforcement which as a critical factor for achieving change.

8.2.7 THE RELEVANCE OF THE MCKINSEY AND PROSCI FRAMEWORKS

In both the McKinsey and Prosci frameworks:

- Different perspectives are offered.
- Structure is outlined to manage change.
- Processes are explained.
- The combination of these models could provide a comprehensive understanding of individual and organisational change.
- A roadmap can be drawn up to plan a change programme.
- The Change Agent and/or Change programme manager can check the relevance of each approach for the contribution made.
- Both models are easy to understand.

- The use of models can be used to examine change programme factors and thereby assist individual and organisational learning.

8.2.8 KÜBLER-ROSS FIVE STAGE TRANSITION CYCLE

Originally developed to explain the human process of grief (Kübler-Ross, 1969), this model was later expanded include any form of personal loss (or transition), such as the death of a loved one, the loss of a job or income, major rejection, the end of a relationship or divorce, drug addiction, incarceration, the onset of a disease or an infertility diagnosis, and even minor losses, such as a loss of insurance coverage (Kübler-Ross & Kessler, 2014). Kübler-Ross examines the 'response to change'. It is worthwhile combining the thinking of Lewin's change management model with Kübler-Ross so that the impact of change can be understood from a psychological perspective.

You must know already that change is often hard to accept, but little is actually known about how significant changes affect individuals in organisations. In simple terms, significant change causes turbulence.

Knowing *what* is significant and *how* it is significant becomes important, but rarely this is managed well.

In realistic terms, change causes distress. Consequent anxiety then affects the organisational climate and working culture, especially when the change is sudden and imposed without adequate warning or consultation. The work of Kübler-Ross (1969) and Kübler-Ross and Kessler (2014) attempts to account for how people are affected by impactful change to their psyche.

The work is based upon just two parameters: mood and time.

The model (Figure 20) shows how mood changes overtime as a result of imposed change, especially when it is unwelcome news as this creates a shockwave which in turn leads to individual vulnerability.

Figure 20: Kübler-Ross five stage transition model

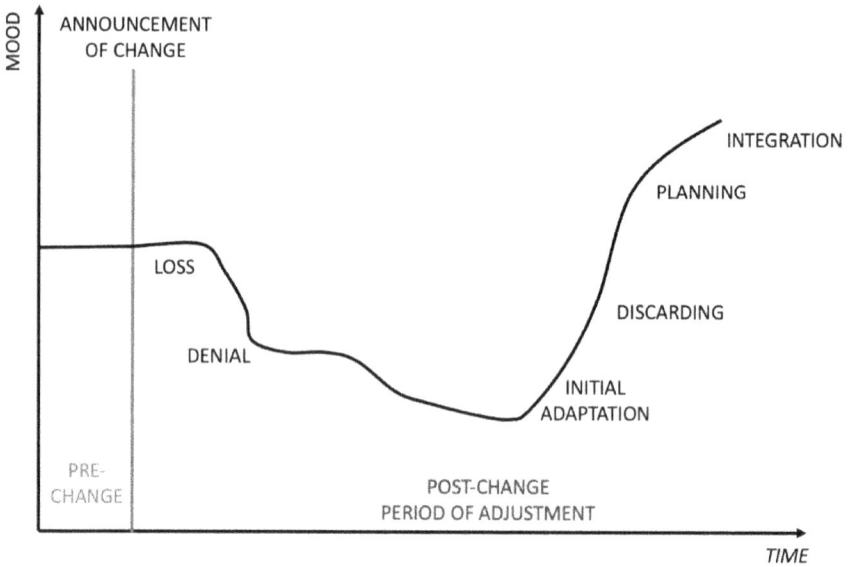

The five Stages in this transition are:

1. Denial.
2. Initial adaptation.
3. Discarding.
4. Planning.
5. Integration.

The inspiration as well as a metaphor for the essence of this model is a bereavement process where sudden loss leads to a series of emotional reactions, where the time taken to adjust and integrate again is not always easy to predict. This can be appreciated in the typical characteristics of each of the five stages in the Kübler-Ross curve (Figure 21).

Figure 21: Characteristics of the Kübler-Ross five stages

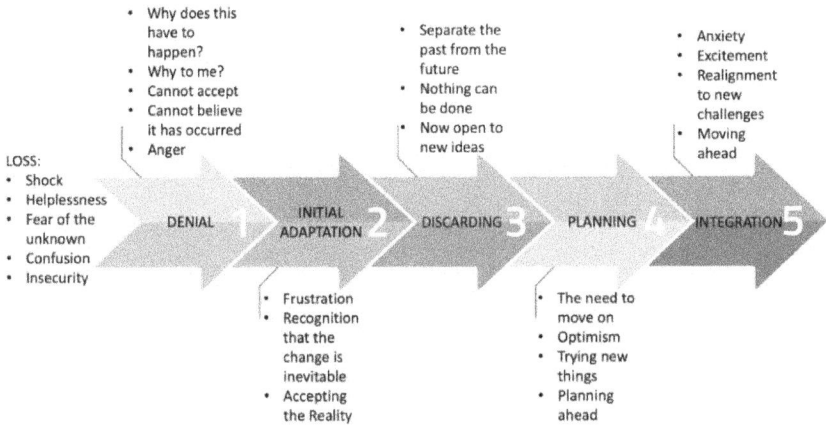

8.2.9   KANTNER'S BOLD STROKES AND LONG MARCHES

Moss Kanter (2004) takes another perspective on change. She claims change can be accomplished through:

- *Bold strokes* - strategic level change which is directed top down and then cascades down the organisation. Different levels in the organisation will filter the needed change and adopt that which is appropriate.

- *Long marches* - operational level changes, that change the way people work, the organisational climate and the work-based culture provided there is 'buy-in' from all relevant employees.

It could be argued that these two classifications may need to work together rather than be independent. The underlying purpose here is to deal with large scale of transformational change. However, incremental change will need to take much smaller steps to effect change.

Despite the somewhat unusual terms to explain strategic and operational change, Moss Kantner's (2004) work is valuable because she outlines 10 steps which apply to both categories of change. These are helpful and offer practical advice to the practising manager:

1. *Analyse the organisation.* The purpose is really to know where change is needed. The analysis seeks to confirm the real need for change. This provides a rationale and underlying purpose for change.

2. *Inspire a shared vision.* Change should be aspirational and inspirational to all stakeholders. A vision binds the change programme together to help to visualise the eventual outcomes and help to achieve a common sense of purpose. This is essential to communicate change to all involved.
3. *Separate from the past.* People 'hang on to the past', which inhibits change because their mindsets live in the past. There is fundamental need to embrace change for the future and sever the psychological attachment to things which until now were familiar.
4. *Create a sense of urgency.* To help to separate from the past, urgency is an important tool to coerce people to fall into new patterns of working. The consequences of not taking action will support this sense of urgency.
5. *Strong leadership.* Change must be lead! Championed from a position of power in the hierarchy. This means top management involvement, commitment and action.
6. *Secure 'political' sponsorship.* This is needed to overcome any meaningful resistance to change.
7. *Craft the implementation plan.* A road map for change is needed together with project managed implementation.
8. *Create enabling structures.* Structure to support and make change is a well-known cliché.
9. *Communicate.* This is needed to build trust in the change and commitment for the change. Transparency is essential. Human Resource Engagement is the key.
10. *Reinforce the change.* New Policies, Procedures, Processes and People will be required to institutionalise the change.

As you can now see, the advice is good, it presents a set of essential conditions which should prevail over a planned time period to achieve the change. However, Moss Kantner's (2004) steps ignore the need for monitoring and review to track the progress being made. These steps, while good, appear mechanistic. Each stage has to be managed by well-appointed 'change agents' who have the responsibility to drive the change plan with an appropriate level of authority to act.

8.2.10 KOTTER'S EIGHT STEPS

The work of Kotter (2012, 2014) is similar to Moss Kanter (2004) and he proposes eight steps to manage change:

1. Create a sense of urgency.
2. Form a guiding coalition.
3. Create a vision.
4. Communicate a vision to secure buy-in.
5. Empower others to act.
6. Create quick wins.
7. Build on the change, do not let up.
8. Institutionalise the change.

It is worth noting that the introduction of the idea of 'quick wins', now a common management jargon term.

Of course, the reason for this is to report and celebrate success. This will motivate subsequent change. However, recognise that transformational change is a long-term process, and this will require more than a series of quick wins to secure the desired outcome.

There are clear messages in Kotter's work:

1. There is a need to create a climate for change.
2. It is essential to engage with the organisation and then enable the organisation for change.
3. Change must be implemented and then be sustained.

8.3   QUESTIONS

1. In which areas of the organisation that you currently work for (or one that you are familiar with) are there prevailing inadequacies which impact organisational performance? Now prioritise these as an actionable agenda to be addressed before transformational change is envisioned.
2. Thinking about the inadequacies you noted previously, to what extent are those inadequacies contributing to performance gaps similar to gaps ① and ② in Figure 16?
3. What is your perspective on action research? Where and how can you see it potential application to your own performance and to issues in your own organisation or an organisation you are familiar with?
4. Motivation is a key element of the Burke-Litwin model. Reflect upon your experience and then list and classify significant sources of demotivation in the workplace. Then consider the impact these may have upon a transformational change agenda.

5. Consider the Kübler-Ross Model and take time to reflect upon it through your own life experiences. Based on your reflection, how important do you consider the Kubler-Ross work?

9. STRATEGIC INTERVENTIONS

"The announcement is the easy part; it makes the manager look bold and decisive. Implementation is more difficult, because no matter how good and compelling the data, there will always be active and passive resistance, rationalisations, debates, and distractions – particularly when the changes require new ways of working or painful cuts. To get through this, managers have to get their hands dirty, engage their teams to make choices, and sometimes confront recalcitrant colleagues."

Ron Ashkenas and Rizwan Khan

9.1 CHAPTER OVERVIEW

This chapter explores strategic change interventions at the individual, group and organisational levels.

The key concepts we consider are strategic interventions and management styles.

On completing this chapter, you should be able to:

1. Implement appropriate strategic change interventions.
2. Adopt a management style that aligns to the interventions you are implementing.

9.2 STRATEGIC INTERVENTIONS DEFINED

Strategic interventions (Peysha & Peysha, 2014) happen at individual, group and organisational levels. Each are implemented in the mission to achieve meaningful change, which may range from a small-scale operational scope to transformational change.

Strategic interventions are hence the actions that are taken to enable change through people taking action.

In this respect, there is a current trend to align people to jobs which have been defined in advance. This 'job profiling' and 'people profiling' become aligned simply to improve organisational performance. Training of course to some extent is a way to achieve this. However emerging trends in recruitment and selection, mentoring and coaching are all targeted at the individual to then achieve needed change at operational level.

At group level, a team-based approach is taken owing to the scale and nature of the change to be achieved. Where consensus is achieved then a more powerful agenda for change can be accomplished. By working together and thinking together a 'culture for change' can achieve an organisational climate for change. Therefore, at Group level, team-working and team building to overcome conflict and achieve change is a powerful intervention strategy. Often through a team-based approach at group level, synergy is created.

The ambition to bring about change by using the team processes enables, for example:

- Reviewing operational processes and performance.
- Achieving a common accord.
- Improving interpersonal engagement.
- Re-defining roles and responsibilities.
- Resolving issues, challenges and prevailing problems.
- Easing communications for decision taking.

Within the context of group level interventions, individuals will also achieve change by adopting.

- Personal strategies for learning within the environment needed.
- Improvements in interpersonal communications.
- A more participative role (including as a member of a team).

For some, personal development at individual level will not only contribute to organisational development at group level, but also potentially affect life transitions through career advancement. Therefore, strategic interventions both at group and individual level are very difficult to separate.

At the organisational level, then larger scale strategic interventions achieve change. Such interventions need, for example:

- Leadership
- An appropriate management style.
- Human process interventions.
- Human resource management intervention.
- Techno-structural intervention.
- Structural change at the organisational level.

9.3   MANAGEMENT STYLES IN CHANGE

Management styles need to be appropriate to effect successful change within a defined organisational domain, organisational climate and operating culture. Unless the organisation is newly created, then much of the fabric of established management style is in place.

It is wise to consider would be to consider the range of styles along a continuum of extremes, then realise the prevailing management style and its appropriateness for the organisation to achieve change, e.g.,

AUTOCRATIC STYLE ←————————————→ PARTICIPATIVE STYLE

Which shows the extent of democratic processes in place when strategic intervention for change is needed.

ACTIVE STYLE ←————————————→ REACTIVE STYLE

There may be bi-polar extremes to drive the type of strategic intervention ... is the organisation forward thinking and taking action to anticipate the need for change ... or is the organisation reacting to a situation which has been discovered and this responding to the need for change (or face untoward consequences)?

One could argue that such managerial mindsets will predict the nature of the strategic intervention, however, depending upon the scale of the change it is not uncommon to find both active styles and reactive styles working together.

9.4   CHANGE AT THE ORGANISATIONAL LEVEL

To move from individual level to group level has been discussed but now intervention at organisational level must be considered to complete the hierarchy of strategic interventions.

There remains a common theme for change at organisational level, namely 'benchmarking' and the related search for best practices in the belief that this is the formula for 'staying ahead' or even 'remaining in the game'.

It is often not appreciated that such managerial practices within an industry simply erodes competitive differentiation as all organisations will eventually appear similar (not a smart move).

Maybe organisational learning from dissimilar industries could provide insights for potential application, e.g., using international bank service culture and systems to transform service in a private hospital would be a more creative and beneficial route to achieve the ambition for benchmarking outcomes.

Typically change at organisational level seems to follow prevailing trends contemporary to a given time period, for example:

- Business process re-engineering
- Total quality management
- Customer centricity
- Right sizing the organisation
- Insourcing and outsourcing
- Flat organisation structure
- Strategic alliances to achieve strategic fit
- Human capital management
- Talent management system
- Performance management
- Learning organisation

The underlying motive is to formulate organisational development through transformations which are normally led by top management who feel that there is pressure on the organisation to sustain competitiveness, which is an understandable fact of organisational life.

9.5   HUMAN PROCESS INTERVENTIONS

Interpersonal relationships and group dynamics are the backbone for this category of intervention.

Human Process Interventions are aimed at improving the way in which people work together, mainly through coaching, training and professional development. Team building has a large part to play.

Process consultation is also used to achieve mutual understanding on specific issues and challenges to achieve a behavioural change outcome.

In situations of consultant-client relationships, process consultation is a common approach used to enable change through jointly achieved solutions to process problems.

Ultimately change cannot happen without human intervention, 'the process' approach recognises the need of shared values and shared behaviour to achieve shared outcomes.

9.6 TECHNO-STRUCTURAL INTERVENTIONS

This bold jargon is simply a focus upon organisational effectiveness through people development achieved through structure and technological or technical domains.

Structure relates to the dynamics surrounding the organisation. This would include, for example:

- Changes to the actual structuring of the organisation.
- Systems embedded in the organisation which are subject to the need for change.
- Re-alignment or re-engineering of business process.
- Change to office design, use of space.
- Management processes.
- Introduction of knowledge management.

'Techno' has a wide interpretation and therefore can relate to the 'man–machine interface' also known as socio-technical systems. Hence the domain of technology change at all levels would fall under the classification, e.g.,

- Technical processes.
- Information and communications technologies.
- Technology-based innovations.
- The IT backbone of the organisation.

It is important to understand that in any organisation even the most trivial change or action ripples through the organisation and outside it. Socio-technical systems are complex and adaptive.

9.7 PEOPLE AND CULTURE INTERVENTIONS

As organisations move from the era of personnel management to human resource management to human capital management, the contribution of the People and Culture function has moved from an administrative role to a more strategic role. This means that People and Culture interventions are on-going. Moreover, their role and value to the organisation has strengthened over recent times.

The underlying agenda is to develop the organisation to develop the business through People and Culture interventions. Why? Because organisational performance and productivity have become an important agenda to which change and change management is attached.

Currently Leadership Development Interventions are common in the belief that the development of formal and informal leaders will contribute to competitiveness and organisational sustainability.

As organisations and business become increasingly global, transparent and visible, as industries move towards a commodity platform, then people are the only way to achieve differentiation. Hence the importance of People and Culture interventions. To offer some examples:

- Executive development through mentoring and coaching.
- Action learning projects.
- Performance management.
- Talent management systems.
- Training.

Collectively the People and Culture intervention agenda aims to deliver an underlying agenda of human capital acquisition and retention.

'The employer of choice' is a theme which is now pervasive. It is based upon the needs, wants, values and expectations of employers which are anchored to employee value propositions which collectively achieve a bond between the organisation and the individual through a 'psychological contact'. This contact is the means by which organisations are held together and a working culture is embedded.

Now the importance of People and Culture interventions can be appreciated.

9.8   EXTERNAL ENVIRONMENTAL INTERVENTIONS

The external organisation environment is always subject to change and uncertainty simply because it is usually beyond the boundaries of organisational influence and control. It comprises macro environmental factors that we have seen before when looking at strategy, such as

- Political.
- Economic.
- Social.
- Technological.
- Ecological.

- Legal.

Known through the acronym PESTEL, these factors should guide external reviews and auditing, supplemented by general market trends and competition (which we have also covered previously).

It is the impact of these factors on the organisation which contribute to the change agenda and the associated need for intervention.

Moreover the 'pace of change' in the external environment will act as a driver for change. Customer life cycles, product life cycles, industry life cycles have also to be factored into this equation when accounting for the impact of the external environment upon the organisation.

Well-conceived organisations, which take a proactive view for planning interventions will 'scan' the external environment for emerging trends in order to be a ready for needed change.

This requires an 'outside-in' approach to organisational management which leads to an agenda of 'remaining relevant' within an industry domain.

The value of strategic interventions in organisations can be assessed in a number of ways, for example:

- The need for organisational agility to be able to achieve change.
- The need to achieve and sustain market relevance.
- The need to acquire and retain talented staff.
- The importance of a well-acknowledged corporate or organisational identity.
- Industry and market positioning.
- The maintenance of a working organisational culture for performance outcomes.
- The fundamental requirement to meet shareholder value expectations.

Change is inevitable, interventions are needed at strategic and operational level, there is no escape.

It is the planning for and implementation of such interventions which is critical to organisational cohesion, vibrancy and success.

9.9 QUESTIONS

1. Think about your own organisation or an organisation you are familiar with. What sort of fads can you identify with? What has been their impact? How useful were they?
2. Where might you apply human process interventions in your own organisation or an organisation you are familiar with?
3. From a leadership perspective with an agenda for organisational transformation, what is the purpose to be achieved by strategic intervention?

10. LEADING CHANGE

"As dealing with change becomes a regular activity, leading it becomes a skill to hone, an internal capacity to master."

Arnaud Henneville

10.1 CHAPTER OVERVIEW

This chapter aims to develop readers' understanding of leading the process of change and leading stakeholder change.

The key concepts we cover are change processes, stakeholder change and forcefield analysis.

On completing this chapter, you should be able to:

1. Plan change.
2. Create a forcefield analysis.
3. Analyse stakeholder systems.
4. Execute a change management strategy involving stakeholders.
5. Identify points of resistance to change.
6. Develop strategies to facilitate stakeholder support.

10.2 LEADING THE PROCESS OF CHANGE

To lead planned change, the following 5-Step Road Map is a starting point from which to appreciate some of the essentials required to effect change from a leadership standpoint.

Step 1: Establish the Purpose

1. Clarify the real need
2. Analyse the impact of doing nothing
3. Create a vision
4. Communicate and secure support for the vision
5. Confirm what needs to change

Step 2: Develop the Momentum

1. Communicate, communicate, communicate
2. Align people behind the change
3. Involve people
4. Provide leadership and teams
5. Create urgency and instil a sense of urgency

Step 3: Plan the Change

1. Set milestones for achievement
2. Establish measures for success
3. Identity and secure resources
4. Allocate and delegate responsibilities for planning and implementation
5. Prepare for contingencies
6. Provide support

Step 4: Lead the Implementation

1. Inspire others
2. Communicate throughout
3. Seek early success and celebrate it
4. Monitor, control, review
5. Deal with the unexpected
6. Plan for continuous growth

Step 5: Monitor the Change

1. Ensure effective oversight of the change
2. Ensure that the project management of the change is effective
3. Review the impact upon organisational climate and culture
4. Progressively review the impact of change
5. Deal with the unexpected
6. Plan for continuous improvement
7. Celebrate real results

10.3 POLITICAL DIMENSIONS OF CHANGE: FORCEFIELD ANALYSIS

As change in most organisations is rarely appreciated, the motivation for it as well as the power base behind it has an important role play.

The dynamics of organisational politics have to be factored into the change equation so that resistance can be anticipated and managed.

It is for this reason that forcefield analysis was designed by Lewin (1943, 1951)to analyse the nature of resistance and the force of resistance to transformational change. Reference to Figure 22 shows how resistance to change can be assessed.

Figure 22: Forcefield analysis canvas

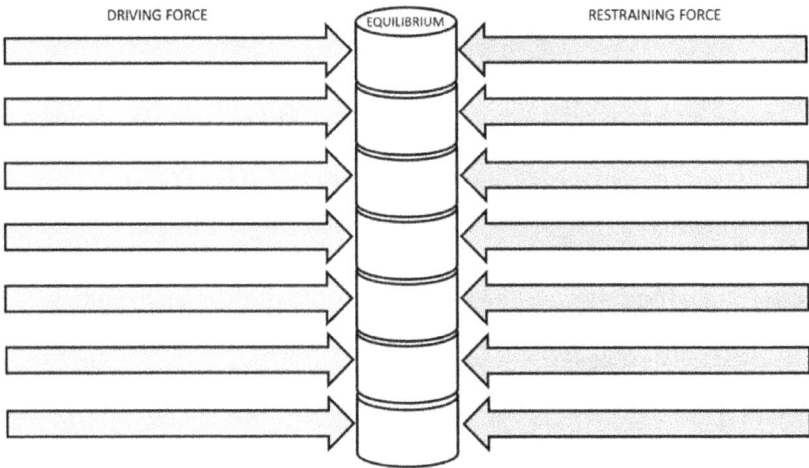

The purpose is to assess the collective 'weight' of resistance and set this against the 'weight' of support for the change. In this way, any disequilibrium can be assessed. The ambition is to reset the equilibrium, should the political faces in evidence from changes intended disturb the status quo.

Forcefield analysis helps change agents embedded in the process of strategy change to better target fields of opposition so that attention is devote to appropriate forms of communication aimed at 'bringing opponents 'on-board' to effect smooth transition.

10.4 LEADING STAKEHOLDER CHANGE: STAKEHOLDER ANALYSIS

Stakeholders for any organisation are derived from a multitude of sources as they are a collective group of individuals or organisations have interest in and are affected by the performance outcomes achieved.

Stakeholder analysis is a process of locating the individuals as well as groups who can influence the organisation's performance as well as be affected by it.

Therefore, stakeholder analysis has the purpose of:

1. Categorising those who will impact the organisation.
2. Those who will be impacted by the organisation.
3. The extent of this impact for both groups.

Stakeholder analysis is a process of locating the individuals as well as groups who can influence the organisation's performance as well as be affected by it.

The purpose to be achieved is to use this analysis in policies, plan design and execution, and any form of significant action to be taken before it happens.

The intention is to ensure all stakeholder interests have been taken into account.

To take this analysis further then the nature of the stakeholder interest held, the power attached to it and the risks arising of such interests cannot be overlooked or mishandled. Stakeholders may be further grouped into those who have favourable or unfavourable predispositions. This has to be accounted for and managed accordingly and it may be useful through the process of stakeholder analysis to form distinct stakeholder groups (Figure 23):

Figure 23: Stakeholder groups

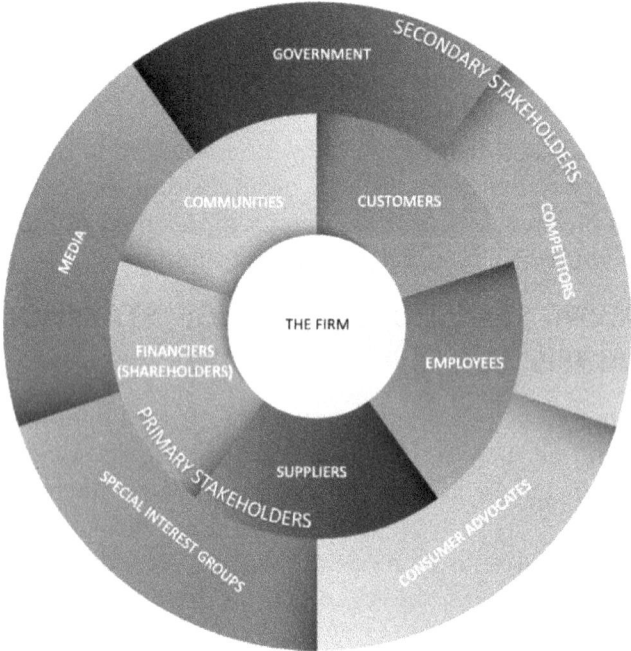

- *Primary stakeholders* comprise groups or individuals who are directly affected, either positively or negatively by the organisation's actions and performance outcomes.

- *Secondary stakeholders* comprise groups or individuals who are indirectly affected but cannot be ignored.

Another part of this analysis is called stakeholder salience mapping whereby the power and influence exerted by individuals or groups can be aligned to the above classifications.

The objective of mapping stakeholder salience is to identify the importance of stakeholder groups to a specific organisation (Mitchell et al., 1997). The salience or covalence model uses three dimensions: legitimacy (A), power (B), and urgency (C), with eight regions each associated to a specific stakeholder type (Figure 24).

Figure 24: Stakeholder salience

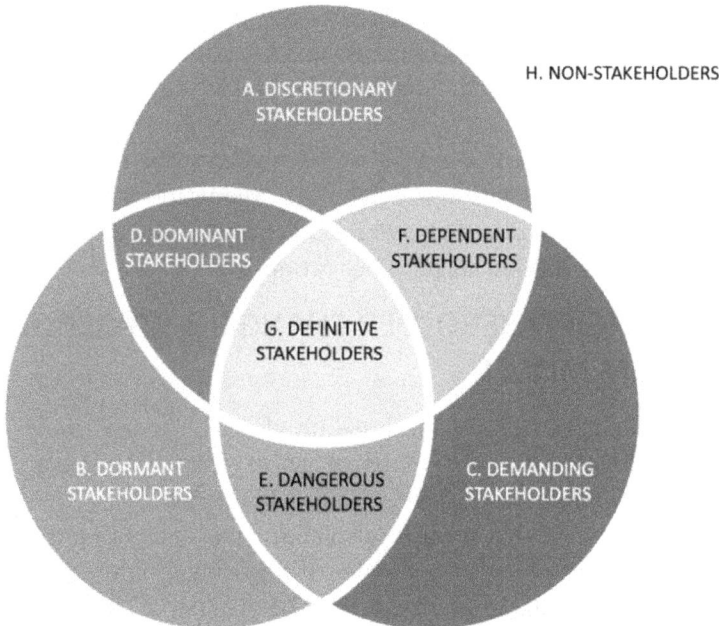

A.   Discretionary stakeholders have little urgency or power and are unlikely to exert much pressure. They have legitimate claims.

B.   Dormant stakeholders have much power but no legitimacy or urgency and therefore are not likely to become heavily involved.

C.   Demanding stakeholders have little power or legitimacy but can make much "noise" because they want things addressed immediately.

D.   Dominant stakeholders have both formal power and legitimacy, but little urgency. They tend to have certain expectations met.

E.   Dangerous stakeholders have power and urgency but are not genuinely pertinent to the project.

F.   Dependent stakeholders have urgent and legitimate stakes in the project but little power. These stakeholders may lean on another stakeholder group to have their voices heard.

G.   Definitive stakeholders have power, legitimacy and urgency and therefore have the highest salience.

H.   Non-stakeholders have no power, legitimacy or urgency.

The reason why this is important is that each stakeholder has a 'stake' in what the organisation does or the outcomes of what action has been taken. Hence, stakeholders have a 'real interest' because they may depend upon the business performance for their own interests.

In turn the organisation will depend upon its stakeholders to realise their mission and objectives. Through this dependency and mutual interdependency stakeholders can be powerful advocates for the organisation.

One significant organisational goal is to balance the forces of various stakeholder groups in the need for organisational development. Any form of strategic planning will need actionable assumptions about the behaviour of multiple stakeholder groups.

10.5 LEADING STAKEHOLDER CHANGE: A STAKEHOLDER SYSTEM MODEL

Using the stakeholder groups outlined previously, we can 'model' the system of stakeholders and also identify sub-systems to produce a classification by defining a systems boundary (Figure 25).

It may be the case that groups of or individual stakeholders have 'boundary spanning' roles into a realm of non-stakeholders (Figure 26).

Sub-systems of stakeholders can then be grouped to build a system map or model of the system of stakeholders (Figure 27).

Should there be a requirement to understand their inter-relationships and dependencies then the systems model can display these relationships (Figure 28).

Such relationships would need to be explained, and for example, could be based upon power, urgency, legitimacy, political Influence and ownership for the change ... and so on. This will depend upon the perspective or series of perspectives being taken.

Figure 25: Stakeholder system model

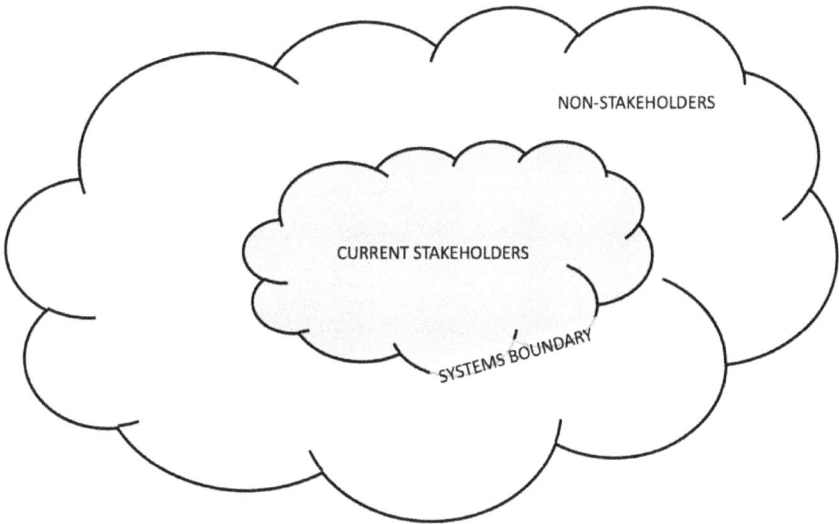

A change planner, when considering the dynamics of change management will need to manage stakeholder groups, and the systems map seeks to model the stakeholders into classification for a clearer understanding. Moreover, the boundaries of control and influence should be understood to support the change management leadership.

Figure 26: Boundary spanning stakeholders

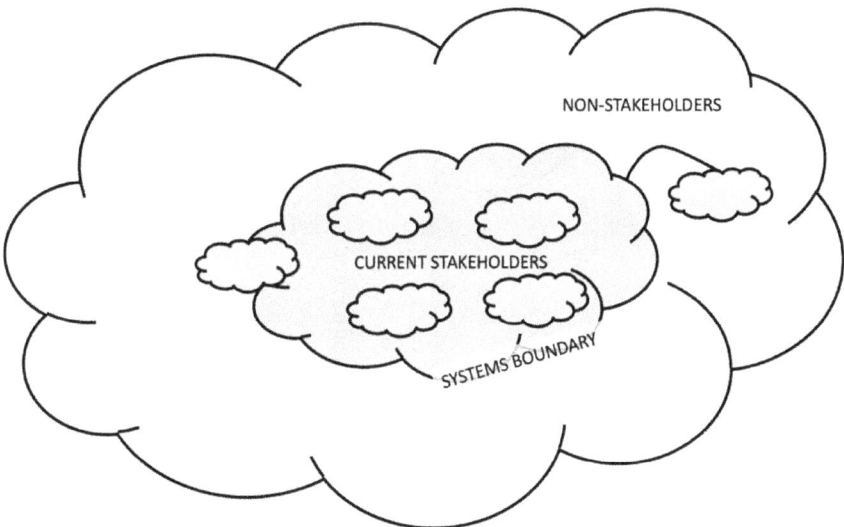

Figure 27: Stakeholder systems map

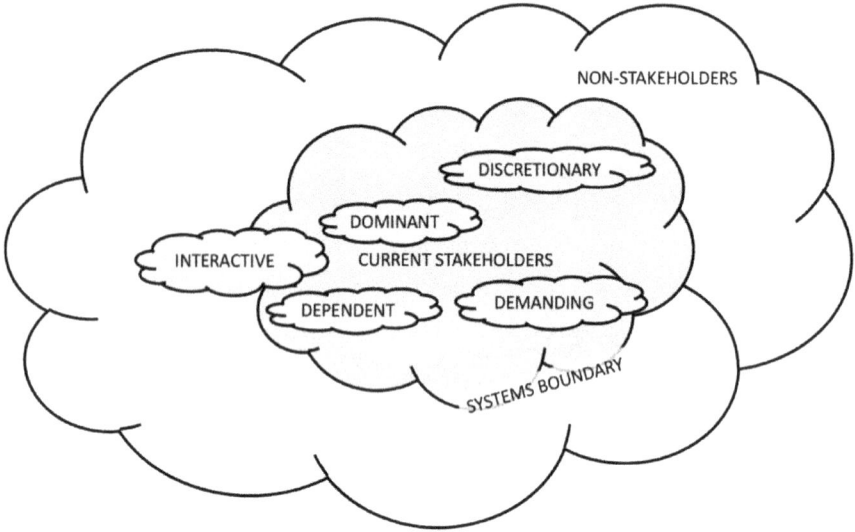

Figure 28: Stakeholder relationships and dependencies map

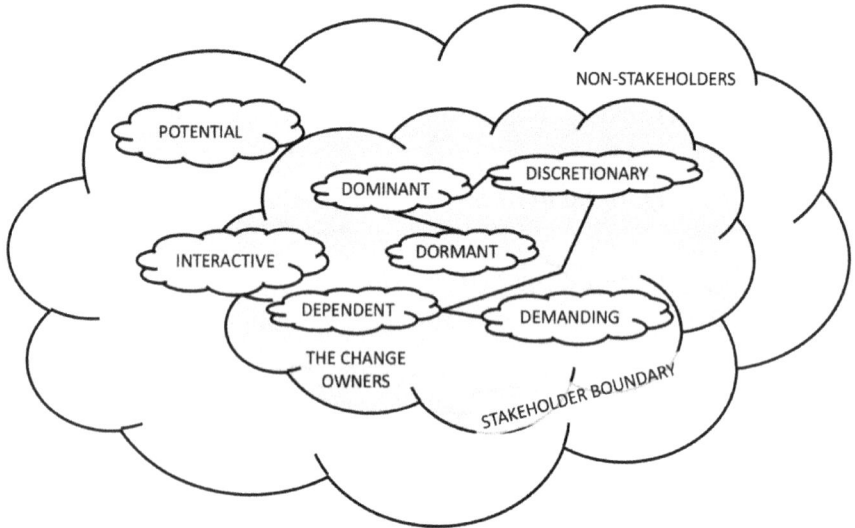

It is clear that with strategic level change, the complexity is such that the use of a systems model to visualise the dynamics of stakeholder upon the change can be very useful to determine the 'stakes' being claimed, which could be economic, or equity stake and influence stake and so on.

10.6 LEADING STAKEHOLDER CHANGE: THE INPUT 'TRANSFORMATION' OUTPUT (ITO) MODEL

Appreciating that stakeholders have different roles in this model may provide useful as an insight for the need to involve them.

It is common to define stakeholders solely as those groups that enjoy output from the model - benefitting from the change or customers of it.

However, in an ITO model, stakeholders may also provide inputs and lead or manage transformations: resourcing, owning or managing the change.

Once ITO groups are identified, analysis may be conducted in terms of roles and responsibilities.

This approach is an effective way of realising how stakeholders are involved in the total process of change. Where change is transformational, the impact of such stakeholder analysis can be very useful.

The involvement of stakeholders has to take into account the convergent and divergent views which need to be managed through appropriate communication plans.

The development of a team-based approach to communication which involves the key stakeholders is strongly advocated because there is often a need to influence prevailing opinion towards support for the change.

In turn the profile of the change becomes heightened, awareness levels rise, providing the opportunity for developing and securing commitment to the change and what it involves.

10.7 LEADING STAKEHOLDER CHANGE: INVOLVING STAKEHOLDERS IN CHANGE MANAGEMENT STRATEGY

Clearly there is no way of avoiding stakeholder involvement in change management strategies, especially where transformational change is involved.

The stakeholder spiral is a simple, but effective tool to reinforce the value and importance of stakeholder expectations when introducing change.

Figure 29 outlines the cycle which is perpetual because change is always present within the operating environments of any active organisation.

The key to using the stakeholder cycle is engagement to get their 'buy-in', interest, commitment and where appropriate, investment to embrace the change, by sharing the plans for change.

To achieve this, the following initiatives can be applied:

- One-to-one discussion.
- Group briefings, meetings and consultations.
- Team building.
- Coaching and training if needed.
- Delegation and empowerment.
- Celebration of progress achieved.

Figure 29: The stakeholder spiral

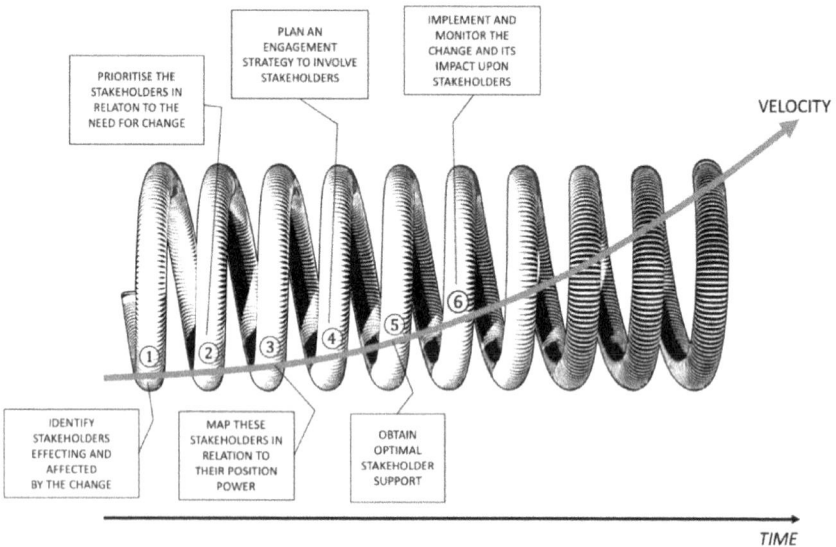

10.8 LEADING STAKEHOLDER CHANGE: STAKEHOLDER MAPPING

From the list of stakeholders, the achievement of the stakeholder map is achieved by positioning the key stakeholders in a system or network to indicate important relationships, their motivations and challenges.

Patterns of interdependence will emerge.

The value is that the stakeholders are 'mapped out' and visualised, which is a huge benefit.

Figure 30 is a stakeholder map of a typical retail store.

Figure 30: Stakeholder map of typical retail store

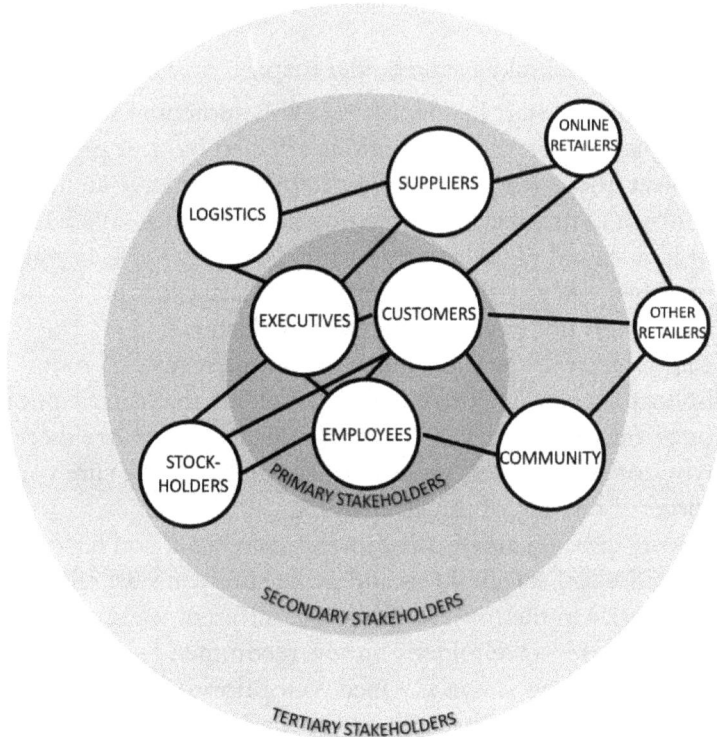

Once you are familiar with this simple analysis tool, there are a number of important points which emerge:

1. The stakeholder groups may be independent, but the actions taken can affect other stakeholder groups.
2. Actions taken by the organisation can have a pervasive effect upon widely distributed stakeholder groups.
3. Stakeholder maps may become more complex overtime.
4. The web of stakeholder relationships can become a challenge to manage as diversity extends to new groups, and here is a need to manage response time so it is effective and reliable and predict likely outcomes proactively.

In simpler terms, the use of a cliché, opportunities and threats from each stakeholder group may work well as a framework for managing the 'texture' of the stakeholder map as well as the complexity.

The use of the stakeholder map, even as a piece of static standalone analysis is useful because it provides a statement of reality of 'what exists'. This tool can also be used for assessing the impact of change before it is introduced.

Here is how you build a stakeholder map:

1. *Brainstorming.* Start by identifying all the potential stakeholders (people, groups, or organisations affected by your product or project, those who have influence over it, or have an interest or concern in its success). Write down their names on a whiteboard or in a shared virtual space. At this point, try to be as granular as possible; you can always eliminate duplicates or those who actually do not have 'skin in the game' later.

2. *Categorisation.* Now it is time to group the results of your brainstorming. Are there any stakeholders that can be put into one category? How can you name this category? Are there any types of stakeholders you forgot about? To make sure you didn't forget about any of the key players.

3. *Prioritisation.* To create a communication plan, you have to prioritise key stakeholders and make sure you start talking to them early in the project. There are different ways you can prioritise the stakeholders, but we recommend salience analysis.

4. *Stakeholder communications.* Once your priorities are defined, it is important to come up with a plan for engaging all the major stakeholders. There is no single recipe that can fit all possible situations, but here are some best practices that can help you create transparency and accountability for your project:

   - You should have a lot of face-to-face communication with high-power, highly interested people. Building trust with them first is critical for your project.
   - If someone is opposed to the project, you can get a buy-in from someone with the same level of power first and then ask the latter to persuade the former.
   - Communicating early and often is also important, because people will need time to think before making a decision.

- Give each stakeholder a right amount of information depending on their interest. Some people need just an executive summary, while others will want to dive deeper.

10.9 LEADING STAKEHOLDER CHANGE: UNDERSTANDING TRANSFORMATIONAL CHANGE VULNERABILITY

Having mapped stakeholders, this analysis could be taken further to understand how transformational change exposes the organisation to strategic vulnerability.

An assessment of how vulnerable the organisation is as a result of implementing change is important. How can this be achieved?

Vulnerability analysis involves a series of steps all related to what underpins the organisation (especially stakeholders) and upon which the organisation really depends to function. Examples of such underpinnings include:

- Customer demand.
- Customer loyalty.
- Customer goodwill.
- Corporate identity.
- Channels.
- The resource base.
- The customer base.
- Costs.
- Values.
- Product or service range.
- Networks.
- Staff loyalty.
- Technology infrastructure.
- Critical components in the business model.
- Supplier relationship.
- Trusted networks.
- Financial health.

Each, and others in context, have a part to play in the organisation's performance outcomes and sustainability.

The steps to be taken then would be:

1. To confirm the Critical Underpinnings which support the organisation and upon which it depends.
2. Examine how the removal or challenge to each of these underpinnings as a result of change would impact the organisation.
3. From '2' above estimate best and worst-case scenarios based upon the change bring introduced.
4. Project the company's response and ability to cope with the consequences.

5. From step '4' determine the scale of vulnerability and work towards a target scenario for sustainability.

Once again, the mindset for vulnerability (and risk) maybe as useful as the adoption of the technique. This will lead to understanding the extent to which the organisation is 'prepared' for change and hence assess 'readiness'. Note that in extreme cases an organisation may be vulnerable and defenceless.

From a managerial perspective, vulnerability analysis helps to focus on:

1. The underpinnings upon which the organisation depends for sustainability.
2. Changes planned or imposed that can destroy the basic underpinnings.
3. Knowing what can impose a serious threat and the impact created.
4. How vulnerable the organisation is.
5. The company's ability and agility to sustain the organisation.

Asking the right questions of the right people at the right time will expose a significant agenda in the organisational transformation Agenda, that is vulnerability.

10.10 LEADING STAKEHOLDER CHANGE: EXECUTION

10.10.1 CHANGE AGENTS AND CHANGE CHAMPIONS

All significant change requires leadership, energy and momentum. Change needs to be driven and hence the role of the change agent is to enable the process required to effect the desired change.

Within stakeholder groups, there needs to be a champion for the cause, hence the term Change Champion. This person or group are custodians of the change from their area of concern or involvement and it is possible to have more than one change champion for planned transformational change.

To achieve change through managing resistance to it will involve people, process and technology. The role of the Change Champion to drive and facilitate the essential processes cannot be ignored.

10.10.2 COMMUNICATING THE CHANGE VISION

To achieve the needed support and active commitment to change, there must be a mechanism to inspire stakeholders.

A change vision of what the eventual outcome will be showed also be a statement to which stakeholders aspire to become attached to.

In this way, the need for a well-communicated to change, there must be a mechanism to inspire stakeholders.

10.10.3 FOCUS ON THE POSITIVE OUTCOMES

The change vision may provide an overall picture of what will be achieved. This constitutes of a series of benefits which are cascaded down through the organisation.

To overcome resistance at different organisational levels then communication must focus upon the positive outcome which collectively will achieve the change vision.

Through this process and by using the findings of the forcefield analysis, then the needed support of all the key players in the entire process of change is essential.

10.10.4 IMPLEMENTATION TRAINING

To build the needed confidence for achieving the change there will be a need to adjust mindset among key stakeholder groups. This can be achieved through mentoring and coaching as needed, but the need for training for the implementation is to be considered as a key role to be discharged.

A programme of training with a well-communicated training calendar is needed. It also will help to address resistance because it informs stakeholder groups that the 'change is real' ; the organisation is fully committed for implementation.

10.10.5 A PLAN FOR CHANGE

One further important feature which cannot be ignored in the battle against different levels of resistance is to plan the change and achieve the change to the designed plan. Hence, a significant organisational goal is to balance the forces of various stakeholder groups in the need for organisational development.

Any form of strategic planning will need actionable assumptions about the behaviour of multiple stakeholder groups falling under the following categories:

- Customers
- Employees and departments
- Top management
- Suppliers (including Creditors)
- Distribution Channel Members
- Competitors
- Shareholders
- Societal groups
- Regulators
- Special Interest Groups
- Unions
- Accreditation agencies
- Local and National Government
- The media
- IT Vendors
- The local community
- Religious groups
- Taxation authorities
- Changing the reward structures

In some cultures, the inducement of financial reward is a powerful source of motivation and while this may be viewed as a coercive method to overcome resistance, it can certainly be considered as the means to facilitate support for the implementation plans for change.

10.10.6   AN ENLIGHTENED PERSPECTIVE

Resistance is there for a reason of which there may be many which obstruct change. However, a more enlightened perspective is that it is an opportunity to learn. Resistance may arise from doubt about the viability of the change become stakeholders are sceptical. If the reason for scepticism is known through a research process (or dialogue) then such discoveries can be accommodated within the change communication plan and execution.

However, if the mood for the change is based upon cynicism, then this is more serious because this amounts to a fundamental disbelief in management ability to achieve the change or simply distrust their motive for the change.

Disbelief combined with mistrust is a powerful formula for undermining the organisation's stability.

Any basis for cynicism must be tackled at root cause level to achieve any change plans being delayed or even sabotaged. Managing such resilience will require a deep searching process to discover the motive and the power base from which cynicism has developed. In such cases, the 'readiness for change' has to be reviewed, because change management will require the shaping and conditioning of attributes & beliefs to favourably support the change.

This again will reinforce the need to:

1. Communicate the need for change.
2. Engage meaningfully with the stakeholder groups to achieve support.
3. Instil, when appropriate a sense of urgency.
4. Take a strategic approach to communicate direction followed by a task approach of what needs to be done and when. Both the strategic and tactical approach will need engagement through interpersonal relationships to build morale, cohesion and alliances so all are aligned to the change purpose and vision.

10.11 QUESTIONS

1. The road map in section 9.2 is intended to outline the essential processes needed and present them in a form of a progressive checklist which the leader may find useful in the workplace environment. We cannot however, as Moss Kanter suggests, overlook the 'human element'. Organisations are 'human activity systems' and therefore we must also consider the response to change. How would you approach dealing with colleagues who negatively respond to proposed change?
2. The calibration of a force field analysis may be more valuable as a concept than a calculated outcome which may be more subjective than objective. What is your appraisal of the strengths and weaknesses of force field analysis in approaching change management?
3. What are the essential factors in effectively managing stakeholders in a change project?
4. Have a go at mapping the stakeholders of your company or a business that you are familiar with. Were there any surprises or surprise relationships? How might these affect planned change in the organisation?

ENABLING ORGANISATIONAL TRANSFORMATION

"Change will not come if we wait for some other person or some other time. We are the ones we've been waiting for. We are the change that we seek".

Barack Obama

11. STRATEGY AND PERFORMANCE

"However beautiful the strategy, you should occasionally look at the results."

Sir Winston Churchill

11.1 CHAPTER OVERVIEW

This chapter explores the strategy to performance gap and performance management.

The key concepts we cover are gap analysis, organisational underachievement, performance management and performance assessment.

On completing this chapter, you should be able to:

1. Evaluate gaps between planned strategic and actual performance.
2. Identify factors underlying organisational achievement.
3. Assess and manage organisational performance.

11.2 WHY CHANGE?

The need for change is driven by one of two phenomena: something substantial has happened or something substantial hasn't happened. The key questions for leaders are:

- What might happen if we do not respond (can we do nothing or more pointedly do we have a choice)?
- What is the evidence that supports the need for a response?

From here the question is back to our friends the six honest servants:

- What do we need to do?
- Why do we need to do it?
- When do we need to do it?
- How do we need to do it?
- Where do we need to do it?
- Who needs to do it?

If the current strategy is not working, we need to quickly grasp the size of the existing and forecast strategy to performance gap. It crucial that we understand the realities and 'hard' facts? Decision-making is always subjective, but the more data we have the better the chances are that we make decisions that have positive outcomes.

We should source evidence a range of sources, including but not limited to:

- Thinking strategically and systematically.
- Strategic planning.
- Contextual statistics.
- Periodic reviews.
- Internal discussions.

Wherever data comes from we need to be assured of its reliability and validity and we should ensure that we have a mandate from the board to act.

11.3 THE STRATEGY TO PERFORMANCE GAP

The business environment impacts upon strategy achievement as a constant challenge for organisations needing to achieve business performance targets for shareholder value enhancement and stakeholder benefit (Kaplan & Norton, 1992, 1993, 1996a, 1996b, 2004, 2008).

It is not unusual for pre-determined strategies to underachieve or overachieve; this is known as "the strategy to performance gap". It becomes a key driver for the organisational transformational adjustments to be made in order for performance to stay on track. The nature of such adjustment will depend upon the extent of the emerging and forecast performance gaps.

Change is required to bridge the performance gap through adjusted strategies, strategic and operational interventions, new value creation, value capture with dedicated leadership.

11.3.1 HOW DOES THE NEED FOR TRANSFORMATION ARISE?

Organisations which have strategic planning systems in place with monthly and quarterly reviews conducted using variance analysis. It is at this time that the strategy to performance gap is usually revealed. In turn this periodic review process will create a managerial mindset for the strategy to performance gap. However, without such conventions of systematic performance tracking, it may require a crisis to drive transformational change. This may happen during conditions of environmental turbulence.

11.3.2 HOW ARE PERFORMANCE GAPS DISCOVERED?

Actual results from past and current strategy implementation will be the key indicator for assessing performance and to highlight what is not working well.

Performance management systems are designed to periodically review strategy results (Kaplan & Norton, 1992, 1993, 1996a, 1996b, 2004, 2008). Such management protocol establishes a mindset for results attainment through the regular rituals and routines which form part of the system for internal control and accountability, without which correction action cannot be taken.

11.3.3 WHERE ARE THE KEY GAPS IN PERFORMANCE?

Usually, performance gaps originate from one of two sources:

- Financial gap analysis
- Non-financial gap analysis

The discovery of these performance gaps will often be based upon pre-determined metrics for assessing performance (Kaplan & Norton, 1992, 1993, 1996a, 1996b, 2004, 2008). These must be in place and reviewed for relevance.

11.3.3.1 Financial Gap Analysis

Here the focus will be upon the variables such as revenue, operating cost, cashflow, gross margin and profitability, assessed through a wide range of financial health metrics to monitor actual achievement. These financial management imperatives directly impact shareholder value projections. In addition, the size of the anticipated gap will be analysed as part of a business forecasting process. Such internal management accounting requirements are commonplace (Kaplan & Norton, 1992, 1993, 1996a, 1996b, 2004, 2008). From a leadership perspective, the need for change and the nature of the changes needed cannot be neglected.

11.3.3.2 Non-Financial Gap Analysis

Here the focus will be upon overall organisational performance because this is the fundamental enabler for financial health (Boxall & Macky, 2007; Garavan et al., 2020). Financial results are only achieved through the efficiencies and effectiveness of the organisation, its leadership and cohesion (Kaplan & Norton, 1992, 1993, 1996a, 1996b, 2004, 2008).

11.3.3.3 Combining the Analysis

It is through combining these analyses, a leader can understand and locate 'root causes' and define the real nature of the performance gap. Research shows that non-financial components usually drive financial performance in many strategy to performance gap scenarios.

11.3.4 TYPICAL SOURCES OF ORGANISATIONAL PERFORMANCE GAPS

From research undertaken (Boxall & Macky, 2007; Garavan et al., 2020; Kaplan & Norton, 1992, 1993, 1996a, 1996b, 2004, 2008), the following sources are typical, but many more may exist:

- Service delivery.
- Organisational cohesion.
- Inadequate leadership.
- Internal and interpersonal communication.
- Poor sense of direction.
- Social intelligence of staff.
- Strategy execution inefficiencies.
- Poor implementation planning.
- Enterprise resource adequacy and deployment.
- Non-compliant culture.
- Employee disengagement.
- Insufficient transparency.
- Competency shortfalls.
- Poor employee value propositions.
- Legacy information systems & technologies.
- Low organisational agility.
- Quality gaps.
- Ineffective strategy into action decision taking.
- Customer loyalty erosion.
- Supplier relationship challenges.
- Channel constraints.
- Business model relevance.
- Under valued customer segment experience.
- Competitor value addition.

- Erosion of relationship capital.
- Inefficient business processes.

- Stakeholder engagement in the workplace.
- Internal control inefficiency

The potential for underachievement and even failure is high and it is clear that the strategy to performance gap is a managerial reality. Why do you think this occurs?

How can we manage underachievement?

The domain of non-financial analysis is complex. Accordingly, a systemic approach to organisational transformation is required to embrace, contain and control organisational performance. Conceptual modelling is required to produce a central point of reference for organisational performance leadership.

Figure 31 presents a classification of organisational underachievement.

Figure 31: Organisational underachievement

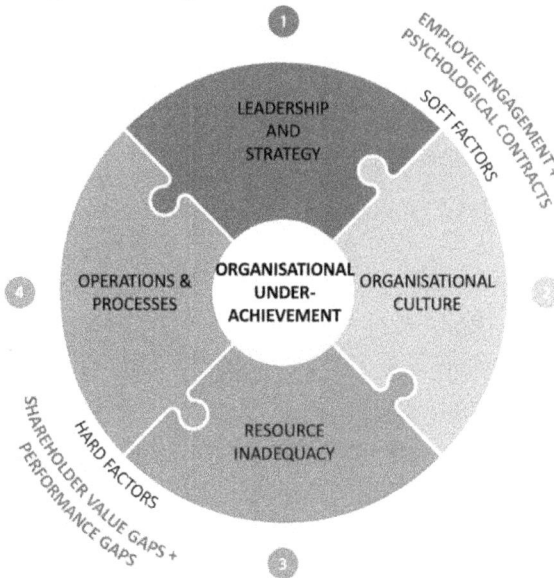

From a top management perspective, a major challenge is to translate well conceived strategy into targeted performance. From an operational perspective, how the results are achieved is a day-to-day challenge.

Results only be achieved through effective realistic planning supported by effective, disciplined, execution processes and leadership which collectively deliver needed solutions to convert strategy into action.

11.4 QUESTIONS

1. Consider the typical sources of non-financial performance gaps presented in this Chapter and then add others driven from your own organisational experience. Now add previous inputs from Chapters 1 to 3 and 4 to 6. Can you determine a way to classify these sources of organisational under-achievement? What conclusions can you draw? What does this imply for leaders?
2. What the main learning points from the concepts around performance management which have resonated with you?

12. ENGAGEMENT AND CULTURE

"Customers will never love a company until the employees love it first."

Simon Sinek

12.1 CHAPTER OVERVIEW

This chapter explores employee engagement and culture change.

The key concepts we explore are employee engagement and culture change.

On completing this chapter, you should be able to:

1. Define employee engagement.
2. Explain the major influences on employee engagement.
3. Identify what constitutes a well-engaged employee.
4. Define organisational culture.
5. Explain the formation of organisational culture.
6. Explain the role of culture in organisational life.

12.2 WHAT IS EMPLOYEE ENGAGEMENT?

Organisational transformation can only be achieved effectively if the level of organisational engagement permits planned change. Organisations globally are now aware of the need to track, monitor and review organisational engagement as one of the most critical factors for sustainability to deliver stakeholder value.

Employee engagement is workplace jargon widely used but not widely understood. Employee engagement is in fact a metric which calibrates the extent to which employees are fully involved in their work and that they are committed to 'on the job' performance for their employer (Harter & Blacksmith, 2009; Harter, Schmidt, Agrawal, Blue, et al., 2020; Harter, Schmidt, Agrawal, Plowman, et al., 2020). Engagement by definition suggests a level of disengagement!

This in turn implies that a percentage of staff may be disengaged, disintegrated, unproductive with a low level of morale. These people may leave for other employment or be retrenched; it is just a matter of time. In the meantime, this group may comprise a disruptive influence.

In July 2020, the highly influential Gallup global survey of employee engagement recently found that [8]

"The percentage of 'engaged' workers in the USA (those who are highly involved in, enthusiastic about, and committed to their work and workplace) reached 38%. This is the highest it has been since Gallup began tracking the metric in 2000. However, their measurement from June 1-14 (following the killing of George Floyd in late May 2020 and subsequent protests and riots on top of a pandemic, unemployment, and attempts to re-open some businesses) finds that 31% of the working population are engaged. Taking into consideration three Gallup measures of employee engagement this year, the overall percentage of engaged workers during 2020 is 36%.

The percentage of workers who are 'actively disengaged' (those who have miserable work experiences and spread their unhappiness to their colleagues) remained at approximately the same engagement level. It was 14% in June compared to 13% in early May. This drops the ratio of engaged to actively disengaged employees from 3.0-to-1 to 2.2-to-1 in the U.S., the lowest ratio since 2016."

It is common that levels of employee engagement are measured through periodic opinion surveys to monitor the 'organisational climate' in order to detect behavioural modification in the workforce which may not be visible to top management and organisational leaders.

Such surveys with usually research and track common themes, for example:

- Job satisfaction
- Working environment satisfaction
- Pride as an employee
- Satisfaction with the employer in terms of compensation, recognition and reward
- Job scope and challenges that are valued
- Relationships with next line of managers, peers and subordinates
- Understanding the contribution made to the organisation for the job role
- Career prospects
- Employee benefits
- Intention to remain as an employee
- Relationship with 'the boss'
- Performance feedback and encouragement
- Opportunities for meaningful work challenges
- Personal growth

As can be appreciated employee engagement is about a wide array of factors over and above compensation for the job role and role profile. Which brings us to the puzzle of motivation.

12.3 THE PUZZLE OF MOTIVATION

Pink (2009) connects motivation and performance. He explains why rewards rarely boost productivity and that "autonomy, mastery and purpose" are the only factors that truly motivate people[9].

Duncker (1945) created the 'candle puzzle', a cognitive science exercise that asks participants to adhere a candle to a wall so that, when lit, wax won't drip on a table below. Participants have access to a candle, a box of thumbtacks and matches. The solution is: tack the thumbtack box to the wall, place the candle in it and then light the wick. The test examines participants' 'functional fixedness', that is, their ability to view the thumbtack box as a candleholder rather than its prescribed purpose as a container.

Rewards, by their very nature, narrow our focus, concentrate the mind; that's why they work in so many cases.

Glucksberg (1962) conducted a variation of the candle experiment to test the influence of incentives on work productivity. In his study,

---

[9] Adapted from
https://www.ted.com/talks/dan_pink_the_puzzle_of_motivation?language=en, accessed 23 April 2021

one group of participants garnered rewards according to how fast they solved the puzzle. A second group received none. Surprisingly, the group with incentives found the solution more slowly. Studies around the world produced similar results. However, when researchers asked participants to conduct the experiment when the tacks were already outside the box, the incentives worked. Thus, while rewards do boost productivity for rote tasks, they do not promote the conceptual, creative thinking required to find solutions and pave new ground in the 21st-century business environment. Yet the business world relies on offering carrots and sticks, rewards and punishments, to raise performance and productivity. Pink (2009) notes that clearly "there is a mismatch between what science knows and what business does".

The solution is not to do more of the wrong things, to entice people with a sweeter carrot or threaten them with a sharper stick. We need a whole new approach.

Research finds that that three intrinsic human desires, "autonomy, mastery and purpose", drive productivity (Baard et al., 2004; Chirkov et al., 2003; Deci & Ryan, 2008; Devine et al., 2008; Gagné & Deci, 2005; Green, 2006; Seligman, 2004, 2012).

3M, Google and Atlassian, an Australian software company, use this knowledge with incredible success. They each give their engineers a day every few months to pursue an idea of their choosing. Several solutions and products have resulted from allowing employees free rein[10].

Ressler and Thompson (2008) created another workplace model called the "Results Only Work Environment (ROWE)". Employees work where, when and how they want, as long as they fulfil their job obligations. In ROWE workplaces, productivity rises, turnover rates drop and engagement skyrockets. The gap between research and practice is substantial. Business should consider that monetary incentives work only in a narrow set of routine conditions, that "if-then rewards" actually can impede creativity, and that the key to improved performance is not carrots and sticks but "the drive to do things for their own sake".

12.4 THE WELL-ENGAGED EMPLOYEE

A well-engaged employee at any level will display certain characteristics which should be observed when appraising performance:

---

[10] https://en.wikipedia.org/wiki/20%25_Project, accessed 23 April 2021

- A sense of urgency.
- Focus upon determined priorities.
- A committed level of involvement.
- Flexibility.

- Individual initiative by working proactively.
- A team player.
- Results orientation.
- Positive energy.

Key influences for improved levels of engagement include:

- Open trust
- Open communication and transparency
- Channels for feedback from the voice of the employee which are visibly acted upon
- Empowerment with support

- Effective Leadership
- Ease of managing up and managing down
- Appropriate job autonomy
- Learning and development

Above all, it is the 'work environment' that counts the most. This drives organisational energy.

Each individual needs a role identity connected to a sense of purpose, so their contribution is known across the organisation.

12.5 WHAT MAKES US FEEL GOOD ABOUT OUR WORK?

What motivates us to work? Contrary to conventional wisdom, it is not just money. But it is not exactly joy either. It seems that most of us thrive by making constant progress and feeling a sense of purpose.

Ariely (2016) finds that the assumption that people work only for a paycheque is inaccurate. The forces that motivate are much more complex (Ariely et al., 2009; Woolley & Fishbach, 2015).

Consider why some individuals subject themselves to the rigour and pain of mountain climbing. Although the ascent is often miserable, they find meaning in the challenge and eventual accomplishment. If you think about mountain climbing as an example, it suggests all kinds of things. It suggests that we care about reaching the end, a peak. It suggests that we care about the fight, about the challenge.

Ariely et al. (2008) devised an experiment to study the importance of meaning in work. In the first variation, the "meaningful condition," they offered participants $3.00 to build a Lego structure. After subjects finished building, testers placed the structure under the table and explained that it would be disassembled. They then offered less pay for a second structure. They continually lowered the pay-out per structure until participants declined because the offer was no longer worthwhile to them. The next variation tested the "Sisyphic condition", named after Sisyphus, who was doomed to fruitless toil. These subjects received the same decreasing pay-outs, but testers disassembled the structures visibly and immediately before reoffering them to the participants. People completed more projects in the first variation though the process felt only slightly less futile than in the second. What's more, in a third variation where subjects heard a description of the first two experiments, they accurately predicted that meaning would be important, though they underestimated the degree.

Ignoring the performance of people is almost as bad as shredding their effort in front of their eyes.

If people feel their work is futile, it saps their commitment and productivity. Thus, when cancelling a project, CEOs who understand the "essence of meaning" will strive to find other ways to use or acknowledge a team's work and input. An additional experiment supports this idea. Ariely (2016) reports asking three groups of subjects to find pairs of identical letters among random letter groupings on paper. Of the three groups, only one received brief acknowledgement for their work, and this group worked the longest. The group whose work was ignored performed almost as poorly as the group whose work was directly shredded.

The good news is that adding motivation does not seem to be so difficult. The bad news is that eliminating motivations seems to be incredibly easy, and if we do not think about it carefully, we might overdo it (Ariely, 2016).

People also enjoy work more, and feel more ownership, when challenged. Furniture store IKEA caters to this trait by requiring self-assembly of its wares (Mochon et al., 2012; Norton et al., 2012). Similarly, in a study where participants constructed origami, they found their creations more valuable and attractive than outside observers did, and the effect increased with difficulty (Mochon et al., 2012; Norton et al., 2012). Therefore, companies that want a happier, more productive workforce must stop viewing paycheques as the sole motivator and incorporate "meaning, creation, challenges, ownership, identity [and] pride" (Ariely, 2016).

12.6 ORGANISATIONAL CULTURE CHANGE

12.6.1 THE FORMAL AND INFORMAL ORGANISATION

Organisations are made up of these two basic components (formal and informal) where formally goals are set, strategy is determined, structures are built supported by systems and processes to achieve financial results through asset deployment. But how this all happens will depend upon the 'informal organisation' which constitutes power, politics, conflict, values, attitudes, beliefs as well as norms of behaviour. This, through leadership styles and organisational behaviour, makes up the 'way things are done', i.e., the *organisational culture*.

There are in fact a multitude of definitions of culture which may provide an insight to the complexities of this phenomenon which constitutes organisation life, but what matters is how and why organisational transformation requires cultural change.

When the common ingredients which constitute organisational culture can be understood then the need for change and the location of this change is more easily determined.

Furthermore, these cultural ingredients must be applied to a specific organisation context.

Against this backdrop, the desired cultural characters for defined organisational transformation must now be considered, for example to achieve:

1. A performance-based organisation.
2. A customer focused business.
3. Team-based orientation.
4. Improved organisational stability.
5. People-centric orientation.
6. Innovation-based climate.
7. Transition towards privatisation.
8. Risk aversion through progressive corporate governance.
9. An entrepreneurial orientation.
10. Organisational evolution.

Once these characteristics are pre-set as the drivers for change, then assessed ingredients for culture change can be prioritised for adjustment to thereby achieve the organisational transformation desired. Transformational change may be a substantial agenda.

12.6.2 HOW CAN WE DEFINE ORGANISATIONAL CULTURE?

Common ingredients of organisation culture which may require adjustment for organisational transformation include:

- Identity (corporate brand).
- Visible artefacts and symbols.
- Behavioural patterns.
- Organisational rituals and processes.
- The management team leadership.
- Organisation structure.
- Power bases and roles.
- Beliefs, values, attitudes.
- Ethics.
- Existence of sub-cultural groupings.
- Organisational energy.
- Routines.
- Control systems for performance.

12.6.3 HOW DOES ORGANISATIONAL CULTURE CHANGE?

In short, with considerable difficulty, this is owing to the fact that organisational dynamics will interplay between desired change as mandated and emergent change which is what actually happens.

This may therefore represent a very real culture change gap.

It is therefore important to establish the real need for change, to get the level of 'buy-in' needed, but this could be frustrated by:

- A lack of shared values.
- Different organisational assumptions held.
- The inability to define where change is needed arising from the difficulty in 'reading' the organisation culture.
- A lack of trust in the proposed changes.
- Insufficient communication or soliciting of prevailing views among those affected.
- A lack of ownership for the changes.
- Low levels of employee engagement.

It is advisable before considering how organisation achieve change is to complete an organisational climate survey or by using an Organisational Culture Assessment Instrument (Cameron & Quinn, 2011) to answer the question "Where are we now ?" . . . as a place to begin to better understand the cultural landscape. Diagnostic tests or surveys will provide useful inputs.

The complexity of culture change is considerable. The reality may be that a cultural change gap may have to be managed progressively through a series of iterations for alignment with the cultural changes desired because

- Of the impact of the organisation's history upon the prevailing culture.
- Patterns of ownership have an impact on culture.
- Of interactions between the formal and informal organisation.
- Of attachment to existing artefacts, processes and procedures.
- All in all, a change of mindset is required.

Unless there is a real crisis, then a revolutionary cultural change can rarely be orchestrated. More often change must be incremental and accomplished step by step.

Ultimately what must emerge is alignment between the outcomes of organisational transformation and the cultural adjustments which are needed. Otherwise, there is a mismatch between future ambitions of the organisation and their ability to achieve them.

12.6.4 WINNING PERFORMANCE CULTURES

To achieve significant organisational transformation, a winning performance culture will be an enduring ambition.

The conditions for such culture include:

- Effective levels of employee engagement.
- A valued psychological contract between the organisation and employees with enduring employee value propositions.
- Valued recognition and reward.
- Strong cascaded leadership for a winning performance culture.
- Attribution to the 'people agenda' to determine a basis for HR engagement.
- HR relationship partners working in the business units as a conduit for information flows.
- Performance is defined and understood at all levels of the organisation.
- Expectations and accountability are understood.
- Empowerment.
- Positive attitudes.
- Energised organisational climate in the workplace.

- Performance management systems aligned to business objectives.
- Learning and development aligned to competency needs.
- A talent inventory of high performing staff to take up key positions.
- Trust and teamwork.

12.7 QUESTIONS

1. Consider the following:
   a. As a leader, what behaviour is most noticeable from a well-engaged employee?
   b. Do you know what conditions in the working environment have contributed most to this level of employee engagement?
   c. Is this behaviour sustained?
2. Consider the following:
   a. What the factors restrict levels of organisational engagement in the workplace?
   b. What are the main contributing conditions for non-productive levels of engagement in the workplace?
   c. As a leader seeking significant organisational transformation, what are the things that must be done to ensure superior levels of employee engagement?
3. Consider the following:
   a. What is the organisation culture?
   b. How is it formed?
   c. How long does it take to establish?
   d. What part does it play in organisational life?
   e. How can it be understood?
   f. How can it be defined?
   g. Why must it change to achieve organisational transformation?
   h. Is culture change difficult?
   i. How can culture change be achieved?
   j. How will culture change remain and not revert?
   k. What other culture-based questions must be asked for leading organisational transformation?

4. Consider the following:
   a. Should cultural change lead transformation or be a progressive outcome of organisational transformation which has been pre-determined?
   b. Is organisational culture, under conditions of transformation, also impacted by national cultures and sub-cultural groupings?
   c. To what extent, does cross-cultural management play a part in achieving transformational change?
   d. Therefore, can cultural change become a sensitive agenda?
5. Consider:
   a. Is it possible to achieve a road map for culture change?
   b. Where would you start?
   c. What will enable change, implement it and then secure it?
   d. If the process of cultural change is difficult and potentially slow, what can be changed so that realistic rather than optimistic outcomes can be achieved?
6. Now also give thought to:
   a. Adjustment in the workforce composition
   b. Structural change and human resource deployment
   c. Top management action
   d. Change management systems
   e. Internal communication
   f. Information flows
   g. Recruitment and selection policies
   h. Ethics and compliance
7. It is necessary to understand why the existing culture has prevailed until now. This will provide a more solid foundation for change and the cultural risk which may be faced in seeking to implement a cultural change agenda. Recognise as well that power, politics and authority have an important part to play. Developing your thinking further:
   a. What other observations do you have?
   b. What leadership insights do you have?
8. As a leader, how will you address an agenda for a winning performance culture?
9. From a leadership perspective with an agenda for Organisational transformation, what is your assessment of the importance of employee engagement and organisational culture?

13. STRUCTURE, PROCESS AND RELATIONSHIPS

"Every company has two organisational structures: The formal one is written on the charts; the other is the everyday relationship of the men and women in the organisation."

Harold Geneen

"If you can't describe what you are doing as a process, you don't know what you're doing."

W. Edwards Deming

"Many relationship problems are rooted in a communication breakdown. These can be as simple as not really hearing what the other person is saying, because we get caught up in our own fixed perspectives."

Sumesh Nair

13.1 CHAPTER OVERVIEW

This chapter aims to develop readers' understanding of organisational structure, processes, business process reengineering and relationship management

The key concepts we cover are organisational structure, processes, business process reengineering (BPR) and relationship management.

On completing this chapter, you should be able to:

1. Demonstrate you understand the concept of organisational structure and its appropriate implementation.
2. Explain what processes are and the contribution they make in organisations.
3. Outline the principles of business process reengineering
4. Demonstrate and understanding of the principles of relationship management.

13.2 ORGANISATION STRUCTURE

To lead planned change, the following 5-Step Road Map is a starting point from which to appreciate some of the essentials required to effect change from a leadership standpoint.

Step 1: Establish the Purpose

1. Clarify the real need
2. Analyse the impact of doing nothing
3. Create a vision
4. Communicate and secure support for the vision
5. Confirm what needs to change

Step 2: Develop the Momentum

1. Communicate, communicate, communicate
2. Align people behind the change
3. Involve people
4. Provide leadership and teams
5. Create urgency and instil a sense of urgency

Step 3: Plan the Change

1. Set milestones for achievement
2. Establish measures for success
3. Identity and secure resources
4. Allocate and delegate responsibilities for planning and implementation
5. Prepare for contingencies
6. Provide support

Step 4: Lead the Implementation

1. Inspire others
2. Communicate throughout
3. Seek early success and celebrate it
4. Monitor, control, review
5. Deal with the unexpected
6. Plan for continuous growth

Step 5: Monitor the Change

1. Ensure effective oversight of the change
2. Ensure that the project management of the change is effective
3. Review the impact upon organisational climate and culture
4. Progressively review the impact of change
5. Deal with the unexpected
6. Plan for continuous improvement

7. Celebrate real results

Organisations need to adapt, evolve and change structures to meet with anticipated or actual environmental turbulence. It is important to guard against structural inertia.

The need for restructuring throughout an organisation's lifecycle is inevitable to allow new energy to flow, otherwise organisations stagnant and productivity diminishes.

13.3 PROCESSES

A business process is a set of logically related tasks performed to achieve a defined business outcome (Davenport, 1993). Processes are the means by which transformation takes place. A strategy can be created but without an implementation process in place for execution it simply remains a 'great idea'.

Without processes businesses simply cannot function.

13.3.1 PROCESS READINESS

Any strategy has to be lead, but it also has to be 'thought through' from end to end to ensure organisational capability, competency and resourcing . . . and process readiness.

A useful input is to apply process mapping to ensure processes are both relevant and efficient to support the change agenda.

Value can be created from new strategies, but it can only be captured through well-conceived, time efficient, adequately resourced processes.

13.3.2 PROCESS REVIEWS

A critical periodic review is recommended to assess process effectiveness and process efficiency, and where appropriate, metrics and measurement tools are required as a basis for setting standards and monitoring performance.

New Processes need consultation often on a team basis to diagnose and prescribe what is really needed, then these will need to be tested, refined and mandated within levels of authority agreed for action, review and performance. Such protocols will achieve a sense of process discipline, provided all communication remains transparent.

13.4 BUSINESS PROCESS REENGINEERING

The original focus for business process reengineering (BPR) was to achieve radical improvements in costs, quality and service by going back to the drawing board and rebuilding business processes from scratch (Champy, 1995; Davenport, 1993; Hammer, 1990; Hammer & Champy, 1993; Hammer & Stanton, 1995). BPR seeks to help companies radically restructure their organisations by focusing on the ground-up design of their business processes.

BPR must be based upon an established need. Such need is often driven by crisis, or economic or business downturn where the need for survival becomes a powerful driver for organisational transformation. Key questions to be faced include:

- Why are things done this way?
- What assumptions form the basis of why things are done this way?
- Are these assumptions valid today?
- Do our core assumptions need to be changed?
- If so, does the business need to be re-engineered for relevance and sustainability?
- If this is required, do the business core processes need to be challenged in the same way to improve efficiency?
- Do we need a new business formula for cost optimisation, quality, competitiveness, customer connectivity, speed and profitability?

13.4.1 THE PROCESS REENGINEERING LIFECYCLE (PRLC)

Guha et al. (1993) offer a comprehensive methodology (Figure 32).

13.4.1.1 Envisioning New Processes

Reengineering is revolutionary, and an organisation's leadership must be its champions. Leaders start by examining how they would run their company if they had no constraints, requiring the creative re-examination of current work practices against optimal work practices. This initial stage involves the crucial component of aligning corporate goals and strategies with the reengineering effort. In this stage, management commits to the project, and the project team identify vital business processes and examine IT enablers.

Figure 32: Business processes reengineering lifecycle

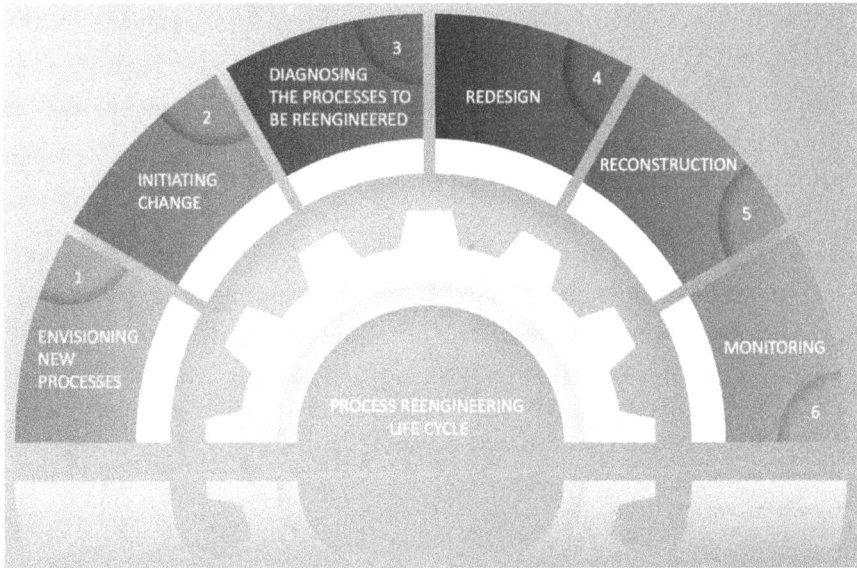

13.4.1.2 Initiating Change

The initiation stage ensures the conduct of careful preparation anticipating organisation-wide radical change. The right team members must staff reengineering projects to sustain the effort. The project should have definite performance goals justified against forecast costs that can later provide the metric for judging success. It is conventional to establish an in-house public relations campaign to inform employees about the redesign project. It is also customary for the CEO to communicate the need, scope, commitment, and leadership of the project to employees.

13.4.1.3 Diagnosing the Processes to be Reengineered

With the staffing issues and performance goals determined, the multifunctional team begins an in-depth investigation of the business process selected for reengineering. The diagnose stage is critical because it clarifies the existing process and uncovers hidden pathologies.

Documenting the Existing Process

To redesign a business process, the organisation must clearly understand how the existing process works. In documenting a current process:

- Depict the process from start to finish, covering several functions, departments, users, and external linkages.
- Identify components of the process (e.g., IS, human, physical, and other process resources).
- Document the performance of the existing process in terms of customer satisfaction, inventory turnover, cycle time, waiting queues, defect rates, activity times, transfer rates, priority rules, and other relevant measures.
- Decompose an extensive process into a set of subprocesses and assign team members to the appropriate subprocesses according to their expertise.

Interview participants in a process to reveal the flow of information and linkages. The value-added may be determined by the nature of the data processed, how it is processed, and the resources used during processing. The time required for information processing, moving, and waiting should be recorded to indicate costs and act as a process improvement benchmark. The performance measures of the existing process should reflect the organisation's goals and missions.

Uncovering Pathologies

Process pathologies are workflow activities, business policies, bureaucracies, and non-value-added roles that constrain or fragment the overall effectiveness of a business process. A critique of the current value and non-value-added workflow activities uncovers such pathologies; this involves:

- Identifying undesirable sequential activities and unnecessary bureaucratic steps.
- Identifying functional information systems for potential integration in a single process-wide system.
- Questioning the need for various forms, approvals, and reports and identifying all paper float and redundancies.
- Identifying dysfunctional policies and rules, formal as well as informal.

One way of uncovering such pathologies is to graph the performance variables set in the initial stage for each activity in the current process. For example, suppose the goal is to reduce time and cost. In that case, it is beneficial to draw the incremental costs, elapsed time, bottleneck delays, labour requirements, and other qualitative measures for each activity of the process. Performance-measurement charts enable comparison with the redesigned process in the next stage (monitoring the project), enabling reengineering teams to select the optimal process configuration.

Organisations typically use process design tools that generate PERT charts or process-activity network diagrams. Such techniques, which have been in use in manufacturing process design, may be applied in analysing business processes and their input used to develop simulation models of the process. Numerous products are available that allow the development of unified data, process, and logic models. Reengineering teams can then use these models to create business solutions and specifications for designing and implementing information systems during the redesign and reconstruction stages.

13.4.1.4 Redesign

Business process redesigns achieve performance improvements in the areas of time, cost, productivity, quality, and the amount of committed capital. In pursuing such enhancements, existing concepts of organisation or process designs should not constrain the reengineering team. Wildly different procedures that employ IT in ways that increase efficiency and effectiveness are often uncovered by 'brainstorming'. A systematic approach that uses the diagnosis stage inputs to eliminate pathologies and redesign effective process configurations follows.

Exploring Alternative Designs

Exploring process design alternatives involves creativity and a radical approach that questions every procedure and principle that currently governs task activities, approvals, and workflow. The reengineering team should develop and investigate alternative process redesign solutions and consider IT applications that may support each alternative.

Alternate solutions entail different workflow activity, staffing, and cross-functional support. The IS reengineering team members should continually educate fellow team members about the opportunities that IT may provide for alternative designs. Selection of the best process design is crucial before the final choice of supporting technology. Without this step, the result could be force-fitting new technologies to existing procedures.

Designing New Processes

The key to successful redesign is to constantly question the reason for completing a specific task, identify better ways of doing it, who is responsible, and which information technology best supports the redesigned process. Uncovering pathologies in the diagnosis stage answers most of these questions. In selecting the redesigned process, there are fundamental elements for consideration, including:

- Pattern breaking. Breaking conventional principles and rules.
- Aligning with performance goals. Ensuring that performance goals align with process outcomes.
- Job assignment. Designing a person's job around the goals and objectives of the process, not a single task.
- Elimination of hierarchies. Replacing bureaucratic hierarchies with self-organised teams working in parallel.
- Elimination of identified pathologies. Questioning the activities and roles used to relay information where information technology can substitute.
- Improving productivity. Moving focus from work fragmentation and task specialisation toward task compression and integration.
- Appraising information technology. Considering the appropriate IT configuration that can support and enable the redesigned process.
- Redesign focuses on leveraging time. Redesigned processes and the application of IT improves processing, transporting and waiting time. Eliminating multiple approval levels and noncritical control checks, integrating data processing into the work that produces the information, removing wait buffers and integrating multiple tasks saves vast amounts of time.

A significant redesign possibility involves the substitution of sequential activities for simultaneous ones. Substitution reduces the waiting time involved in processes. Applying online databases and information networks across the process enables concurrent information access at every node.

Separate tasks within processes should be integrated as much as possible into one job description to keep important information from being lost as responsibility transfers across inter-organisational boundaries. Redesign enables immediate problem resolution by directly providing line workers with the appropriate information, including direct, timely feedback on performance. Using IT platforms that support enterprise-wide information access, individual jobs designs enable parallel tasks and allow workers to make more informed decisions.

People and Culture

Reengineering a company is not limited to its processes; recasting the organisational structure to match process efficiencies is also essential. Indeed, the subunit divisions of an organisation should support the processes as much as possible. Reorganising subunits to minimise unit interdependencies holds potential for reducing costs and improving productivity. Improving the alignment of objectives, tasks, and people in a single subunit minimises interdependencies between subunits. A well-designed people and culture architecture should support a free exchange of information, refocusing decision making and actions at the individual and work-group levels.

Inevitably, reengineering may cause significant changes in the organisational structure and people and culture architecture. The redesign stage should include a people and culture component that incorporates the following:

- Redefinition of job titles and positions affected by changes in cross-functional processes.
- Team-based management techniques include establishing self-motivated teams assigned to specific business processes based on unique skills individuals possess.
- Continual organisational learning through on-the-job training with an emphasis on quality, time, and output.
- Performance evaluation based on team productivity and measured by group effectiveness.
- Incentives and reward structures based on group performance and an individual's contribution to the team.

- Modification of management structures that require managers to be leaders as well as equals to team members.
- Continuous reengineering project communication to all employees who provide feedback on progress.

Prototyping

Prototyping has been widely used in traditional systems development because it creates rapid feedback that helps determine systems requirements. Prototyping techniques are beneficial for reengineering projects because they demonstrate proposed redesigns that would otherwise be difficult for people to comprehend. Computer-aided software engineering (CASE) tools and 3D printing enable rapid prototype development.

Prototypes should be reviewed and evaluated by the reengineering team; they provide management with a vehicle to make judgments toward a final process design choice.

Selecting an IT Platform

Integration, cooperation, ease of migration, adaptability to new technologies, and enterprise-wide information access and sharing are among the factors that influence the selection of an IT platform to support the redesigned process. The IT base must support communication between corporate systems and decentralised divisional systems, as well as tie suppliers, vendors, and customers using WANs. The need for cooperation may result in downsizing mainframe-based systems to LAN-based open systems using object-oriented technology. Some reengineering consultants believe that only an object-oriented infrastructure will allow developers to integrate and implement systems fast enough to meet the reengineering time frame.

The critical need for information sharing and access determines the corporate database design requirements, leading to developing an enterprise-wide information architecture or distributed databases. The IT platform selected must outline hardware decisions (e.g., mainframe, minicomputer, or workstation-based configurations), software decisions (e.g., operating systems), and a data architecture at all levels of systems implementation. It must also detail the appropriate software systems implementation at every level, such as developing a decision support system at the executive level and several integrated work-group applications for transaction processing. Decisions on IT deployment of third-party software, in-house software development kits to support applications development, software reengineering plans, documentation, and training programs are required. The selection of an IT platform for a particular process can be related to the enterprise-wide IT architecture.

13.4.1.5 Reconstruction

This next stage is the actual implementation of the change. As with any major organisational change, a methodical process should be adopted that takes advantage of small-scale pilot projects, user training, and extensive user feedback. When problems arise in this stage of reengineering, those involved must retain their commitment to the main ideas generated during process redesign yet must be amenable to changes required to facilitate the installation.

13.4.1.6 Monitoring

This stage has two distinct components that focus on performance measurement of the process and quality improvement.

13.5 RELATIONSHIP CAPITAL

One critically important enabler for organisational transformation is the relationship capital which has to be built to provide a sound platform for sustainable business relationships. From this basis of trust and dependable working relationships the processes of change can be built.

Relationship capital is built from the sum total of relationships throughout the business network, comprising customers, suppliers, employees, partners, regulating bodies and more. This intangible component of business cannot be neglected and yet it is difficult to measure, assess and resource.

Relationship capital anchors the stability of the organisation. It is the basis of trust within and between key stakeholder groups. Insufficient relationship capital in business will stall sustainable futures.

The goodwill which has been created throughout the organisational history is the fundamental component upon which organisational transformation depends, provided that the 'engagement dynamics' remain positive, valued and effectively integrated.

Felt relationships are complex opportunities to learn through mutual emotional exchanges which build dependencies and trust. Forming relationships and then sustaining relationships requires energy and commitment.

13.6 NEW STAKEHOLDER RELATIONSHIPS

It is well-accepted that new relationships may move through a series of dynamics which are acknowledged sometimes difficult to read, understand and leverage. These dynamics can be seen as stages in relationship building (Tuckman, 1965; Tuckman & Jensen, 1977):

- Forming.
- Storming.
- Norming.
- Performing.
- Adjourning.
- Mourning.

This simplistic causal process is a classical model but may not be so sequential as proposed, moreover the time component is an important element and cannot be predicted.

Consider how relationships are formed. At this forming stage, stakeholders intending a working relationship are independent. As the relationship builds overtime and shared performance is achieved then a stage of mutual interdependence emerges.

If this dynamic is secure, this state will hold for the desired future. However, if the conditions which surround the relationship change, it is feasible that the state of mutual interdependence moves to total dependence upon one stakeholder from the other or breaks down.

13.7 STAKEHOLDER GROUPS AND RELATIONSHIP MANAGEMENT

When planning Organisational Transformation from a relationship management perspective, a simple but effective analysis tool should be applied for addressing the need of stakeholder groups before the process of transitioning begins.

The following step-by-step approach will be useful:

1. Identify all stakeholders
2. Decide key influential stakeholders

3. Map the relationship among these stakeholders
4. Consider the impact of planned organisational transformation upon
   a. Each stakeholder
   b. Stakeholder relationships

   And then consider this impact in terms of

   c. Future Opportunity
   d. Future Threats for Relationship Management.
5. Now review the opinion leadership forces key stakeholder groups exert on the organisation.
6. Develop and lead a relationship strategy based upon the net value provided by each stakeholder group.

N.B. The above analysis may be based upon assumptions, these assumptions should be minimised so that the analysis is based upon verified hard facts. Further, the step-by-step approach may be easy to lay out but be much more complex to implement. Mapping the influence and inter-relationships of key stakeholder groups is a wise move!

13.8 TRUST BONDS

Trust is the foundation for everything we do in social exchanges (Blau, 1960, 1964; Emerson, 1962; Homans, 1958; Kelley & Thibaut, 1978; Macaulay, 1963; Thibaut & Kelley, 1959). But what do we do when it is broken?

The dynamics of organisational transformation dislodge individuals and even teams to often create a situation of disequilibrium, uncertainty and even insecurity because the status quo has been destabilised. If this is known in advance, then the impact can be minimised by building trust and confidence in the changes which are needed.

The role of the leader here is to build, secure and retain trust bonds with all key stakeholder groups through open transparency with frequent planned communication (Lambe et al., 2001).

In a climate of suspicion or mistrust, change will be slow to occur (Schilke et al., 2015).

The value of organisational transformation has to be 'felt', this can only be based upon trust, a shared vision for the future and strongly bonded relationships (Shanka & Buvik, 2019). Developing trust bonds for organisational transformation is complicated (Figure 33). We have to move from a situation of uncertainty, engage with colleagues and promote confidence. In other word we need to move from a position where trust is something we aspire to achieve to a position where it is secured. In this model trust is a product of individual and collective identity, rational and emotional personality factors (individually and in groups) developed over time.

Figure 33: Trust bonds for organisational transformation

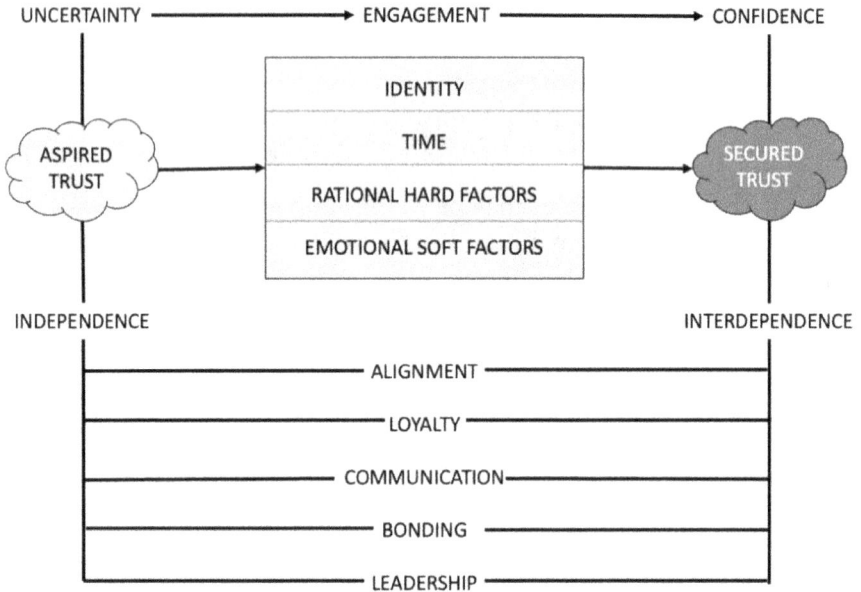

We move from a position of independence to interdependence governed by processes of alignment, loyalty, communication, bonding and leadership

Barriers to trust will emerge, e.g., sense of loss, individual self-interest, lack of team spirit, poor organisational cohesion, lack of connection with the benefits to be gained, and so on. Therefore, secure leadership is needed, with position power, to orchestrate the needed change as well as to build the levels of commitment required.

It is important to remember that trust is a most sensitive emotion, it takes time to build and only moments to lose.

13.9 QUESTIONS

1. Consider the following:

a. How many organisations undertake process mapping to ensure that core processes can absorb new strategy implementation or are equipped for additional load?
b. Are processes audited for performance adequacy?
c. Where does the responsibility and authority lie in the organisation for process reviews?

2. Consider:
   a. As a leader, where can relationship capital become potentially eroded?
   b. As a manager, can your relationship dependencies which prevail in the workplace?
3. Consider:
   a. How does behaviour change through the process of relationship building?
   b. What are the consequences for organisational transformation?
   c. How do organisational transformations face difficulties in forming, storming or when it does not proceed beyond storming, instead moving straight to adjourning?
   d. How do organisational transformations face difficulties at the performing stage, leading to early adjournment?
4. How can you develop the trust bonds for organisational transformation model further?

BUSINESS MODEL TRANSFORMATION

"You can't build an adaptable organisation without adaptable people--
and individuals change only when they have to, or when they want to."

Gary Hamel

14. BUSINESS MODELS

"Having the ability to be brutally honest with yourself is the greatest challenge you face when creating a business model. Too often we oversell ourselves on the quality of the idea, service, or product. We don't provide an honest assessment of how we fit in the market, why customers will buy from us, and at what price."

Mark Cuban

14.1 CHAPTER OVERVIEW

This chapter introduces business models and our '5D' approach to their development.

The key concepts we cover are business models, the 5D approach and defining business models.

On completing this chapter, you should be able to:

1. Explain what a business model is.
2. Describe the 5D approach in outline.
3. Define a business model.

14.2 INTRODUCTION TO BUSINESS MODELS

There are some key questions we need to ask in any business:

1. Do we really know what a business model is, what purpose it serves, how to build and review it?
2. Is the business model known and shared?
3. Does it really feature in your organisational life? Or
4. Is 'business model' just management jargon where the assumption is that everyone knows, but they actually do not?

So, do you know what you do not know about your business model?

Again, there are a series of questions to be asked:

1. Where does the business model fit into the life of an enterprise?
2. How does the business model help organisational leadership?
3. What value does the business model bring to the enterprise?

Where should the business model fit into the life of an enterprise? We need to look at business models as part of organisational strategic intent and where we need to change organisational logic (Figure 34).

Where the logic changes, we need to review the business model architecture, develop it further and then prepare it for transformation.

Figure 34: Strategic intent and business modelling

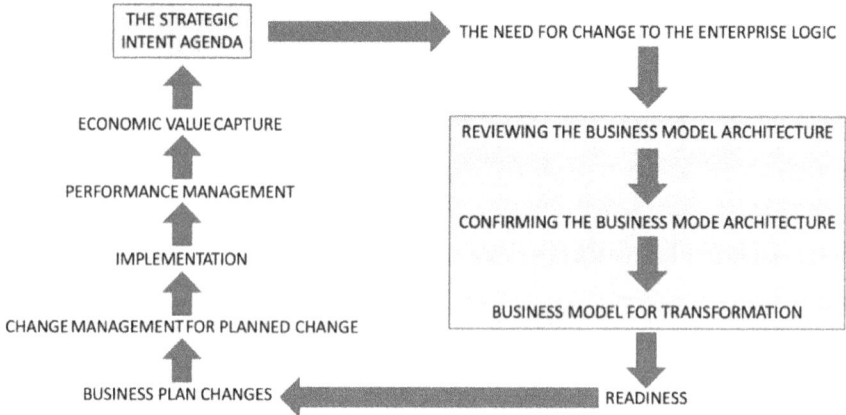

From a leadership perspective, there is a need for:

- Collective understanding.
- Assessment.
- The adoption of business models as a framework for achieving business results and to achieve transformational change.

Why does a strategic intent agenda drive transformational change?

- Shareholder value gap.
- Strategy to performance gaps.
- Survival, continuity, sustainability.
- Competitive resilience.
- Preserving pride and heritage.
- Business history and heritage - needing to leverage the legacy
- New top management leadership.

A methodology is needed to build and also assess business model relevance to achieve significant adjustments to the strategic intent. It is for this reason that the '5D' approach was created.

14.3 THE 5D APPROACH

What is the 5D approach?

- An approach to reframe the way in which business is perceived and led.

- An innovative approach to business sustainability, especially in times of economic turbulence.
- The 5D approach is intended to accelerate progress.

This innovation for business model creation will:

- Challenge the status quo.
- Convince you of the importance of the business model for new value creation and new economic value capture.
- Provide new perspectives on business leadership.
- Offer a platform to review business logic.
- Show a route to innovation and advancement for those who are unaware.

The 5D approach is a step-by-step progression to understand and apply a methodology to create a new business model or to review an existing business model (Figure 35).

14.4 DEFINING THE BUSINESS MODEL

Business Models are not commonly understood. It is also often difficult to agree on a common model, based on prevailing misunderstandings, which in turn are often based upon flawed assumptions. Clarity is required.

Figure 35: The 5D framework

There are commonly differing views of the purpose that business models serve:

- 'How the business makes money'
- 'How business is conducted'
- The logic of the enterprise
- 'How the enterprise works'
- 'What business gets paid for'

Clearly, something more definitive is needed:

> *A Business Model is an energised rationale to prescribe and achieve contextually relevant, risk assessed, value creation, value delivery and*

value capture activities for sustaining time-conscious competitive organisational performance capabilities, superior relationships and effective leadership. It is the business formula for achieving future financial performance ambitions driven by changing enterprise environments.

The core purposes served by the business model are that it provides:

- A framework to contain the essence of the business.
- A common source of reference for business decision making.
- A basis for analysis, discussion and review.
- A foundation for competitive strategy.
- An anchor for business planning.
- A value management platform.
- A dynamic enabler for transformation.
- A mechanism to accelerate business performance.

There is no doubt that without these imperatives any business would face difficulties.

The outcomes of defining the business model include:

- Managerial mindset realignment.
- A unique holistic perspective for the business.
- Mindset change from knowing more about the way the business works.
- Strategic management value.
- Assessment of the routes to shareholder value.
- Evaluating business logic.
- Auditing performance.
- Challenging the routes to value creation.
- Strategic review.
- Reviewing business cohesiveness for achieving strategic intentions.

14.5 DETERMINING THE UNDERLYING BUSINESS MODEL LOGIC

The business model needs to demonstrate:

- Strategic logic - to create value through relationships
- Linkage logic - to confirm business activity synergies

- Resource logic - to ensure capability and capacity is relevant and adequate

Now it can be seen that without a business model the organisation is at a distinct disadvantage.

14.5.1 A CONCEPTUAL FORMULA FOR DETERMINING THE BUSINESS MODEL

Strategic logic + Linkage logic + Resource logic = Projected returns - Opportunity costs - Collaboration costs - Execution risk
= Strategy net present value
= Economic logic
   Now apply this formula to determine:

- A stress test for the current business model
- Cohesiveness
- Risk
- The strategic realisation for change
- The strategic value of the current business model

Stress test any significant changes to the business logic attributed to organisational transformation to thereby determine and confirm revised business model strategy. The economic logic will locate the value and speed of returns. The stress test will help determine a route for winning.

14.5.2 A STRATEGY FORMULA FOR VALUE ADDITION

Strategic logic + Linkage logic + Resource logic = Projected returns (= VALUE CREATION)
- Opportunity costs - Collaboration costs - Execution risk
= Strategy net present value (= NET VALUE CAPTURE = VALUE ADDITION TO THE BUSINESS)
= Economic logic
   Hence, the basis for business model determination has progressed to a value-based platform.

14.6 DESIGNING THE BUSINESS MODEL

The business model design should feature sources of value creation that enable incremental value capture.

To assist this imperative, a business model template is required (Figure 36).

Figure 36: 5D business model template

		CORE ACTIVITIES		
THE COMPANY		TRUSTED IDENTITY	**THE COMPANY**	
CORE ACTIVITIES			CUSTOMER SEGMENTS	
DISTINCTIVE COMPETENCES				
CORE VALUE	ENERGY		SUPERIOR VALUE PROPOSITIONS	
RESOURCES			END TO END CUSTOMER EXPERIENCE	
NETWORKS		STRATEGIC INTERVENTIONS	CUSTOMER PROCESSES	
PARTNERS	COLLABORATION			
RISK ASSESSMENT			CHANNELS	
		VALUE CAPTURE		

COSTS	BUDGET	REVENUE STREAMS	CASH FLOW	PROFIT	CUSTOMER VALUE
		FINANCIAL PERFORMANCE MEASUREMENT			

In adapting the generic business model template there are three imperatives:

1. Review the value delivery enablement components for contextual relevance.
2. Then adapt the template accordingly to achieve the business model for your organisation.
3. Then confirm the template for management application.

This, when secured by top management will serve as a platform for leadership.

14.7 AN ALTERNATIVE: THE BUSINESS MODEL CANVAS

The *Business Model Canvas* (BMC) is a template used for developing new business models and documenting existing ones (Figure 37). You will easily find a full-scale version online. It visually summarises elements describing a firm's value proposition, infrastructure, customers, and finances, assisting businesses to align their activities by illustrating potential trade-offs.

14.7.1 THE BUILDING BLOCKS

Developed by Osterwalder and Pigneur (2010), the BMC is built on nine "building blocks". The following descriptions are based largely on the 2010 book *Business Model Generation*.

Figure 37: The Business Model Canvas

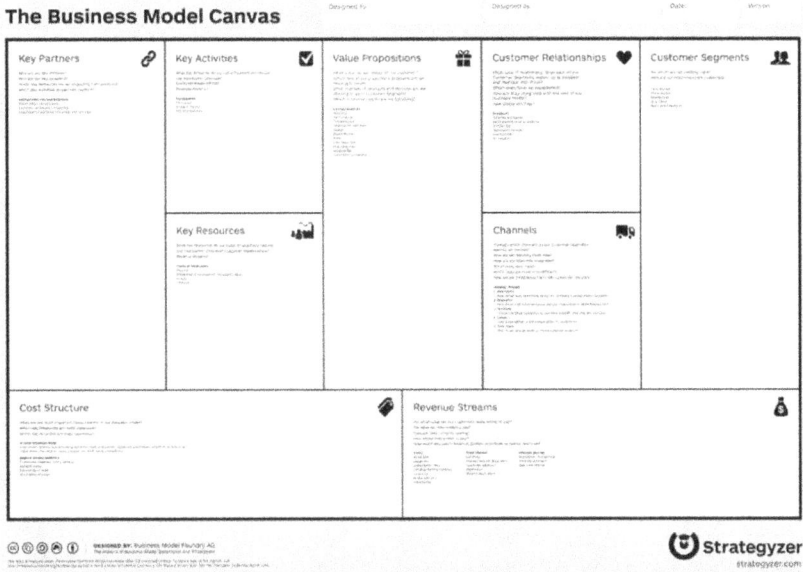

Customer segments. To build an effective business model, a company must identify which customers it tries to serve. Various sets of customers can be segmented based on their different needs and attributes to ensure appropriate implementation of corporate strategy to meet the characteristics of selected groups of clients. The different types of customer segments include:

- Mass market. There is no specific segmentation for a company that follows the mass market element as the organisation displays a wide view of potential clients, e.g., a car.
- Niche market. Customer segmentation based on specialised needs and characteristics of its clients, e.g., Rolex.
- Segmented. A company applies additional segmentation within existing customer segment. In the segmented situation, the business may further distinguish its clients based on gender, age or income, or a combination of any three.
- Diversified. A business serves multiple customer segments with different needs and characteristics.
- Multi-sided platform. For smooth day-to-day business operations, some companies will serve mutually dependent customer segments. A credit card company will provide services

to credit card holders while simultaneously assisting merchants who accept those credit cards.

Value propositions are collections of products and services a business offers to meet the needs of its customers (Osterwalder et al., 2014). A company's value proposition is what distinguishes it from its competitors. The value proposition provides value through various elements such as newness, performance, customisation, fit-for-purpose, design, brand, status, price, cost reduction, risk reduction, accessibility, convenience or usability. Value propositions may be:

- Quantitative – price and efficiency
- Qualitative – overall customer experience and outcome

Channels. A company can deliver its value proposition to its targeted customers through different channels. Effective channels will distribute a company's value proposition in ways that are fast, efficient and cost-effective. An organisation can reach its clients through its own channels (store front), partner channels (major distributors), or a combination of both.

Customer relationships. To ensure the survival and success of any businesses, companies must identify the type of relationship they want to create with their customer segments. That element should address three critical steps on a customer's relationship: How the business will get new customers, how the business will keep customers purchasing or using its services and how the business will grow its revenue from its current customers. Various forms of customer relationships include:

- Personal assistance in a form of employee-customer interaction. Such assistance is performed during sales or after sales.
- Dedicated personal assistance is the most intimate and hands-on personal assistance in which a sales representative is assigned to handle all the needs and questions of a special set of clients.
- Self-service is the type of relationship that translates from the indirect interaction between the company and the clients. Here, an organisation provides the tools needed for the customers to serve themselves easily and effectively.
- Automated services are similar to self-service but more personalised as it has the ability to identify individual customers and their preferences. An example of this would be

Amazon.com making book suggestions based on the characteristics of previous book purchases.

- Communities' creation allows for direct interactions among different clients and the company. The community platform produces a scenario where knowledge is shared and problems are solved between different clients.
- In co-creation a personal relationship is created through the customer's direct input to the final outcome of the company's products or services.

Revenue streams are the ways a company makes income from each customer segment. There are several variations:

- Asset sale (the most common type). Selling ownership rights to a physical good, e.g., retail.
- Usage fee. Money generated from the use of a particular service, e.g., courier services.
- Subscription fees. Revenue generated by selling access to a continuous service, e.g., Netflix.
- Lending, leasing or renting. Giving exclusive right to an asset for a particular period of time, e.g., leasing a car.
- Licensing. Revenue generated from charging for the use of a protected intellectual property.
- Brokerage fees. Revenue generated from an intermediate service between two parties, e.g., a broker selling a house for commission.
- Advertising. Revenue generated from charging fees for product advertising.

Key resources are necessary to create value for the customer. They are considered assets to a company that are needed to sustain and support the business. These resources could be human, financial, physical and intellectual.

Key activities are the most important activities in executing a company's value proposition. An example for Bic, the pen manufacturer, would be creating an efficient supply chain to drive down costs.

Key partnerships. In order to optimise operations and reduce risks of a business model, organisations usually cultivate buyer-supplier relationships so they can focus on their core activity. Complementary business alliances also can be considered through joint ventures or strategic alliances between competitors or non-competitors.

Cost structure describes the most important monetary consequences while operating under different business models. Structures are cost-driven (focused on minimising all costs with no frills) or value-driven (focused on creating value for products and services). The characteristics of cost structures are:

- Fixed costs, unchanged across different applications, e.g., salary, rent.
- Variable costs that vary depending on the amount of production of goods or services.
- Economies of scale, where costs go down as the amount of goods are ordered or produced.
- Economies of scope, where costs go down due to incorporating other businesses which have a direct relation to the original product.

14.8 DISCOVER THE PERFORMANCE GAPS

Using the business model template, an adapted template or the business model canvas you may:

- Locate performance gaps between intended value creation and actual value captured.
- Discover if there is an effective performance management system installed which can be applied to the business model?
- Realise the consequential inadequacies.

The business model can be used for auditing business performance and it should be! This step will require a critical review of what exists, what is missing and to discover inherent weaknesses to which the business is exposed.

There are critical questions at the strategic level:

- What distinctive capabilities do we have (or do we need) to achieve business model sustainability for the longer term?
- Where is the business vulnerable?
- Have our resources been audited for adequacy?
- Do we really know where the organisation produces value and who needs to know?

- Have we tested the assumptions upon which value is created, are these still valid?
- Which relationships produce strategic value and are these relationships still dependable?
- Where does accountability for the total customer experience reside?
- How do we know our business model is relevant for tomorrow?

Working with the business model canvas we have some specific questions for each of the building blocks (Osterwalder & Pigneur, 2010, pp. 20-41):

- *Customer Segments.* For whom are we creating value? Who are our most important customers?
- *Value Propositions.* What value do we deliver to the customer? Which one of our customers problems are we helping to solve? Which customer needs are we satisfying? What bundles of products and services are we offering to each customer segment?
- *Channels.* Through which channels do our customer segments want to be reached? How are we reaching them now? How are our channels integrated? Which ones work best? Which ones are the most cost efficient? How are we integrating them with customer routines?
- *Customer Relationships.* What type of relationship does each of our customer segments expect us to establish and maintain with them? Which ones have we established? How costly are they? How are they integrated with the rest of our business model?
- *Revenue Streams.* For what value are our customers really willing to pay? For what do they currently pay? How are they currently paying? How would they prefer to pay? How much does each revenue stream contribute to overall revenues?
- *Key Resources.* What key resources do our value propositions require? Distribution channels? Customer relationships? Revenue streams?
- *Key Activities.* What key activities do our value propositions require? Our distribution channels? Customer relationships? Revenue streams?

- *Key Partnerships.* Who are our key partners? Who are our key suppliers? Which key resources are we acquiring from partners? Which key activities do partners perform?
- *Cost Structure.* What are the most important costs inherent in our business model? Which key resources are most expensive? Which key activities are the most expensive?

Metrics and measurement tools are essential for each component of the business model and used to periodically review component effectiveness and cross-component efficiencies. A business model dashboard is recommended for performance monitoring and review.

14.9 DECIDING ON YOUR NEW BUSINESS MODEL

From the identified performance gaps, the following actions will need to be decided:

- Transformational change agenda
- Prioritise interventions
- Re-check the business model logic based upon the transformations
- Plan the change processes
- Lead the change execution
- Ensure execution happens for new value creation and value capture
- Manage periodic reviews
- Know how the transformed business model will be effectively value managed
- Ensure readiness structures, processes, people, technology and ownership to embrace change

14.9.1 HOW TO DECIDE THE ROUTE TO NEW VALUE CREATION

This requires:

- Search for new opportunities to move current value delivery to new value creation additions
- Search across the business model components for links to integrate opportunities for value creation
- Search resource intersections for value creation

- Ensure that all value creation is securely anchored to a trusted identity
- Screen value creation opportunities for technology strategic fit, desirability, feasibility, viability and 'do-ability'
- Set a timeframe for value addition
- Review the consequences of value creation adoption (or deferment)
- Ensure measured outcomes
- Check that value addition to the customer does not erode value capture for the company
- Remember to audit the business model for business sustainability on the basis of the total customer experience, the operating culture, the resource base, structure and processes, and technology
- Audit the change management system
- Periodic review strategies for needed change
- Lead the needed change well and with confidence

14.9.2 HOW TO DECIDE ON PLANNED TRANSFORMATIONAL CHANGE

This requires:

- A change management model
- Transitioning
- A review of the human capital development implications
- Focussed outcomes
- Momentum
- Communication
- Realignments
- Institutionalisation of changes

Deciding planned change will also require a performance management backbone which should comprise:

- A new value chain for value-adding activity
- New key result areas
- New KPI's

- New oversight systems for reporting the actioning of transformational change
- Governance for the changes, which should include essential modifications to existing systems, accountability, ownership, cohesiveness, effective reporting and leadership

14.9.3 HOW TO DECIDE THE DESIRED RESULTS FOR ECONOMIC VALUE ADDITION

This will include:

- Contribution to strategic intent
- Changes to the enterprise logic
- Incremental shareholder value gains
- Cost efficiencies
- Net revenue streams
- Customer value enhancement

Ultimately this will impact brand equity which is at the epicentre of the business model and strategic realignment will be achieved.

14.10 LONG-TERM VALUE CREATION

14.10.1   SHAREHOLDER VALUE THEORY

The earliest incarnation of modern value creation theory in business is the shareholder value added (SVA) model (Rappaport, 1997) (first published in 1986). SVA is a company's worth to shareholders minus liabilities and capital costs, expressed as its net operating profit after tax minus capital costs from stock and bond issues (Figure 38). Dividends increase and stock issues lower SVA.

Figure 38: Shareholder value added

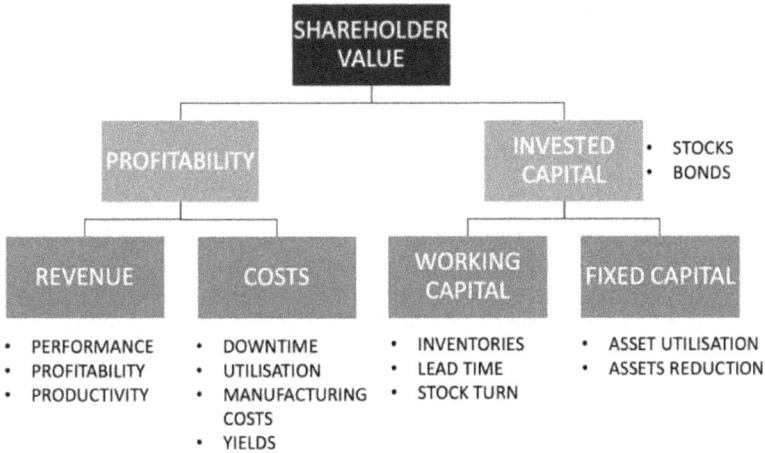

SVA reflects a company's performance in a way that is meaningful to shareholders. In its purest application, it reflects (Friedman, 1970). In other words, pure SVA implies that any company's primary goal is to increase shareholders' returns, rather than create value for the company. Anyone seeking ever-higher SVA believes that management should make decisions for the company that primarily cater to shareholder interests.

The adoption of SVA in the 1980s was a reaction to corporate managers' prior, common habit of focusing on generating rapid quarter-by-quarter earnings results, driving bonus schemes. Management self-interest over shareholders' returns is an example of the principal-agent problem (Figure 39).

Figure 39: The principal-agent problem

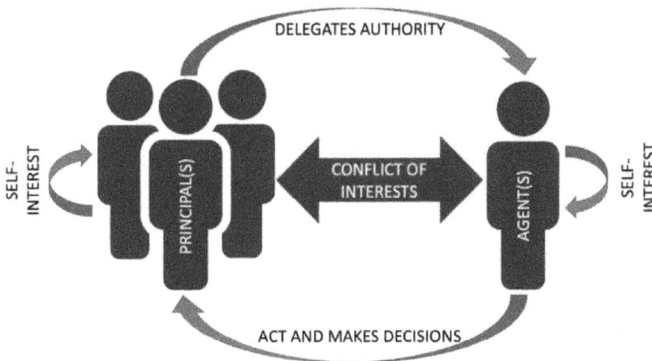

The problem follows from a conflict in priorities between a person or group (principals - the shareholders) and representatives (agents – the managers) authorised to act on their behalf. A principal-agent problem occurs when an agent acts against the principal's best interests (Jensen & Meckling, 1976). Using SVA counters the problem, forcing managers to look ahead and fulfil their stockholders' best interests (Rappaport, 1997).

SVA theory further argues for long-term SVA over short-term SVA, preferring steady growth over quick returns

SVA theory, like the shareholder primacy norm (SPN) (Smith & Rönnegard, 2016) insists that corporations should have no role in social activism. They should only be work with other stakeholders, where this serves the best interests of shareholders. Indeed, SVA theory argues, only a little dramatically, that costly 'activism' (presumably working with stakeholders) aimed at furthering political agendas will eviscerate competitiveness.

Like Friedman (1970), Rappaport (1997) insist that executives fundamental right and duty is keeping their companies competitive. Further, he contends that doing 'less' (breaking shareholder primacy) will destroy a company or set it up for takeover (or merger). Rappaport (1997) surmises that executives who keep their companies financially healthy are socially responsible.

14.10.2   STAKEHOLDER VALUE THEORY

Acceptance of the importance of accommodating the needs of wider groups of stakeholders to firm performance (Freeman, 1994) is now well-established. However, until relatively recently, the concept of value in shareholder remained relatively under-developed (Harrison & Wicks, 2013, p. 98) (Figure 40).

Figure 40: Stakeholder value added

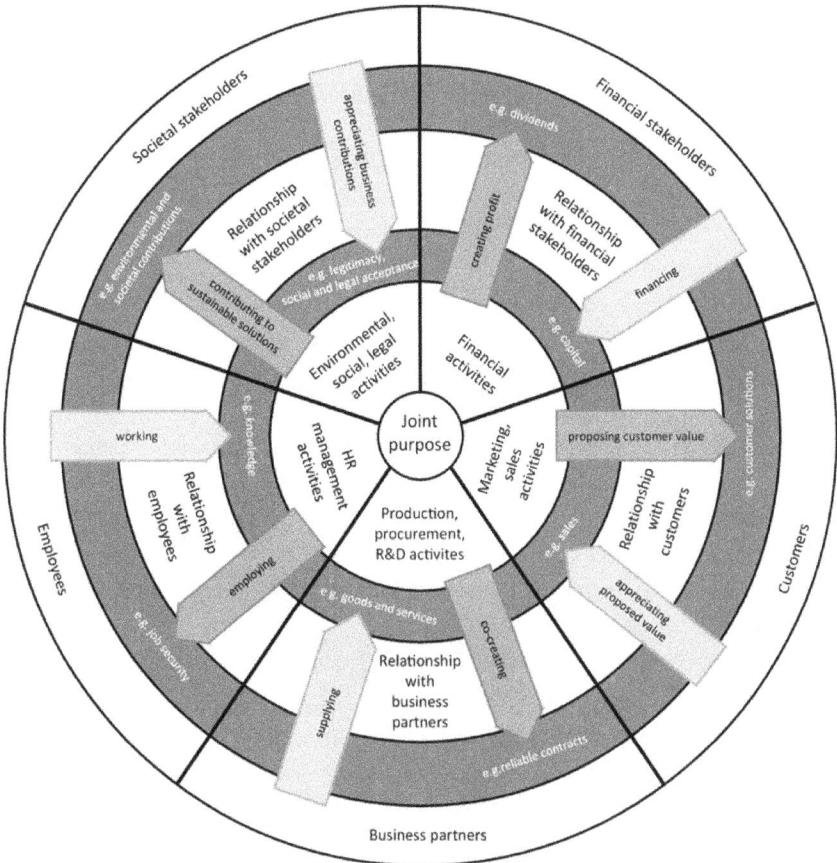

Developing a stakeholder-based perspective of value is essential (Freudenreich et al., 2020). Managers focus on matters that yield higher performance based on what gets measured (Kaplan & Norton, 1992, 1993, 1996a, 1996b; Sachs & Rühli, 2005, 2011). Stakeholder-based performance measures do not primarily focus on economic measures of performance. Instead, adopting the perspective of stakeholders involved in creating value, managers are forced to examine value creation much more broadly. Marketing and sales activities, production, procurement, R&D, people management activities and the relationship with societal stakeholders are all sources of value (Freudenreich et al., 2020). It is important emphasise that these are not just 'potential' sources, they are genuine. Moreover, accessing these sources offers managers information that better enables stakeholder engagement. Further, informational and stakeholder insights enhance creative, managerial abilities that, in turn, create more value. This virtuous spiral multiplies stakeholder well-being for all involved in a firm's value creation 'ecosystem' (Harrison & Wicks, 2013, p. 98).

Establishing stakeholder-based performance measures does not require onerous research by businesses. Owners and managers commonly use metrics associated with primary stakeholders (Harrison & Wicks, 2013, p. 115) to measure firm performance (Kaplan & Norton, 1992, 1993, 1996a, 1996b; Sachs & Rühli, 2005, 2011) Figure 41).

Similar measures can be adopted to assess performance relating to secondary stakeholders.

14.10.3   BLUE OCEAN STRATEGY AND VALUE INNOVATION

Paralleling the development of thinking around shareholder value theory is the development of Blue Ocean Strategy theory (Kim & Mauborgne, 2005a). At the heart of this market-creating strategy theory lies the concept of value innovation (Figure 42) (Kim & Mauborgne, 1997, 1999, 2005b), squarely focused on value creation for the firm and its customers (buyers).

Value innovation is the simultaneous pursuit of differentiation and low cost, creating a leap in value for both buyers and the company. Value to buyers comes from a product or service's utility minus its price. Companies generate value from their products or services' prices minus their costs. Value innovation occurs only when the whole system of utility, price, and cost is aligned.

Figure 41: Stakeholder-based performance measures

EMPLOYEES	• COMPENSATION AND BENEFITS • WORKPLACE BENEFITS • LEGAL ACTIONS OR, IF UNIONIZED, GRIEVANCES • PRODUCTIVITY MEASURES • INCLUSION ON LIST OF BEST COMPANIES TO WORK FOR • INTERNAL PROMOTIONS TO TOP MANAGEMENT TURNOVER • HEALTH AND SAFETY CONCERN OR STRENGTH • WORKFORCE REDUCTIONS • PENSION/BENEFITS CONCERN OR STRENGTH • CASH PROFIT SHARING
CUSTOMERS	• GROWTH IN SALES • CONSUMER REPORTS ON PRODUCTS/SERVICES • REPUTATION RANKINGS • PRODUCT SAFETY CONCERN • MARKETING OR CONTRACTING CONTROVERSY • QUALITY RANKING OF PRODUCTS • R&D/INNOVATION RANKING
SUPPLIERS	• DAYS PAYABLE • LONGEVITY OF SUPPLIER RELATIONSHIPS • LEGAL ACTIONS
FINANCIERS (SHAREHOLDERS)	• SHAREHOLDER RETURNS • PRICE-TO-EARNINGS RATIO (P/E) • RISK ASSOCIATED WITH RETURNS • NUMBER OF SHAREHOLDER PROPOSALS • COMPENSATION LEVELS OF TOP MANAGERS • OWNERSHIP CONCERN
COMMUNITY	• TAX BREAKS OR OTHER ADVANTAGES PROVIDED TO THE FIRM • NEW LOCAL REGULATIONS THAT AFFECT FIRM LEGAL ACTIONS • TAX DISPUTES OR INVESTMENT CONTRO- VERSIES • NEGATIVE ECONOMIC IMPACT • GENEROUS GIVING

Figure 42: Value innovation

COST SAVINGS ARE MADE BY ELIMINATING AND REDUCING THE FACTORS AN INDUSTRY COMPETES ON.

COST

VALUE INNOVATION

BUYER VALUE IS LIFTED BY RAISING AND CREATING ELEMENTS THE INDUSTRY HAS NEVER OFFERED.

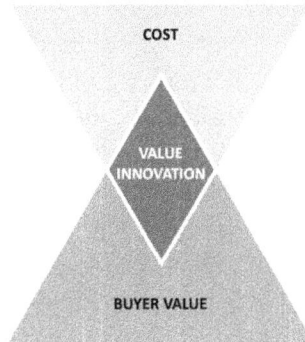

BUYER VALUE

Applying the 'four actions framework' (Figure 43) (Kim & Mauborgne, 2005a, pp. 29-37) break the value-cost trade-off, and asks:

- Which of the factors that the industry takes for granted can be eliminated?
- Which factors should be reduced well below the industry's standard?

- What factors should be raised well above the industry's standard?
- What factors should be created that the industry has never offered?

Figure 43: Four actions framework

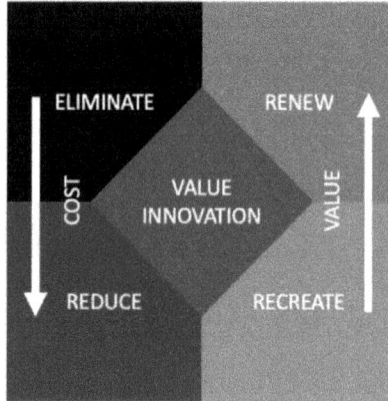

14.10.4 STAKEHOLDER VALUE INNOVATION

How might we involve stakeholders in value innovation?

The answer lies in revising a firm's business model through responding to the four actions' questions mentioned above. Using the business model canvas (Osterwalder & Pigneur, 2010) means that the majority primary stakeholder groups are already engaged to some extent. Arguably, communities do not directly feature in the template, and some of the other stakeholder groups are implicitly involved. However, the different building blocks of the template are sufficiently broad to include all stakeholder groups (primary and secondary).

Hence, involving stakeholders in value innovation entails seeking their opinion on the four actions' questions.

14.11 QUESTIONS

1. Does your organisation have a business model?
2. Does your organisation need a business model?
3. Is there a need to define the business model for common managerial understanding?
4. Is it time to change?

5. What the main learning points from the concepts around the two business model templates which have resonated with you?
6. What the main learning points from the concepts around business model performance that have resonated with you?

STRATEGIC PLANNING

"Always plan ahead. It wasn't raining when Noah built the ark."

Richard Cushing

15. A STRATEGY FRAMEWORK

"A vision without a strategy remains an illusion."

Lee Bolman

15.1 CHAPTER OVERVIEW

This chapter considers what is strategic planning, who strategic leaders are, values, culture, power, vision, mission and objectives.

The key concepts we cover are strategic planning, strategic leaders, values, culture, power, vision, mission and objectives.

On completing this chapter, you will be able to:

1. Summarise the strategic planning process.
2. Explain the principles of strategic leadership.
3. Articulate the role of values culture and power in strategy.
4. Evaluate an organisation's vision, mission and objectives.

15.2 STRATEGIC PLANNING IN CONTEXT

15.2.1 THE GREAT ACCELERATION

"There are decades where nothing happens; and there are weeks where decades happen."

Vladimir Ilyich Lenin

The weeks leading up to and immediately following the 11 March 2020, the day on which the World Health Organisation declared COVID-19 a pandemic, imposed decades-worth of changes in our lives and in businesses. (Galloway, 2020, p. xvi).

In weeks, many of us moved out lives online and businesses went virtual (Galloway, 2020, p. xviii).

At the beginning of 2020, approximately 16% of retail sales transactions occurred digitally. Eight weeks after the pandemic reached the United States, digital retail transactions jumped to 27%. They are not going back. The United States registered a decade of eCommerce growth in eight weeks (Galloway, 2020, p. xvii).

Take any social business or personal trend. Forecast 10 years ahead. Even if your business is not there yet, consumer behaviour and the market is now at the 2030 point on the trend line, positive or negative.

If your business had a weak balance sheet, insolvency beckons. Essential retail goods are more essential than ever. Discretionary retail is more discretionary than ever (Galloway, 2020, p. xvii).

Investors calibrated the value of technologically disruptive companies based not on the next weeks or years, but an assumption of the firm's position in 2030. It took Apple 42 years to reach a trillion dollars in value. In the 20 weeks from March to August 2020, Apple's value doubled to two trillion dollars. In the same period, Tesla became not just the most valuable car company in the world, but more valuable than Toyota, Volkswagen, Daimler, and Honda combined (Galloway, 2020, p. xviii).

Negative trends may have accelerated at a greater rate. For decades economists have warned that our economic inequality is deepening and economic mobility declining. Economies with uncomfortable underlying trends moved towards dystopian crises.

Prior to COVID-19, one commentator had pointed to our being in a "decade of disruption" (Church, 2017, pp. 1-12), posing substantial challenges to businesses of all size. The pandemic seems to have condensed and multiplied the trend. We are in decades of disruption.

Wholly different strategies to the leading businesses through this 'great acceleration' are required. Do we stick, pivot or shift our business models? The rate of change prior to the pandemic was already challenging; now it is off the charts (Luffman et al., 1991, p. 3).

Furthermore, compounded by the rate of change, there is the issue of the investment in technology and people required to shift strategies. And that's before we consider which market we want to be positioned in (Luffman et al., 1991, pp. 3-4).

While some products and services will remain unaltered, serving familiar markets, many more will not. How will those whose value propositions or markets have been disrupted survive the great acceleration?

15.2.2 STRATEGIC DECISIONS

Strategic decisions are concerned with a whole organisation, not a division of the organisation or one of its functional areas. However, many strategic approaches and analytical tools are appropriate for use by organisational units, when seeking to determine their long term future within the context of the organisation in which they operate (Luffman et al., 1991, pp. 6-7).

Much of the time of operating managers is concerned with activities in the short or medium term. However, corporate issues and decisions are concerned with the long term. It is important in all sizes of business for leaders to ensure that their leaders regularly review the long-term prospects of their business, identifying major opportunities and threats as early as possible. This is especially true in the disruptive times in which we live (Luffman et al., 1991, pp. 6-7).

It follows from the long-term holistic nature of strategic decisions that they are almost always unique. That is, given that the environment and the firm changes, a business's operating context at a point in time is different from that faced five years ago, last year or sometimes last week, because no two companies are identical, and because the business environment never stands still. And because no two companies are identical in terms of leadership style, products, markets and resources, it is unlikely that experience from other companies will be of any direct benefit in formulating strategy. That stated, there are often similarities over time and between companies, which provide the basis for analysis and comparison. However, the differences in business models and the timing of strategic decisions between competitors mean that in comparison with other decisions there much greater uncertainty surrounding the outcome (Luffman et al., 1991, pp. 6-7).

Strategic decisions are the point from which all of the decisions and activities in a company emanate. They provide direction and motivation. Most people prefer to know the purpose and objectives of an organisation to which they belong (Luffman et al., 1991, pp. 6-7). 'Doing nothing' is a strategic decision. To ignore information from the environment, which might afford significant opportunities or threats is a decision to 'do nothing', even though the matter may not have been discussed at a board meeting, or by senior leadership (Luffman et al., 1991, pp. 6-7).

Organisational strategic decision-making integrates activities across the organisations business model (Osterwalder & Pigneur, 2010) and allocates resources. As part of the reason for a given set of resources and activities being combined to create a company to gain maximum benefit from their interaction, it is important that all parts of the organisation work to the same end, that there is no unnecessary conflict. Hence, integration and allocation become key outcomes of strategic decisions (Luffman et al., 1991, pp. 6-7).

15.2.3 THE TASK OF STRATEGIC ANALYSIS

A highly formalised system of strategic planning is no guarantee of success. Equally, leaving things to chance, constitutes the best possible guarantee failure. The essence of success is not so much in the adoption of a formal approach to strategy formulation, but rather the quality and consistency of the implementation, coupled with an organisation's ability to adapt to an ever-changing business environment (Luffman et al., 1991, p. 7).

The task of the business strategist is to (Luffman et al., 1991, p. 7):

- Understand the position of the company, with respect to its internal strengths and weaknesses, and the opportunities and threats that emerge from the analysis of its external environment.
- Bring to bear, other functional business knowledge relevant to the strategic steps the company should take.
- Evaluate the feasibility of strategic options.
- Select from among the options and persuasively argue why the company should follow the selected path.

The role of the strategist is to understand the current position of the company and the strategic modes available to such firms in such situations, and then evaluate those moves (Luffman et al., 1991, p. 8).

15.3 STRATEGIC LEADERSHIP STRUCTURE

Strategic decisions are concerned with the direction of the whole of an organisation in the long term. This the responsibility of the board of directors and the chief executive of the organisation There are basically six board structures (Luffman et al., 1991; Tricker, 2012):

1. All-executive director boards,
2. Majority executive-director boards,
3. Majority non-executive director boards,
4. All non-executive director boards,
5. Two-tier boards, comprising a supervisory board working with a management board, and
6. Advisory boards.

15.3.1 BOARD FUNCTIONS

In a publicly listed company, the board of directors is appointed or elected by the shareholders to manage the assets in the interest of the shareholders by (Luffman et al., 1991; Tricker, 2012):

- Ensuring the long-term success of the company through attention to mission, objectives, strategies and policies of the company,
- Disseminating such information to appropriate stakeholders,
- Reviewing and publishing at regular intervals the financial performance of the company,
- Employing appropriate senior personnel to achieve these tasks, and
- Reviewing periodically, the business model of the organisation to ensure the implementation of the strategic plan.

The boards of private companies are usually small and consist of the owners and a company secretary. They may also choose to have an advisory board of external directors or may choose to join a 'mastermind' group that acts as an advisory board.

Incorporated associations have a similar board structure to listed companies, although the directors are usually elected directly by the association's members.

In listed companies and associations, a key question is to what extent the board actually has any power? It is been suggested that boards are best described as decision-taking rather than decision-making, institutions. In many cases, there is no doubt that senior management can engage in manipulative strategies, with the aim of getting a proposal through the board, by giving any generalised estimates at the costs involved and minimum expectations of outcomes. The key resides in the power of the senior management to control information. Provided no contrary information is placed before the board, it is often difficult for the board to object to proposals. These tactics require effort at pre-board meetings to prepare the cases, and often summaries of board papers so that the board can digest them at one sitting (Luffman et al., 1991; Tricker, 2012).

15.3.2 BOARD STRUCTURE AND MEMBERSHIP

15.3.2.1 Board Structure

There are basically six board structures (Tricker 2012):

1. All-executive director boards,
2. Majority executive-director boards,
3. Majority non-executive director boards,
4. All non-executive director boards,
5. Two-tier boards, comprising a supervisory board working with a management board, and
6. Advisory boards.

15.3.2.2 Types of Director

There are three types of directors (Tricker, 2012):

1. Non-executive directors are not employed by the organisation but have a financial interest in the organisation. Their fees have a performance element (e.g., performance-related fees or share options), which compromises their independence.
2. Independent non-executive directors are not only not employed by the organisation, but also have no conflict of interests with the organisation other than being a director.
3. Executive directors are senior executives within the company, with day-to-day managerial responsibilities who have a parallel role on the board.

15.3.2.3 Chair

The choice of board chair is vital. They may be an executive director or a non-executive. Where they are chair and an executive director, known as an executive chair, the role is often combined with that of chief executive officer (CEO) or managing director (MD). This is considered poor practice in most listed companies, because:

- An increase in executive pay generally gets the attention of company shareholders. Increases come at the expense of shareholder profits, although most understand that competitive pay helps to keep talent in the business. However, it is the board of directors that votes to increase executive pay. When the CEO is also the chairman, a conflict of interest arises, as the CEO is voting on his or her own compensation. Although a board is required by legislation to have some members who are independent of management, the chair can influence the activities of the board, which allows for abuse of the chair position.

- One of the board's main roles is to monitor the operations of the company and to ensure that it is being run in conjunction with the mandate of the company and the will of the shareholders. As the CEO is the management position responsible for driving those operations, having a combined role results in monitoring oneself, which opens the door for abuse of the position. A board led by an independent chair is more likely to identify and monitor areas of the company that are drifting from its mandate and to put into place corrective measures to get it back on track.

- In most jurisdictions, there is a requirement that the audit committee consists of only external board members. This means that no member of management can sit on the audit committee. However, because the committee is a sub-group of the board of directors and reports to the chair, having the CEO in the chair role limits the effectiveness of the committee

Hence, it is considered best practice that there is a non-executive chairman and a CEO.

15.3.2.4 Non-Executive Directors

What is their role?

Non-executive directors:

- Should bring independence and objectivity to the board. Subordinate managers will always find it difficult to speak openly in front of their immediate superiors,
- Can provide specialist advice or skills (e.g., knowledge of government procurement), and
- Can form special committees, for example, a remuneration and risk committee.

What proportion should be non-executive?

Current best practice recommends that a majority of directors on listed company boards be independent non-executive directors.

What qualifications and quality should they have?

Credibility is important, and so is the time to commit themselves to the company. As our qualifications as a board director.

How are they appointed?

It is usually the case that they are appointed by the chairman and ratified at the Annual General Meeting. However, increasingly boards are setting up nomination committees made of non-executive directors to advise the chair.

This prevents the constant appointment of 'friends'. However, it does not help the situation where there are no non-executive directors in the first place.

The appointment of directors of public companies remains problematic.

15.3.3 RESPONSIBILITY AND ACCOUNTABILITY

The board is responsible for the overall governance, management and strategic direction of the organisation and for delivering accountable corporate performance in accordance with the organisation's goals and objectives (AICD, 2016; Tricker, 2012).

This responsibility is usually set out in the organisation's constitution or in the enabling legislation under which the organisation is registered or incorporated (AICD, 2016; Tricker, 2012).

In performing its role, specific responsibilities commonly reserved to the board either in its constitution, its board or governance charter or by cultural practice include (AICD, 2016; Tricker, 2012):

- Providing strategic direction to the organisation and deciding upon the organisation's strategies and objectives in conjunction with the CEO.
- Monitoring the strategic direction of the organisation and the attainment of its strategies and objectives in conjunction with the executive.
- Monitoring the operational and financial position and performance of the organisation generally.

- Driving organisational performance so as to deliver member value or benefit.
- Assuring a prudential and ethical base to the organisation's conduct and activities having regard to the relevant interests of its stakeholders.
- Assuring the principal risks faced by the organisation are identified and overseeing that appropriate control and monitoring systems are in place to manage the impact of these risks.
- Reviewing and approving the organisation's internal compliance and control systems and codes of conduct.
- Assuring that the organisation's financial and other reporting mechanisms are designed to result in adequate, accurate and timely information being provided to the board.
- Appointing and, where appropriate, removing the CEO, monitoring other key executive appointments, and planning for executive succession.
- Overseeing and evaluating the performance of the CEO, and through the CEO, receiving reports on the performance of other senior executives in the context of the organisation's strategies and objectives and their attainment.
- Reviewing and approving the CEO's and, in conjunction with the CEO, other senior executive remuneration.
- Approving the organisation's budgets and business plans and monitoring major capital expenditures, acquisitions
- and divestitures, and capital management generally.
- Ensuring that the organisation's financial results are appropriately and accurately reported on in a timely manner in accordance with constitutional and regulatory requirements.
- Ensuring that the organisation's affairs are conducted with transparency and accountability.
- Overseeing the design, implementation and periodic review of appropriate and effective policies, processes and codes for the organisation, which depending on the organisation, may include with respect to ethics, values, conduct, securities trading, disclosure of securities' price sensitive information, employment, remuneration, diversity and otherwise.

- Ensuring sound board succession planning including strategies to assure the Board is comprised of individuals who are able to meet the responsibilities of directors of the organisation.
- Overseeing member and stakeholder engagement, reporting and information flow.

15.3.4 THE ROLE OF THE BOARD

In practice, the role of the board including governing, directing and monitoring an organisation's business, affairs and operations in two broad areas (AICD, 2016; Tricker, 2012):

1. *Overall organisational performance.* The board must ensure the organisation develops and implements strategies and supporting policies to enable it to fulfil the objectives set out in the organisation's constitution. Commonly the board delegates the day-to-day operations of the organisation to the management team via the CEO but remains accountable to the members and shareholders for the organisation's performance. The board monitors and supports management in an on-going way.

2. *Overall compliance or conformance.* The board must ensure the organisation develops and implements systems, processes and procedures to enable it to comply with its legal, regulatory and industry obligations (complying with the law and adhering to accounting and other industry standards) and ensure the organisation's assets and operations are not exposed to undue risks through appropriate risk management.

The differing emphasis of these two areas of organisational performance and conformance or compliance responsibilities can result in conflicting pressures on boards and their members. Boards must balance these roles and give appropriate attention to both (Figure 44).

Figure 44: Balancing board roles

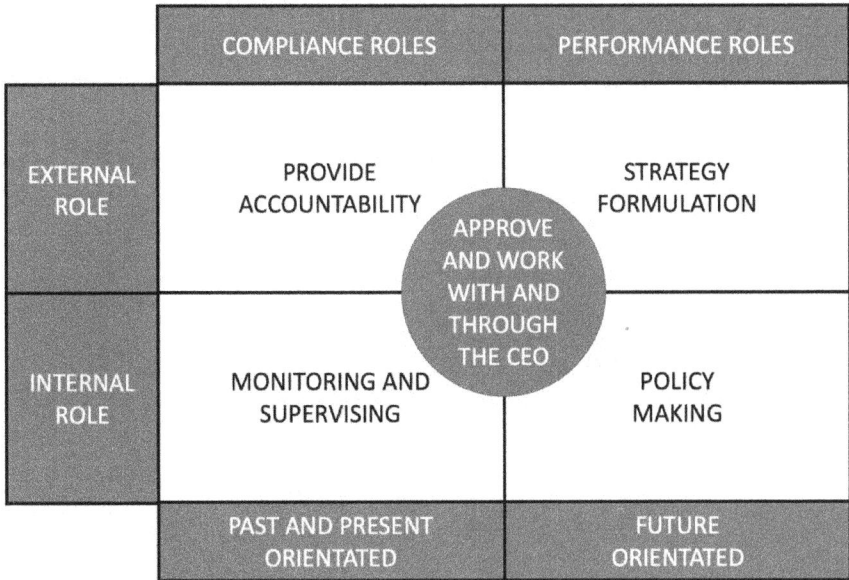

	COMPLIANCE ROLES	PERFORMANCE ROLES
EXTERNAL ROLE	PROVIDE ACCOUNTABILITY	STRATEGY FORMULATION
INTERNAL ROLE	MONITORING AND SUPERVISING	POLICY MAKING
	PAST AND PRESENT ORIENTATED	FUTURE ORIENTATED

APPROVE AND WORK WITH AND THROUGH THE CEO

15.4 A STRATEGIC PLANNING MODEL

There are few organisations that operate in circumstances where the rate of change is so slow that there is no need to consider the future. Their position that what is currently being produced or provided, and sold is likely to provide a formula for success in the long term (Luffman et al., 1991, pp. 13-15).

It follows that some evaluation process is necessary. So, whatever the size of the business, it needs to develop a strategic perspective. This might be achieved through a formal planning system, especially if the company is large, with many markets and products or services to evaluate. Where the rate of change is rapid (that's everywhere at the moment), a strategic perspective could be achieved through the skill and experience of one person, although the evidence of the success of this mode of decision making over the long term is not good. Indeed, a major factor evident in corporate collapse is the 'one-man band' (Luffman et al., 1991, pp. 13-15).

In the short term, results based on the intuition and knowledge of one person can often be spectacular. However, it is often difficult to sustain such success over the long term, whether or not it is initially successful. The resignation retirement or death of these individuals often leads to a large vacuum, as there is rarely been any attention focused on management development and succession (Luffman et al., 1991, pp. 13-15).

The model that we follow here has been described as the rational analytical model or the Harvard design school model. First developed in 1965 by Learned, Christensen Andrews and Guff (Christensen et al., 1978) it remains the most widely taught in business schools worldwide, to this day (Luffman et al., 1991, pp. 13-15) (Figure 45).

Figure 45: Strategic decision-making process

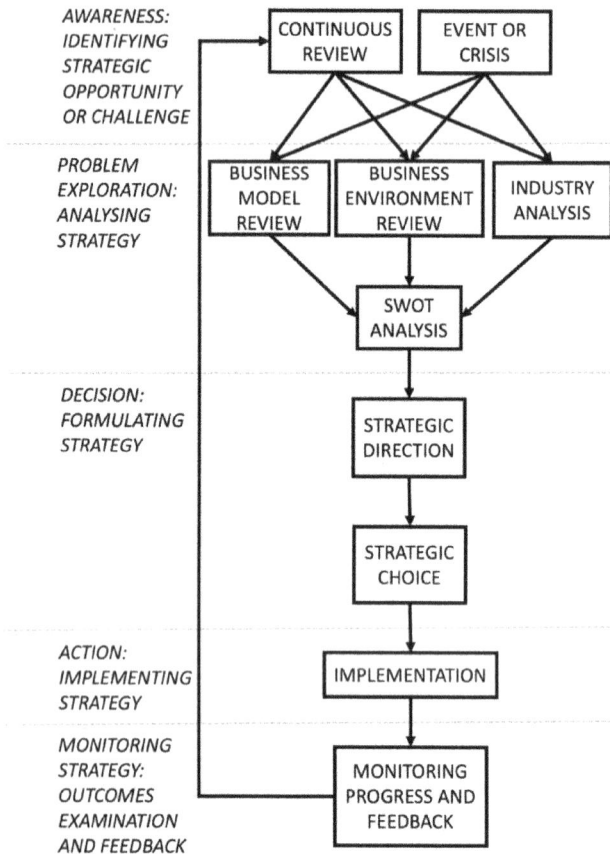

AWARENESS: IDENTIFYING STRATEGIC OPPORTUNITY OR CHALLENGE	CONTINUOUS REVIEW — EVENT OR CRISIS
PROBLEM EXPLORATION: ANALYSING STRATEGY	BUSINESS MODEL REVIEW — BUSINESS ENVIRONMENT REVIEW — INDUSTRY ANALYSIS → SWOT ANALYSIS
DECISION: FORMULATING STRATEGY	STRATEGIC DIRECTION → STRATEGIC CHOICE
ACTION: IMPLEMENTING STRATEGY	IMPLEMENTATION
MONITORING STRATEGY: OUTCOMES EXAMINATION AND FEEDBACK	MONITORING PROGRESS AND FEEDBACK

Most practitioners have their own modification, but few vary from the basic model, which follows any problem-solving situation. In this module, we supplement the design school tradition with the work of:

- Osterwalder and Pigneur (2010), swapping business model analysis for the convention of 'internal analysis', and
- Kim and Mauborgne (2005a), across strategic analysis, direction and choice.

Whether this strategic thinking is done on the back of an envelope by one person or through a formal planning process. These are the necessary steps in the thought process (Luffman et al., 1991, pp. 13-15).

15.5 VALUES, CULTURE AND POWER

An understandable misperception of many people approaching strategic management for the first time is that a strategic planning system is in itself sufficient to ensure that the right questions are posed a correct analysis performed and suitable strategies are developed. In reality, such a view ignores the basic fact that the systems themselves do none of these tasks. They are performed by people. Thus, realistically, organisations make strategic responses to a changing environment through people individually or collectively. It would further compound the misperception if the people part of the strategic equation was seen as the complicating factor. Rather, it should be regarded as the reality of the situation. So, we need to provide an initial insight into the important aspects of these individual and collective behavioural dimensions of the strategic process (Luffman et al., 1991, p. 18).

15.5.1 CORPORATE VALUES

Company values (also called corporate values or core values) are the set of guiding principles and fundamental beliefs that help a group of people function together as a team and work toward a common business goal. These values are often related to business relationships, customer relationships, and company growth.

They often revolve around the classical virtues (Peterson and Seligman, 2004) (Figure 46).

From a business perspective, having a core set of company values makes it easier for a company to make decisions, quickly communicate principles to clients and customers, and hire employees with the right attitude. Here are some great guidelines for developing values from David Darmanin at Hotjar[11]:

Figure 46: Virtues and character strengths

6. TRANSCENDENCE	APPRECIATION | GRATITUDE | HOPE | HUMOUR | SPIRITUALITY	
5. TEMPERANCE	FORGIVENESS | HUMILITY | PRUDENCE | SELF-REGULATION	
4. JUSTICE	TEAMWORK | FAIRNESS | LEADERSHIP	
3. HUMANITY	LOVE | KINDNESS | SOCIAL INTELLIGENCE	
2. COURAGE	BRAVERY | PERSEVERANCE | HONESTY | ZEST	
1. WISDOM	CREATIVITY | CURIOSITY | JUDGMENT | LOVE OF LEARNING | PERSPECTIVE	

1. Creating a business is similar to creating a community. If you want the community to act as a group, you need a shared code, vision, identity and ethos that drives who you choose to invite in and how the community functions as a whole. If you do not own, define, and care about the values of your community, they will evolve on their own, potentially in ways that hurt your business.

2. Your company values are the principles that support your company vision. We'll turn to this soon, but a vision statement describes an ideal vision of the impact a company will have on the world. Before you can articulate effective company values, you need to think about what impact your company can have on people (even if it is a tiny niche) and write a sentence that sums up that ideal scenario.

3. We have all heard values like 'think big' or 'be curious' from a handful of giants like Netflix and Amazon; it is not unusual that smaller companies are influenced by them and end up having pretty much the same values. This is not but effective company values should be unique to your company and experience. It is easier to hide behind sweeping formulas that sound great but do

---

11 https://www.hotjar.com/blog/company-values/#:~:text=Company%20values%20(also%20called%20corporate,customer%20relationships%2C%20and%20company%20growth, accessed 29 April 2021

not really apply to you. Use your values to make sure you hire people that think the same, unique way.

4. When your company grows, the values you wrote early on might not be completely relevant to where you have arrived. Dynamics change as the number of employees grows, and different things become more or less important. Re-examine company values as your team grows and get feedback from existing employees to help guide the process.

15.5.2 VALUES AND CULTURE

You will probably be familiar with workplace phrases such as

"The way we do things around here."
"It is not the sort of business we want to get into."
"We're different here."

Such statements are manifestations of organisational values and culture. They are a powerful determinant of how an organisation behaves. There is also much ongoing debate on the effect of national cultures on industrial prosperity. Culture is a major determinant of managerial perceptions, which in turn affects recruitment, resource allocation, management and organisational design; all essential aspects of an organisation (Luffman et al., 1991, pp. 18-19).

A well-known approach to cultural analysis is the McKinsey Seven-S framework (Peters & Waterman, 2004; Waterman et al., 1980), which we outlined in chapter 4. In the McKinsey model, shared values have been termed superordinate goals but, essentially, they are a set of values and aspirations which underpin objective statements, and, and as such are fundamental to and deep-seated within the organisation. Whether formally expressed or not, they are omnipresent, and often drive the other six framework elements.

More recent work has seen culture tied back to the classic virtues and character strengths classification outlined above. Cameron (2012) and colleagues identify the notion of a positive organisational culture where: values are virtuous, the purpose of the business is ethically attuned and well-understood, open communication occurs early and often relationships are well-managed, and leaders set clear expectations.

15.5.3 CULTURE AND STRATEGY FORMULATION

Many researchers have identified topologies of culture and their effect upon strategic decision making (Luffman et al., 1991, p. 19).

Mintzberg (1973) identifies entrepreneurial, adaptive and planning organisations:

1. *Entrepreneurial* organisations tend to be characterised by growth, the search for new opportunities with power held by the chief executive. Such organisations often exhibit dramatic change.
2. Organisations without clear, explicit objectives tend to exhibit *adaptive* strategies which are often a function of conflicting goals, held by senior managers. In this way they react to environmental change in decisions tend to be incremental, and based upon the power complex in the organisation, resulting in pragmatic strategic decisions.
3. *Planning* organisations are characterised by coordinated anticipatory decision making, which results in a number of scenarios about future with different strategies. This tends to provide the values of the organ to the organisation of analysis, analysts.

There is a relationship between the organisation's environment and the strategic culture of the organisation. Developing environments are conducive to entrepreneurial organisations. Volatile, uncertain, complicated and ambiguous environments see organisation adopt the adaptive mode, whereas stable environments are conducive to the planning mode. However, larger organisations offering multiple value propositions across multiple markets may face several different types of environment.

Other researchers have attempted to classify organisations in relation to their behaviour, stemming from their culture, and strategic response, over time.

Miles and Snow (1978) identify four typologies:

1. *Defenders*, tend to be conservative, they like well-tried ideas, low risk.
2. *Prospectors* are immature, accepting higher risks and seeking market opportunities.
3. *Analysers* are strong on monitoring strategy, adopting formal structures.

4. *Reactors* find it difficult to adapt, often lurching into crisis management.

Faced with a similar problem, different organisations will respond differentially. For example, faced with declining turnover, the defender will seek to cut costs and restore margins, 'battening down the hatches'. The prospector will look for new markets and opportunities. The analyser will spend time looking for reasons before changing but may well have anticipated the change. The reactor will do something about it when it begins to hurt.

Grinyer and Spender (1979) find that a manifestation of culture in many organisations strategic decision making is the creation of 'recipes'. These are strongly held beliefs and ideas about 'what works'. They are responses to a changing environment, perceived to have worked well in the past, and subsequently embedded in the organisation. They are rarely questioned since doing so might be perceived as an attack on the values of senior managers who attained their position through the recipes. Like many cultural aspects of an organisation, recipes create a perceptual framework that focuses senior managers' views of the environment and the organisation. They can act as a constraint on strategic action.

15.5.4 STRATEGIC PERFORMANCE AND CULTURE

Given the nature of the relationship between culture and strategy, several inquiries have attempted to discover what relationships exist between performance and control. Deal and Kennedy (1982) researched American companies and find successful companies (above average, long term performance) are those who believe in something that permeates the whole organisation. They further argue that in addition to endemic beliefs, employees ought to be rewarded for behaviour which complies with such beliefs. In essence, the major aspects of culture which appear to contribute towards success are seen to be a close relationship between critical success factors and values, which are well communicated such that they become institutionalised as rituals in the organisation. They are often implanted by visionary managers who set the culture. Strong cultures can assist in prioritising problems and providing a framework for what is expected in people.

Other insights into the relationship between culture and performance are provided by Peters and Waterman (2004) in their classic book, *In Search of Excellence* (originally published in 1982) which we discussed in chapter 4. Peters and Waterman (2004) work has been a catalyst for a number of books in the area. However, care must be taken in using the findings themselves as a recipe for success. If business was that simple, then everybody would be doing it. This raises the issues of

- What constitutes a successful culture?
- Whether successful cultures can be transplanted, or initiated to improve corporate performance?

The limiting factors on these propositions stem from:

- Difficulties in defining culture.
- The receptivity of organisation to new cultures.
- The time it takes to implement cultural change.

It is perhaps easy to change culture when something serious has happened to a company. For example, a loss or a hostile takeover; short, sharp shocks. However, the more incremental methods of cultural change, which inevitably occur and indeed have to occur often take longer. Any organisation is a function of its history and cultural changes take place by:

- Recognition that what is currently in place is inappropriate.
- Defining what should take its place.

15.5.5 CULTURE AND ORGANISATION

Organisational effectiveness is a fundamental concept in strategic planning aspects of organisational design. Handy (1993) provides a framework for explaining this relationship by defining four types of culture, found in organisations:

- Power cultures have strong central authority with few rules. Typically, entrepreneurial high risk, run by powerful individuals,
- Role cultures are less personality run, more bureaucratic, well-defined roles, systems and procedures. They are more risk averse.
- In task culture, problem-solving dominates relying heavily on expertise and teamwork. Personality is less important. They often have a matrix structure.
- Person cultures are based on serving the needs of individual members. This is evident in professional organisations such as

law firms. The culture may be present in other cultural types. It is often difficult to manage individuals as individuals may not be responsive to personal or expert power.

Handy's (1993) types have a lot to do with organisational power, a manifestation of structure, the effect of coalitions or the personality of the entrepreneur.

15.6 POWER

Power is essentially the ability to engage in action. It is important in attempting to effect strategic change. Power has both internal and external implications. External power sits with the business environment (specifically in politics and economics) and in the competitive environment (with dominant competitors, new entrants, suppliers and buyers). We'll return to these themes later (Luffman et al., 1991, pp. 22-23).

Any discussion of power in organisations has to take account of further concepts of authority and control. Power has a contextual or relationship serving circumstance. For example, authority is the final power vested in specific roles or positions in an organisation. Often it is delegated from the top. hence, the amount of authority a manager has may well depend on how much their CEO is willing to delegate (Luffman et al., 1991, pp. 22-23).

Clearly, there may be advantages in the marriage of power and authority within an organisation, and many systems such as rewards are geared to this relationship. But often, they can be divorced from each other, particularly in terms of informal power relationships. Informal power occurs because of expertise or specialisation, historical evidence of being right, claims of internal politics, or a host of other reasons. Strategically, the problem is that if power groups become dominant, then they can affect, delay or halt necessary strategic change (Luffman et al., 1991, pp. 22-23).

It is useful to revisit major decisions to examine the sources and extent of power that influenced the decisions. A continuing problem in many organisations is that powerful people control these systems, whereby others gain power and so people get to the top because they adhere to the values of their dominant power group and negate the alternative view or indeed, a better approach (Luffman et al., 1991, pp. 22-23).

15.7 VISION, MISSION AND OBJECTIVES

15.7.1 VISION STATEMENTS

Here is some great thinking and guidance on vision statements from Stephanie Ray[12].

15.7.1.1 What is a Vision Statement?

A vision statement is a document that states the current and future objectives of an organisation. The vision statement is intended as a guide to help the organisation make decisions that align with its philosophy and declared objectives. It is essentially a roadmap to where the company wants to be within a certain timeframe. A vision statement is not only used in business, as non-profits and government offices also use them to set objectives.

Vision statements are not necessarily set in stone. They can be reviewed and revised as necessary. Any changes should be minimal, however, because a vision statement should have been given a great deal of thought before being finalised.

A vision statement does not have any particular length. It can be as short as an aspirational sentence or pages long, depending on how much detail you want to give it. However long it is, the vision statement is formally written and used as a reference in company documents to serve as a guide for actions now and in the future.

15.7.1.2 What is the Purpose of a Vision Statement?

A vision statement is not a pie-in-the-sky document that collects the shared fantasies of the organisation and then is filed away. Similar to a mission statement, it is a living document that is referred to as a compass to lead a company to its next innovation.

Some might think a vision statement is a waste of time, but it fills a vital need for the company. For instance, it sets a broader strategic plan for the organisation. It is very easy to get bogged down on the day-to-day details of running an organisation. The vision statement helps you plan long-term.

You can set whatever goals you want but without motivating your employees to achieve that goal, chances are you are not going to get

---

[12] https://www.projectmanager.com/blog/guide-writing-perfect-vision-statement-examples#:~:text=A%20vision%20statement%20is%20a%20document%20that%20states%20the%20current,and%20declared%20set%20of%20goals accessed 29 April 2021.

anywhere. A motivational vision statement will both motivate existing employees and also drive talent to the company. They'll want to work at a place with vision.

A vision statement almost sounds mystical. But it is not supernatural, far from it. Rather, a vision statement is a foundational business document.

Often confused with a mission statement, the vision statement has a different purpose. A vision statement looks towards the future, but a mission statement talks about what the company is doing in the present.

Because the vision statement is a foundational document that will guide the company's direction for years to come, consider using project planning tools and brainstorming techniques to get input from everyone on the team. That way, you will get greater buy-in from the company, and you'll widen your net for collecting ideas.

A strong vision statement also works to help differentiate your company from others. All companies want to become profitable, but a company that can set an agenda to achieve that goal is going to set itself apart and inspire others. Use a vision statement to focus the efforts of the organisation on the core competencies it needs to achieve its goals.

15.7.1.3 Best Practices for Writing a Vision Statement

There is no template for writing a vision statement. However, a common structure for successful ones includes these traits:

- Be concise. This is not the place to stuff a document with fluff statements. It should be simple, easy to read and cut to the essentials, so that it can be set to memory and be repeated accurately.
- Be clear. A good rule of thumb for clarity is to focus on one primary goal, rather than trying to fill the document with a scattering of ideas. One clear objective is also easier to focus on and achieve.
- Have a time horizon. A time horizon is simply a fixed point in the future when you will achieve and evaluate your vision statement. Define that time.
- Make it future-orientated. Again, the vision statement is not what the company is presently engaged in but rather a future objective where the company plans to be.

- Be stable. The vision statement is a long-term goal that should, ideally, not be affected by the market or technological changes.
- Be challenging. That said, you do not want to be timid in setting your goals. Your objective should not be too easy to achieve, but also it should not be so unrealistic as to be discarded.
- Be abstract. The vision statement should be general enough to capture the organisation's interests and strategic direction.
- Be inspiring. Live up to the title of the document and create something that will rally the troops and be desirable as a goal for all those involved in the organisation.

15.7.1.4 Examples of Great Vision Statements

These examples prove that a vision statement is not a templated document that only differs from another organisation by the branded logo on top of it.

IKEA

> *"Our vision is to create a better everyday life for many people."*

That's aspirational, short and to the point. More than that, it sets the tone for the company and makes it clear that they are in the market to offer low-priced good furnishings that suit everyone's lifestyle.

Nike

> *"Bring inspiration and innovation to every athlete* in the world. (*If you have a body, you are an athlete.)"*

Nobody cared much for sneakers in the past. They were just another piece of sports equipment. But Nike saw a future that had not yet existed, in which they delivered products that inspired and motivated people. Notice how they include everyone as an athlete. It is clever and inclusive.

McDonald's

> *"To be the best quick service restaurant experience. Being the best means providing outstanding quality, service, cleanliness and value, so that we make every customer in every restaurant smile."*

The power of this vision is that it is constructed like a checklist. The word best is a word that requires definition, and McDonald's provides it with qualifiers, making the roadmap to success clearly marked with signposts.

Patagonia

> *"Build the best product, cause no unnecessary harm, use business to inspire and implement solutions to the environmental crisis."*

Talk about inspiring, Patagonia first outlines a product vision of what the best product means for them as a company. Then takes it one step further by stating they'll run their business to carry that environmental policy to a global level.

Oxfam

> *"A world without poverty."*

This may seem to contradict one of the traits of a good vision statement in that it feels unrealistic. But as challenging visions go, it is hard to see how anyone wouldn't be inspired and motivated by this short and powerful one.

15.7.2 MISSION STATEMENTS

Here is some great guidance on writing mission statements from Jason Westland[13].

What is the point of having a mission statement? You it is run a business without a plan, so think of the mission statement as the plan at its highest level, overriding all other directions. It is like a compass you can always turn to and set yourself right if you feel that you've gone off-course.

When you are working on anything, the first thing you should do is create a mission statement. It creates boundaries, and it provides both a pathway to success and a sense of what it is you are doing before you start doing it. The last thing you want is to have to stop in the middle of what you are doing to define what it is you are doing and why.

15.7.2.1 What Is a Mission Statement?

Socrates, according to Plato's account, famously said, "I know that I know nothing." That does not mean throwing up our hands and saying, "Well, I do not know, so why bother?" It means starting at the

---

[13] https://www.projectmanager.com/blog/mission-statement-with-examples, accessed 29 April 2021

beginning and developing a set of ethics to live by based on what you can observe or test as fact against what's important for you as a person.

This applies to any project or any business. At first, you do not know. That is where the mission statement comes in. It is the document that comes from the processes of figuring out what is the reason for your organisation or project.

15.7.2.2 Mission Statement vs. Vision Statement vs. Value Statement

There is usually three of these statements that any business must understand before they start to have a compass leading them forward. There is a value statement, which outlines what the company stands for, and there is a vision statement, which looks towards the future and states where you want to be in five, 10 or whatever number of years.

Then there is the mission statement. It differs from the other two in that it clearly states what it is that your organisation does or why it exists. These are existential questions that might seem odd for a company to have to address but similar to a person, a company must recognise its purpose in order to be successful. This purpose should be succinct and address the present. A mission statement is distilled to the essence of why your company exists, and it is usually only a sentence or two.

Your mission statement is a reflection of you and your company, of course. They can vary wildly from organisation to organisation. But they always answer the following two questions: what does your business do, and who does it benefit?

15.7.2.3 What Makes A Good Mission Statement?

A good mission statement is short, to the point and memorable. It is like a tagline in advertising, something that sticks with a person when they hear or read it. In a true sense, the mission statement is an ad in that it identifies your company as one that a customer would want to work with or support.

That said, the mission statement can differ depending on the business. If your company is already branded and its reason is obvious, then the mission statement is less important. People know already. That does not make the mission statement irrelevant, though, especially if there is competition from which you want to differentiate yourself.

But even if your company stands alone and is so unique that it is unmistakable what its purpose for being is, a mission statement can still be important. That's because a mission statement informs not only your customers who you are and why you are but your employees within your organisation as well. It is surprising how important it is to have that identity clearly defined to maintain quality.

A mission statement motivates employees to work at a certain standard. Far and few between are those companies that generate that sort of excitement in their workforce simply by name alone. Most organisations need a mission statement for definition and to rally the troops around.

15.7.2.4 What Goes into a Mission Statement?

Long-term goals

While not a vision statement, the mission statement will reflect the long-term goals of your company. That includes what the company stands for, making it clear to its employees, its stakeholders and those outside the organisation, such as customers, retailers, etc. Summarize your priorities, and make sure the statement reflects company culture. But take your time; do not rush the process.

Value, inspiration, plausibility and specificity

These four elements are critical to a successful mission statement. All these elements need to be relayed in only a couple of sentences, which illustrate the value of the company and serve as inspiration while remaining plausible and specific.

Ask yourself

What does your team expect from the company? Who are your customers? How can you help them? What values are important to the company? Do you have a set of beliefs or morals? Do you adhere to an ethical standard? What are your founding principles? What do you aspire to? How do you define success? How is your company unique?

Present tense

Remember, vision statements are about the future. Mission statements stay firmly in the present: who you are and what's important to you, now. Be timely, explain who you are today and do so clearly.

Be concise

You are not writing a novel, so there is no need for nuance. It is a short, punchy summary of your company's unique position. One or two sentences is the limit. Add more than that, and you are muddying the waters. Keep paring it down until you have the base elements, but make sure it is still memorable and effective.

Be holistic

The mission statement is not coming from the C-level executives but reflects everyone in the organisation. It is more comprehensive this way and gets buy-in from everyone. Each employee is part of the company process and, therefore, everyone is invested in its success.

Version one

Mission statements are not chiselled in stone. They are meant to reflect the time and place in which they were created. But times change and so should mission statements. Companies evolve and their mission statements need to change with them.

15.7.2.5 Examples of Mission Statements

You probably know a lot of mission statements without realising it. Here is a little bit of inspiration.

Coca-Cola

> *"To refresh the world, to inspire moments of optimism and happiness, and to create value and make a difference."*

Google

> *"To organise the world's information and make it universally accessible and useful."*

The Humane Society

> *"Creating animals, confronting cruelty."*

NASA

> *"We reach for new heights and reveal the unknown for the benefit of humankind."*

Smithsonian

> *"The increase and diffusion of knowledge."*

American Express

> *"We work hard every day to make American Express the world's most respected service brand."*

Nordstrom

> *"To give customers the most compelling shopping experience possible."*

JetBlue

> *"To inspire humanity – both in the air and on the ground."*

PayPal

> *"To build the web's most convenient, secure, cost-effective payment solutions."*

Kickstarter

> *"To help bring creative projects to life."*

Forbes

> *"To deliver information on the people, ideas and technologies changing the world to our community of affluent business decision-makers."*

Sony

> *"To be a company that inspires and fulfils your curiosity."*

Cisco

> *"Shape the future of the internet by creating unprecedented value and opportunity for our customers, employees, investors and ecosystem partners."*

Toyota

> *"To attract and attain customers with high-value products and services and the most satisfying ownership experience in America."*

15.8 OBJECTIVES

"[Objectives] are the road maps that guide you and show you what is possible."

Les Brown

15.8.1 WHAT PRECISELY IS AN OBJECTIVE, AND WHY ARE THEY SO IMPORTANT?

In business and management theory and practice, objectives (also called goals) are forecast futures or desired results that an individual or team envision, plan and commit to achieving (Locke & Latham, 1990). Locke and Latham (1990) developed empirical research in organisational psychology that led to goal-setting theory (Stajkovic et al., 2006). Much of what they wrote is focused on personal goals. However, it is equally applicable to organisations, since as the saying goes "there's no such thing as organisations, just people". They found that

"specific, difficult goals lead to higher performance than either easy goals or instructions to 'do your best,' as long as feedback about progress is provided, [people are] committed to the goals, and the [organisation] has the ability and the knowledge to perform the task"

(Locke & Latham, 1990).

Locke and Latham (1990) found that goals affect performance in four main ways:

1. They direct attention and effort towards activities related to goals,
2. They lead to greater effort,
3. They increase persistence, and difficult goals prolong effort, and
4. They indirectly stimulate interest, promoting the discovery and use of strategies and knowledge relevant to the task.

Positive performance outcomes associated with goals depend first on the importance of the goal and the commitment of the individual and team responsible for the goal. Effective goals require feedback to the individual and team responsible for them. Self-efficacy of individuals and team members enhances goal commitment too.

It is common to try and establish goals (or objectives, a common synonym) as specific, measurable, achievable, relevant and time-bound (SMART). Michael Hyatt, a thought leader in productivity, takes this further, adding evaluation and review to create SMARTER goals[14]. However, not all thought leaders in coaching agree with this (Grant, 2012). The issue is achievability. Locke and Latham (1990), in their theory, recommend the selection of goals in the 90th percentile of difficulty; in other words, stretch goals that may not be achievable.

The use of goal characteristics that help define it and determine someone's motivation to achieve it is a better predictor of goal achievement (Deckers, 2018). Consider:

- Complexity. How many sub-goals are there, and how are goals interconnected?
- Awareness. How aware is a person of a goal?
- Difficulty. How likely is it that the goal will be achieved?
- Importance. What is the qualitative or quantitative value of the goal?
- Specificity. How clearly is the goal stated?
- Schedule. What is the duration of the task(s) leading up to the goal, and what is the deadline?

15.8.2 WILD IMPORTANCE

> *"Nearly everything you do is of no importance, but it is important that you do it."*

Mahatma Gandhi

Building on research in neuroscience and psychology, McChesney et al. (2012) devote almost all of *The 4 Disciplines of Execution* to explaining how to achieve "wildly important goals". As indicated above, science is on their side. Locke and Latham (1990) identify positive performance with the importance of the goal, and a goal's significance is, according to (Deckers, 2018), a key characteristic.

Implicitly building on this, McChesney et al. (2012) advocate for a narrow focus on a small set of goals to overcome the "whirlwind" of business as usual at work. They argue that

> *"Your chances of achieving two or three goals with excellence are high, but the more goals you try to juggle at once, the less likely you will be to reach them."*

---

[14] https://michaelhyatt.com/goal-setting/, accessed 29 April 2021.

They reckon that trying for four to 10 goals above business as usual will yield success in only one to two goals. Going for 11 to 20 goals above business as usual see none bought to fruition.

Why should this be so?

15.8.3 WE ARE BEARS OF LITTLE BRAIN

While some scientists dispute it, the consensus is that the human brain cannot multi-task or at best cannot multi-task very well. The human mind can't perform two tasks requiring high-level brain functions at the same time. An exceedingly small percentage of people with proper training can mimic multi-tasking, but they are actually task-switching rapidly and have been trained at length to do so (pilots are a case in point). Low-level functions such as breathing or pumping blood are autonomic: they operate unconsciously, not requiring high-level brain function. Our inability to multi-task is why it is not only illegal to drive a car and use a mobile phone in your hand at the same time; it is also a dangerous cognitive challenge for most of us.

This inability to cognitively juggle important tasks effectively extends to essential business goals. Even the most brilliant business and science brains adopt this heuristic, focusing on a handful of what McChesney et al. (2012) call "wildly important" products, goals or ideas; further the psychology of learning grounds this idea.

Miller (1956) found that, through experimentation, most adults can store between five and nine elements only in their short-term memory. He labelled this theory the "magic number seven" (plus or minus two items). His thesis is that human memory only has limited storage 'slots' for things. He does not specify how much information each slot can hold. Instead, he suggests that we can 'chunk' information together to store more. However, it is 7 ± 2. That's it.

It is our brain physiology that limits us. The prefrontal cortex, the brain's central 'doorway' is designed only for small amounts of inputs. Multi-tasking weakens and erodes the brain's circuits dedicated to thinking profoundly and reading. The circuitry dedicated to more 'superficial' scanning or skimming tasks is strengthened by multi-tasking. As is the case in so many parts of life, long-term effective performance may be sacrificed to short-term, limited gains. Multi-tasking limits our ability to think creatively and powerfully. Meaningful reasoning is not encouraged by multi-tasking.

Understanding that your brain should focus on one thing at a time still permits you to have a further 6 ± 2 close at hand. However, focusing on one thing at a time is shown repeatedly to lead to excellent results. That applies just as much to teams and organisation as it does to individuals. In fact, it is the foundation of one of the great works on organisational effectiveness and efficiency, Goldratt's (1990) theory of constraints.

If we go back to Locke & Latham's (1990) perspective on how goals affect performance, having a singular goal means:

Our direct attention and effort are singularly focused.

Our effort is focused.

We persist single-mindedly with one challenging goal.

We narrow the strategies and knowledge we are applying to a single goal.

Focusing on goals in this manner is similar to how production engineers apply Goldratt's (1990) theory of constraints. When you find multiple constraints on a production system, you concentrate effort on releasing the single most significant constraint. Then you move to the next one and the next one and so on.

A singular focus enables you to manage complexity better, heightens your awareness and increases the likelihood that you will achieve the goal. It makes it easier to understand the specific goal and allows a focus on meeting deadlines.

15.8.4 HOW DO YOU JUDGE WHAT IS WILDLY IMPORTANT?

We go back to Locke & Latham's (1990) recommendation to choose stretch goals that may not be achievable; this is counter to a great deal of conventional wisdom advising the adoption of SMART goals. However, it does fall in line with the thinking of (Collins & Porras, 2004) in *Built to Last*. They adopted old engineering vernacular ("Big Hairy A***d Goal") and gentrified it: Big Hairy Audacious Goal (BHAG). A BHAG engages people, reaching out and grabbing them viscerally. It is focused energising and tangible. It takes little or explanation. People just 'get it.' It is aspirational, clear and compelling and demonstrates commitment and risk. By definition, it is wildly important.

You will almost certainly have a high-level wildly important goal (let's call them 'WIGs' from now on, acknowledging McChesney et al. (2012)). However, you will need to disaggregate goals such as this to operationalise them. Usually, this will be three, but you might have 'reserves' of another four, based on Miller's (1956) thinking (Figure 47).

Figure 47: WIG hierarchy

The point is that in focusing on the three WIGs supporting your 'over-the-horizon' WIG, you are still following McChesney et al's (2012) heuristic of no more than three. If you succeed with one or more, you roll in one or more from your reserve list. Taking this to the extreme is the 'Rule of Five Ones,' commonly adopted by entrepreneurs and attributed to a variety of people. It is five WIGs arranged vertically: one market, one product, one conversion tool (sales channel), one source of leads in one year. It works.

15.9 QUESTIONS

1. What is a strategic plan?
2. Does your organisation have a strategic plan?
3. Is this a formal document?
4. Is it communicated or circulated and to whom?
5. Have you seen it?
6. Will a strategic plan be needed for organisational transformation or will change be introduced?
7. Corporate boards are an institution that most people have little to do with. Look at the business sections of a recent serious newspaper or have a look back through *The Economist*. What are the stories that you see about boards? What contribution do you think they make?
8. Thinking about the material on strategic leadership structures, what contribution do you think boards should make?
9. What do you understand by the term strategic planning?
10. Think about what you understand as the meaning of values in a business? Identify good examples of corporate values and bad.
11. What do you understand is the meaning of organisational culture? Identify some examples of good organisational culture and bad.
12. What do you understand is the meaning of power in organisations? Identify some examples of good uses of organisational power and bad.

13. What do you understand the meaning of vision in organisations to be? Identify some examples of good and bad organisational vision statements.
14. What do you understand the meaning of mission in organisations to be? Identify some examples of good and bad organisational mission statements.
15. What do you understand by the phrase organisational objectives or goals? What do you think good goals look like? Think about some examples.

16. CHOOSING AND IMPLEMENTING STRATEGY

"In reality strategy is actually very straightforward. You pick a general direction and implement like hell."

Jack Welch

16.1 CHAPTER OVERVIEW

This chapter aims to develop readers' understanding of choosing and implementing strategy.

The key concepts we cover are strategic direction, strategic choice, blue ocean strategy, implementing strategy and the strategic plan.

On completing this chapter, you should be able to:

1. Identify potential strategic directions based on analysis.
2. Choose appropriate directions.
3. Develop a blue ocean strategy based on reviewing the business model.
4. Explain the principles of implementing strategies.
5. Draft a strategic plan.

16.2 STRATEGIC DIRECTION: RED OR BLUE?

Determining strategic direction is covered in detail in chapter 6. However, in summary, it comes down to choosing between generic (red ocean) (Ansoff, 1970; Porter, 1980, 1985) or value innovation (blue ocean) (Kim & Mauborgne, 1997, 1999, 2005a, 2005b) strategies.

16.2.1 GENERIC STRATEGY (RED)

Combining Ansoff (1970) and Porter (1980, 1985), we have a choice between:

1. An *aggressive* strategy - cost leadership + market penetration, leveraging on strengths to pursue opportunities.
2. A *competitive* strategy - differentiation + market/product/service development with more leverageable strengths than major competitions.

3. A *conservative* strategy - segment focus + niche market penetration to consolidate strengths into a superior position in the market where few threats are present or anticipated.
4. An *exit* strategy - diversification into new markets because little potential exists for current business and where weakness and threats far exceed actionable strengths or current market opportunities.

With the exception of an exit strategy, these are conventional 'red ocean' strategies. Organisations stick to what they are good at, pivot to new segments with their existing model or stick to existing segments using disruptive technologies or thinking to change their business model. They rarely genuine shift segments and the rest of the model at the same time. Moreover, they usually stay in the same board competitive arena as always. The red ocean is a metaphor for highly competitive markets, with little space for all of the players. They are unforgiving environments (Kim & Mauborgne, 1997, 1999, 2005a, 2005b).

16.2.2 STORMY RED OCEANS

There are six assumptions on which most companies hypnotically build their strategies keeping companies trapped competing in red oceans, specifically companies tend to do the following (Kim & Mauborgne, 2005a, pp. 47-49):

1. Define their industry similarly and focus on being the best in it.
2. Look at their industries through the lens of generally accepted strategic product or service sectors and strive to stand out in their chosen strategic sector.
3. Focus on the same buyer group be they purchaser, user or influencer.
4. Define the scope of the products and services offered by that industry similarly.
5. Accept their industry's functional or emotional orientations.
6. Focus on the same point in time, often non-current (and certainly not future) competitive threats in formulating strategy.

Competitive convergence is driven by the volume of companies sharing conventional wisdom about how they compete (Kim & Mauborgne, 2005a, p. 48).

Leaving red oceans means companies must break out of accepted competitive boundaries. Managers need to look systematically across them to create blue oceans. They need to look across alternative industries, strategic groups, buyer groups, complementary value propositions, the functional-emotional orientation of their industry, and even across time. Their search must apply value innovation strategy (Kim & Mauborgne, 2005a, pp. 48-49).

16.2.3 VALUE INNOVATION STRATEGY (BLUE)

We have previously discussed this, but it is worth repeating because it is an important strategic concept.

Value innovation is the simultaneous pursuit of differentiation and low cost, creating a leap in value for both buyers and the company. Value to buyers comes from a product or service's utility minus its price. Companies generate value from their products or services' prices minus their costs. Value innovation occurs only when the whole system of utility, price, and cost is aligned. (Kim & Mauborgne, 1997, 1999, 2005a, 2005b) (Figure 48).

Figure 48: Value innovation

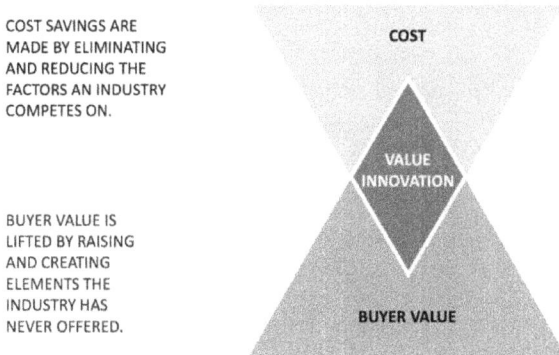

COST SAVINGS ARE MADE BY ELIMINATING AND REDUCING THE FACTORS AN INDUSTRY COMPETES ON.

COST

VALUE INNOVATION

BUYER VALUE IS LIFTED BY RAISING AND CREATING ELEMENTS THE INDUSTRY HAS NEVER OFFERED.

BUYER VALUE

The only interest there is in competitors in firms committed to value innovation is in the position of their business model relative to competitors.

Broadly speaking, the aim of blue ocean strategy, enabled by value innovation is to create uncontested market space and make the competition largely irrelevant.

How do we operationalise this idea?

16.3 STRATEGIC CHOICE

Again, we have covered some of the following previously, but it is worth repeating because of its strategic importance.

We are going to look at an alternative approach that blends blue ocean strategy (Kim & Mauborgne, 1997, 1999, 2005a, 2005b), business model generation (Osterwalder & Pigneur, 2010) and the theory of constraints (Goldratt, 1990).

16.3.1 THE FOUR ACTIONS FRAMEWORK

Applying the 'four actions framework' (Kim & Mauborgne, 1997, 1999, 2005a, 2005b: pp. 29-37) breaks the value-cost trade-off and asks (Figure 49):

1. Which of the factors that the industry takes for granted can be eliminated?
2. Which factors should be reduced well below the industry's standard?
3. What factors should be raised well above the industry's standard?
4. What factors should be created that the industry has never offered?

Figure 49: Four actions framework

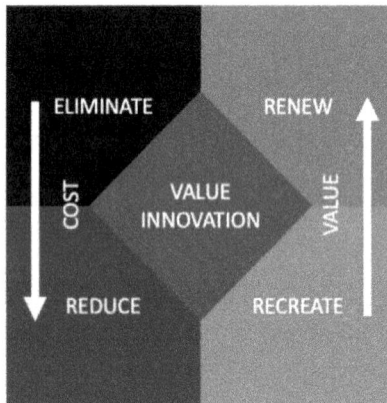

We need to ask these questions across each element of the business model (Figure 50).

Figure 50: Value innovation canvas

	CREATE +	ELMINATE –	RAISE ↑	REDUCE ↓
CUSTOMERS				
VALUE PROVIDED				
CHANNELS				
CUSTOMER RELATIONSHIPS				
REVENUE				
KEY RESOURCES				
KEY ACTIVITIES				
KEY PARTNERS				
COSTS				

For example:

- Which customer factors that the industry takes for granted can be eliminated?
- Which customer factors should be reduced well below the industry's standard?
- What customer factors should be raised well above the industry's standard?
- What customer factors should be created that the industry has never offered?

How are we inspired to identify the factors in these questions?

16.3.2 SIX PATHS TO RECONSTRUCT MARKET BOUNDARIES

Applying each question to each model building block, we look at six paths for inspirations for value innovation (((Kim & Mauborgne, 2005a, pp. 47-49):

1. Look across *alternative industries*. What are the alternative industries to your industry? Why do customers trade across them? By focusing on the key factors that lead buyers to trade across alternative industries and eliminating or reducing everything else, you can create a blue ocean of new market space.
2. Look across *strategic groups* within industries. What are the strategic groups in your industry? Why do customers trade up

for the higher groups? Why do they trade down for the lower one?

3. Look across the *chain of buyers*. What is the chain of buyers in your industry? What buyer group does your industry typically focus on? If you shifted the buyer group of your industry, how could you unlock new value?

4. Look across *complementary products and services*. What is the context in which your product or service is used? What happens before, during and after use? Can you identify the pain points? How can you eliminate these pain points through a complementary product or service offering?

5. Look across *functional or emotional appeal to buyers*. Does your industry compete on functionality or emotional appeal? If you compete on emotional appeal, what elements can you strip out to make it functional? If you compete on functionality, what elements can be added to make it emotional?

6. Look across *time*. What trends have a high probability of impacting your industry are irreversible and are evolving in a clear trajectory? How will these trends impact your industry? Given this, how can you open up unprecedented customer utility?

16.3.3 CONCEIVING NEW MARKET SPACE

By thinking across conventional competitive boundaries, you can see prospective convention-altering strategic moves that reconstruct established market boundaries, creating blue oceans. The process of discovery and creation (through value innovation) is not about predicting or pre-empting industry trends. Neither is it a trial-and-error process of implementing wild new business ideas that happen to come across, managers minds or intuition. Rather it is a structured process of reordering market realities in a fundamentally new way.

Reconstructing existing business model elements across industry and market boundaries liberates businesses from head-to-head competition in red oceans.

16.3.4 KERB YOUR ENTHUSIASM: ONE STEP AT A TIME

It is tempting to take the identified value innovations from this exercise and put them into action all at once. This is dangerous since it will open the business up to complex interactions between several different strategic moves in your business model.

The next step is to identify which of the proposed moves you've identified will have the biggest impact or release the most substantial business constraint (Goldratt, 1990). Feed it back by building a revised business model canvas ... and repeat. The idea is to simulate the impact of a chain of value innovations on your business model, one step at a time, and see where it all takes you.

There is no simple path here, but a path will emerge.

There are some qualifications:

- Do not get too hung up on revenue and costs. Focus on the big picture. Applying Walsh's (2009) thinking seems a long way from finance. However, the score (aka the balance sheet and profit and loss) will take care of itself if the building blocks of the model are right.

- Do not get too close to the here and now. You're looking for newly constructed demand. You have to reach beyond existing demand.

- The path will emerge. However, the reason for repeatedly revisiting the business model canvas is to get the sequencing right, to focus on the constraints in the model as it is refined (Goldratt, 1990).

16.4 IMPLEMENTING STRATEGY

16.4.1 THE BEST LAID PLANS

"The best-laid schemes o' mice an' men / Gang aft a-gley."

Robert Burns, *To a Mouse*

"No plan outlasts the first encounter with the enemy."

von Clausewitz

The point of planning is to get an idea of the steps you need to take in the direction of your goals. Things will get in the way; stuff happens; and plans change. They should be regularly revised as they are implemented.

And so, to implementation or better still execution. Its foundation is that it is future-focused; it is about achieving your organisation's wildly important goals. Then, naturally enough, it is about having a bias to action. If you want what you want, then you have to actively work towards it. Sitting back and waiting for things to happen does not generally lead to achievement, especially of the difficult. When you are in action, you need to be ruthlessly consistent, keep an eye on the score, and you must have a means of being held accountable.

16.4.2 ASPIRATIONAL GOALS ARE THE MOST EFFECTIVE

In another life, Clive was accused of having no interest in the operations of the enterprise he was running. In the mind of at least one of his board members, he was: "all about strategy and plans" with "insufficient attention to operational details".

On mature reflection, this was in Clive's opinion: "complete rubbish". His argument was code for Clive not paying (in his opinion) sufficient attention to cash flow. Cash flow is essential to implementing plans, and yes, Clive actually did monitor it. However, implementing strategies in business and for individuals is not solely about money; it is more complicated than that.

Another interesting case for Clive, was John, a Departmental Manager, one of the four who reported to Clive. The business was in a tight spot. It had good revenue, but the CEO and CFO wanted to use our surplus to pin up other parts of the enterprise for 'strategic reasons'.

Now, the costs were pretty much fixed; easily, the most significant component was staff. What we needed was more revenue and ideas to stimulate it: future-focused, strategic and not operational. Yet, at every meeting, John had his nose in his operating budget spreadsheet, visibly worried and fretting. After two or three sessions observing this behaviour, which went on throughout the meetings, Clive took him aside. "John," he said, "it's not going to get any better." "What do you mean?" he responded. "Your operating budget for this year isn't going to improve. And it isn't going to improve next year either if we do not get more revenue. That's where I need your attention." John was looking back. We needed to look forward.

16.4.3 LOOK FORWARD!

Strategy is about looking forward. I'm going to repeat that: strategy is about looking forward.

The challenge is that too often we try and gauge progress against these strategic objectives by looking at what McChesney et al. (2012) call "lag measures". These are conventional measures that are superficially comforting and familiar: quarterly results, sales numbers, kilograms lost. The issue is that they measure the goal as you move towards it. They do not measure actions leading to the goals. They have happened already, and you cannot do anything to change them; they are not influenceable. Lag measures state that you will go from "X to Y by when". They are not action orientated.

"Lead measures", on the other hand, are predictive and influenceable. If the lead measure changes, so will the lag. They are changeable so that you can influence the outcome.

You need both types of measure.

Here is a WIG with which many people are far too familiar: losing weight. The lag measure shown on the scales; for example, decrease your body weight from 90kg to 80kg by 30 May. However, it needs lead measures too; for example, reducing kilojoules consumed through diet and increasing kilojoules burned through exercise. These strongly indicate that you will lose weight and they are directly influenceable by you.

16.4.4 A BIAS FOR ACTION

A bias for action is "when you have a choice, you choose action over inaction". It is not "just do it", which discounts or ignores issues; a bias for action accounts for them. It means that taking purposeful action is your default state. When you have a bias for action, not doing things is what takes a decision; you automatically do something. It is about energy and enthusiasm focused on execution, the thrill of getting things done, as simply as is possible and then doing the next thing (Bossidy & Charan, 2009; Bruch & Ghosal, 2004; Peters, 2018; Peters & Waterman, 2004).

A goal without a plan is just a wish; so too is a plan without action. Goals and plans simply do not matter if you fail to act. A bias for action is not about you continually doing everything you could possibly do; it is simply the idea that you need to do something. Sometimes you really are too busy to do what it says on the plan. Life does get in the way. Your dynamic centre shifts. When it does, do not just stand there, do something!

Those who have a bias for action (Bruch & Ghosal, 2004):

- Know who they are and who the people they work with are.
- Know their business.

- Are critically and relentlessly realistic about their position and their position at work or of their business. They insist on realism.
- Identify clear goals and priorities.
- Follow-through on actions they start.
- Reward themselves and others based on achievement.
- Learn relentlessly and expand people's capabilities, seeking greatness in others.

They also set up a work environment that matches their ambitions and are evident in their expectations (Walsh, 2009). They look to put the right people in the right place (Bossidy & Charan, 2009).

They are not frantic, desperate or hasty or even slightly unfocused; nor do they procrastinate, postponing work because of a lack of energy or focus. They are not insecure and do not fear failure. Neither are they detached, disengaged, aloof, tense or apathetic. People with a bias for action are purposeful and get the job done; they are highly focused and energetic. They come across as reflective and calm, especially at times of threat, crisis or chaos. It is not a question of being 'simply' well-motivated. A bias for action requires wilfulness: having clarity of intent; conscious choice in relentlessly pursuing that intent; and the ability to protect that intent from distraction, boredom or frustrations. Key to this is the development and improvement of good habits and dismissing bad ones. So too is the pursuit of mindfulness and flow, both essential characteristics of those biased to action. The enemies of action are overwhelming demands on your time, severe constraints on your ability to act and not exploring alternative choices (Bruch & Ghosal, 2004).

Clive's favourite exemplar of a bias for action is one of his early mentors, John Williamson, "JW" as he is known to his colleagues who love him (and the word love is not used trivially). When we first met JW was, not to put too fine a polish on it, implacably and consistently ruthless in shaping Clive. In working on a large-scale commercial IT project, his version was that he saw latent ability, but that Clive's approach was "all wrong." Clive was, with hindsight, a snotty, over opinionated academic, with a superiority complex that he remains ashamed of to this day. What JW needed was a commercially minded project manager who could solve problems and respond to client or project needs, without letting his ego get in the way of pragmatism.

Until JW 'polished' Clive, he would give clients any number of reasons why he couldn't solve something and several more that explained why clients' solutions couldn't possibly work. Clive spent too much time talking, not enough time listening, and nowhere near enough time thinking about practical solutions.

A straightforward exercise was all it took. On one day, JW permitted Clive only to answer his questions with "yes," "no," or "don't know." "Yes" or "no" bought an action for JW or an instruction for Clive. "Don't know" resulted in a singular instruction: "well, go and find out then." It drove Clive slightly mad. By the close of business, Clive was 'bursting for a fight'. JW took one look and said: "right, down the pub then for a natter". Over a beer, JW explained: "now you've learned to listen, ask questions and come up with practical solutions, instead of spouting rubbish without listening to what the client wants or finding their pain points". It was with hindsight a masterclass in having a bias for action.

There are things you can do now to develop a bias for action (Bruch & Ghosal, 2004):

- Be mindful – live in the present moment and focus. Visualise your intent; confront ambivalence.
- Prepare for obstacles and self-distance – if something seems impossible or if you start overthinking, you're less likely to move and act. Pause, mentally step outside, clear your mind, step back, re-engage.
- Break big problems down into smaller ones, so making for smaller decisions.
- Make choices by creating a 'decision-system.' At its simplest, that's a diary and a to-do list linked to a planner. Plan annually, quarterly, monthly, weekly and daily. A little and often.
- Set aspirational, experiential rewards for success.

16.4.5 YOUR SCORECARD

Ideally, you have a bias for action, focused on your wildly important (aspirational) goals (WIGs)to ensure you're making progress against your plans. The question is how do you gauge progress?

You need a 'compelling' scorecard that reflects your goals, plans and actions (McChesney et al., 2012). As noted earlier, it is important that you have lead measures as well as lag measures when you're looking at how you're travelling.

But there is something else we think you need to take into account as you build your scorecard. It should not just be about your goals; it also needs to reflect on some other critical matters that heavily influence organisational performance.

16.4.6 THE BALANCED SCORECARD

One of the most influential business books ever is *The Balanced Scorecard* by Kaplan and Norton (1996a). It outlines a tool, a standard semi-structured report by which managers keep track of the execution of activities by staff and the outcomes of those activities. It pulls together ideas from decades of research by other scholars, as well as Kaplan and Norton themselves. It is intended is to facilitate effective and efficient strategy implementation. It focuses on a mixed set of financial and non-financial measures to summarise actions designed to impact performance and monitor outcomes.

Figure 51 is an example of a strategy map, which takes the scorecard to the next level Kaplan & Norton (2004). In essence, it is a strategic plan on a page.

Figure 51: A strategy map

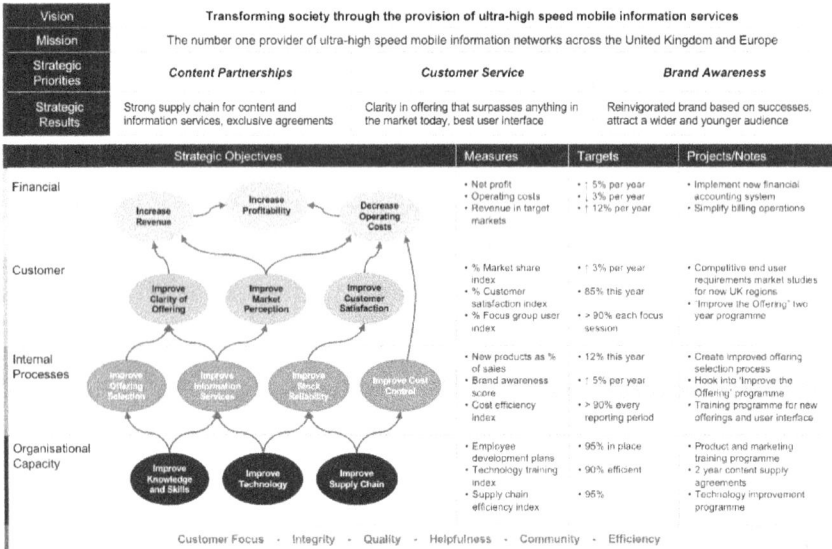

The vision, mission, strategic priorities (a higher-level form of objectives used in some larger organisations) and (expected strategic results) are stated clearly. From there the business objectives, measures, targets and strategic initiatives are recorded (yes there are lead and lag measures). The objectives are causally mapped, across different company perspectives (financial, customer, processes and organisational capacity). The values are neatly stated across the base of the map.

A map gives directions and the tool that enables strategic implementation. The strategy map is the artefact around which all strategic conversations around implementation occurs.

16.5 STRATEGIC PLAN STRUCTURE

A strategic plan, usually based over a three to five-year timeframe, will follow the structure of the planning process:

1. Executive Summary.
2. Business Description.
3. Values, Vision, Mission.
4. Strategic Analysis.
5. SWOT Analysis.
6. Business Model Review (based on the four actions).
7. Business Objectives.
8. Strategy Map.
9. Organisation Structure.
10. Financial Projections (based on analysis).

16.6 QUESTIONS

1. If you haven't put together a business canvas for your organisation, sketch one out quickly. Without taking too much time, experiment with the value innovation canvas. Ask the four questions. Pick a couple of paths. What opportunities or constraints do you see?

17. CLOSING THOUGHTS

Leading transformational change is difficult. If it was easy, many more organisation transformation projects would work. That so many do not, indicates just how crucial leadership is to such undertakings.

In this book we have covered what we think is the essential knowledge and skill set you need in approach change leadership. But the truth is we have only scratched the surface of each of the disciplinary areas we have covered. The book could easily be twice as long! We also cannot instil experience in you through a book. For that you need to *engage*.

Which brings us to the unifying strand across the book: a bias to act, to change. We're both overly fond of two sayings:

> *If you do what you've always done, you'll get what you've always had.*

And

> *You choose how you react to what life throws at you. Choose wisely.*

So, if you are not content with where you find your organisation or indeed yourself in life, choose to change. Our small ambition is for this book to help you with that. Simply put:

> *If you change what you do, you'll change what you get.*

If you are reading this book as part of our course, *Certified Transformational Leader*, then it is likely that your next step will be an applied research project. We wish you well with that work. Do not forget this book when you are developing your theoretical framework for that project.

If you are reading this book out of curiosity or because it was recommended to you, thank you. If you would like to learn more about us and our work in leadership education, take a look at www.iimbas.com.

In closing, we recommend you cultivate the habit of reading a range of books to stimulate your thinking and to encourage challenging the *status quo*. And always remember the wise words of Heraclitus:

> *"No man ever steps in the same river twice, for it's not the same river and he's not the same man."*

Leading change is a 'forever skill'. The more we learn about it, the better our chance of success in leading change.

REFERENCES

AICD. (2016). *Role of the board.* Australian Institute of Company Directors.

Ansoff, H. I. (1970). *Corporate Strategy* (New Impression ed.). Penguin.

Ariely, D. (2016). *Payoff: The Hidden Logic That Shapes Our Motivations.* Simon & Schuster.

Ariely, D., Gneezy, U., Loewenstein, G., & Mazar, N. (2009). Large stakes and big mistakes. *Review of Economic Studies, 76*(2), 451-469.

Ariely, D., Kamenica, E., & Prelec, D. (2008). Man's search for meaning: the case of Legos. *Journal of Economic Behavior & Organization 67*(3-4), 671-677.

Ashcroft, J. (2014). *The Lego Case Study.* John Ashcroft and Company.

Augustsson, H., Churruca, K., & Braithwaite, J. (2020). Change and improvement 50 years in the making: a scoping review of the use of soft systems methodology in healthcare. *BMC health services research, 20*(1), 1-1063. https://doi.org/10.1186/s12913-020-05929-5

Baard, P. P., Deci, E. L., & Ryan, R. M. (2004). Intrinsic need satisfaction: a motivational basis of performance and well-being in two work settings. *Journal of Applied Social Psychology, 34*(10), 2045-2068.

Bandura, A. (1986). *Social Foundations of Thought and Action: a Social Cognitive Theory.* Prentice-Hall.

Bandura, A. (2005). The evolution of social cognitive theory. In K. G. Smith & M. A. Hitt (Eds.), *Great Minds in Management: The Process of Theory Development* (pp. 9-33). Oxford University Press.

Bauman, Z. (1998a). *Globalization: The Human Consequences.* Polity Press.

Bauman, Z. (1998b). *Work Consumerism and the New Poor.* Open University Press.

Bauman, Z. (1999). *In Search of Politics.* Polity Press.

Bauman, Z. (2000). *Liquid Modernity.* Polity Press.

Bauman, Z. (2001). *The Individualized Society.* Polity Press.

Beck, U. (1992). *Risk Society. Towards a New Modernity* (M. Ritter, Trans.). Sage.

Beck, U. (1998). *Democracy Without Enemies.* Polity Press.

Beck, U. (1999). *World Risk Society.* Polity Press.

Beck, U. (2000). *The Brave New World of Work* (P. Camiller, Trans.). Polity Press.

Blau, P. M. (1960). A theory of social integration. *The American Journal of Sociology, 65*(6), 545–556.

Blau, P. M. (1964). *Exchange and Power in Social Life.* John Wiley & Sons.

Bossidy, L., & Charan, R. (2009). *Execution: the Discipline of Getting Things Done* (Second ed.). Crown Business.

Boxall, P., & Macky, K. (2007). High-performance work systems and organisational performance: bridging theory and practice. *Asia Pacific Journal of Human Resources, 45*(3), 261-270.

Brown, T. (2009). *Change By Design.* HarperCollins.

Bruch, H., & Ghosal, S. (2004). *A Bias for Action: How Effective Managers Harness Their Willpower, Achieve Results, and Stop Wasting Time.* Harvard Business Review Press.

Brynjolfsson, E., & McAfee, A. (2016). *The Second Machine Age: Work, Progress, and Prosperity in a Time of Brilliant Technologies.* W. W. Norton & Company.

Burgelman, R. A. (1994). Fading memories: a process theory of strategic business exit in dynamic environments. *Administrative Science Quarterly, 39*(1), 24-56.

Burgelman, R. A. (2002). *Strategy Is Destiny: How Strategy-Making Shapes a Company's Future.* Free Press.

Burke, W. W., & Litwin, G. H. (1992). A causal model of organisational performance and change. *Journal of Management, 18*(3), 529-545.

Burns, J. M. (1978). *Leadership.* Harper Collins Publishers.

Cameron, K. S. (2012). *Positive Leadership: Strategies for Extraordinary Performance* (Second ed.). Berrett-Koehler.

Cameron, K. S., & Quinn, R. E. (2011). *Diagnosing and Changing Organizational Culture: Based on the Competing Values Framework* (Third ed.). Jossey-Bass.

Champy, J. A. (1995). *Reengineering Management,* . Harper Business Books.

Checkland, P. B. (1999). *Systems Thinking, Systems Practice* (Second ed.). John Wiley and Sons.

Checkland, P. B., & Scholes, J. (1999). *Soft Systems Methodology in Action* (Second ed.). John Wiley and Sons.

Chirkov, V., Ryan, R. M., Kim, Y., & Kaplan, U. (2003). Differentiating autonomy from individualism and independence: a self-determination theory perspective on internalization of cultural orientations and well-being. *Journal of Personality and Social Psychology, 84*(1), 97-110.

Christensen, C. R., Andrews, K. R., & Bower, J. (1978). *Business Policy: Text and Cases.* (Fourth ed.). Richard D Irwin.

Church, M. (2017). *Next: Thoughts About Tomorrow You Can Talk About Today.* Thought Leaders Publishing.

Cobb Jr., J. B., & Griffin, D. R. (1976). *Process Theology - An Introductory Exposition.* The Westminster Press.

Collins, J., & Porras, J. I. (2004). *Built to Last. Successful Habit of Visionary Companies* (Second ed.). HarperCollins.

Costanza, R., & Daly, H. E. (1992). Natural capital and sustainable development. *Conservation Biology, 6,* 37-46.

Darwin, C. (1859/2015). *The Origin of the Species.* Wilder Publications.

Davenport, T. (1993). *Process Innovation: Reengineering Work through Information Technology.* Harvard Business School Press.

Dawkins, R. (1976). *The Selfish Gene.* Oxford University Press.

Dawkins, R. (2006a). *The Blind Watchmaker* (Second ed.). Penguin.

Dawkins, R. (2006b). *The God Delusion.* Bantam Books.

Deal, T. E., & Kennedy, A. A. (1982). *Corporate Cultures: The Rites and Rituals of Corporate Life.* Penguin Books.

Deci, E. L., & Ryan, R. M. (2008). Facilitating optimal motivation and psychological well-being across life's domains. *Canadian Psychology, 49*(1), 14-23.

Deckers, L. (2018). *Motivation: Biological, Psychological, and Environmental* (Fifth ed.). Routledge.

Devine, J., Camfield, L., & Gough, I. (2008). Autonomy or dependence—or both? Perspectives from Bangladesh. *Journal of Happiness Studies, 9*(1), 105-138.

Dobbs, R., Manyika, J., & Woetzel, J. (2015). *No Ordinary Disruption. The Four Global Forces Breaking All the Trends.* . Public Affairs.

Duncker, K. (1945). On problem-solving. *Psychological Monographs, 58*(5), i–113.

Dyer, J. (2019). *Critical Thinking. 12 Rules for Intelligent Thinking.* Amazon.

Emerson, R. M. (1962). Power-dependence relations. *American Sociological Review, 27*(1), 31–41.

Ertel, C., & Solomon, L. K. (2014). *Moments of Impact: How to Design Strategic Conversations That Accelerate Change.* Simon & Schuster.

Flanagan, K., & Gregory, D. (2019). *Future Skills: The 12 Skills to Future Proof Yourself, Your Team and Your Kids.* Wiley.

Freeman, R. E. (1994). The politics of stakeholder theory: some future directions. *Business Ethics Quarterly, 4*(4), 409-421.

Freudenreich, B., Lüdeke-Freund, F., & Schaltegger, S. (2020). A stakeholder theory perspective on business models: value creation for sustainability. *Journal of Business Ethics, 166*(1), 3-18. https://doi.org/10.1007/s10551-019-04112-z

Frey, C. B., & Osbourne, N. M. (2013). *The Future of Employment: How susceptible are jobs to computerisation?* Oxford Martin School, University of Oxford.

Friedman, M. (1970, 13 September). A Friedman doctrine: the social responsibility of business is to increase its profits. *New York Times Magazine.*

Gagné, M., & Deci, E. L. (2005). Self-determination theory and work motivation. *Journal of Organizational Behaviour, 26*(4), 331–362.

Galloway, S. (2020). *Post Corona: from Crisis to Opportunity.* Bantam Press.

Garavan, T., McCarthy, A., Lai, Y., Murphy, K., Sheehan, M., & Carbery, R. (2020). Training and organisational performance:A meta-analysis of temporal, institutionaland organisational context moderators *Human Resource Management Journal, 31*(1), 93-119.

Giddens, A. (1984). *The Constitution of Society.* Polity Press.

Giddens, A. (1990). *The Consequences of Modernity.* Polity Press.

Giddens, A. (1998). *The Third Way: the Renewal of Social Democracy.* Polity Press.

Glucksberg, S. (1962). The influence of strength of drive on functional fixedness and perceptual recognition. *Journal of Experimental Psychology, 63*(1), 36–41.

Golder, P. N., & Tellis, G. J. (1993). Pioneer advantage: marketing logic or marketing legend? *Journal of Marketing Research, 30*(2), 158–170.

Goldratt, E. M. (1990). *What is This Thing Called Theory of Constraints and How Should It Be Implemented?* The North River Press.

Gollwitzer, P. M. (1999). Implementation intentions: Strong effects of simple plans. *American Psychologist, 54*, 493-503.

Gollwitzer, P. M., & Brandstaetter, V. (1997). Implementation intentions and effective goal pursuit. *Journal of Personality and Social Psychology, 73*, 186-199.

Graetz, F. (2002). "Strategic thinking versus strategic planning: towards understanding the complementarities. *Management Decision, 40*(5), 456-462. https://doi.org/https://doi.org/10.1108/00251740210430434

Grant, A. (2017). *Originals: How Non-conformists Change the World.* Virgin Digital.

Grant, A. M. (2012). An integrated model of goal-focused coaching: an evidence-based framework for teaching and practice. *International Coaching Psychology Review, 7*(2), 146–165.

Gratton, L. (2011). *The Shift: The Future of Work is Already Here.* Harper Collins Business.

Gratton, L., & Scott, A. (2016). *The 100-Year Life: Living and Working in an Age of Longevity.* Bloomsbury.

Gray, J. (1998). *False Dawn.* Granta Books.

Green, F. (2006). *Demanding Work: The Paradox of Job Quality in the Affluent Economy*

Grinyer, P. H., & Spender, J.-C. (1979). Recipes, crises and adaptation in mature business. *International Studies of Management & Organization, 19*(3), 113-133.

Guha, S., Kettinger, W. J., & Teng, J. T. C. (1993). Business process reengineering: building a comprehensive methodology. *Information systems management, 10*(3), 13-22.

Hammer, M. (1990). Reengineering work: don't automate, obliterate. *Harvard Business Review*(July/August), 104–112.

Hammer, M., & Champy, J. A. (1993). *Reengineering the Corporation: A Manifesto for Business Revolution.* Harper Business Books.

Hammer, M., & Stanton, S. (1995). *The Reengineering Revolution.* Harper Collins.

Handy, C. (1993). *Understanding Organisations* (Fourth ed.). Oxford University Press.

Harari, Y. N. (2011). *A Brief History of Humankind.* Vintage.

Harnish, V. (2002). *Mastering the Rockefeller Habits: What You Must Do to Increase the Value of Your Growing Firm.* Select Books.

Harrison, J. S., & Wicks, A. (2013). Stakeholder theory, value, and firm performance. *Business Ethics Quarterly, 23*(1), 97-124. https://doi.org/10.5840/beq20132314

Harter, J. K., & Blacksmith, N. (2009). Employee engagement and the psychology of joining, staying in, and leaving organisations. In N. Garcea, S. Harrington, & P. A. Linley (Eds.), *Oxford Handbook of Positive Psychology and Work.* Oxford University Press.

Harter, J. K., Schmidt, F. L., Agrawal, S., Blue, A. T., Plowman, S. K., Josh, P., & Asplund, J. (2020). *The Relationship Between Engagement at Work and Organisational Outcomes: 2020 Q12® Meta-Analysis: 10th Edition.* Gallup.

Harter, J. K., Schmidt, F. L., Agrawal, S., Plowman, S. K., & Blue, A. T. (2020). Increased business value for positive job attitudes during economic recessions: a meta-analysis and SEM analysis. *Human Performance, 33*(4), 307-330.

Heath, C., & Heath, D. (2017). *The Power of Moments. Why Certain Experiences Have Extraordinary Impact.* Corgi.

Heifetz, R. A., & Laurie, D. L. (2012). Mobilising adaptive work: beyind visionary leadership. In J. A. Conger, G. M. Spreitzer, & E. E. Lawler (Eds.), *The Leader's Change Handbook: An Essential Guide to Setting Direction and Taking Action* (pp. 55-86). Jossey-Bass.

Hiatt, J. (2006). *ADKAR: A Model for Change in Business, Government and our Community.* Prosci Learning Center Publications.

Hodes, D. V. (2017). *More Than Just Work: The Surprising Power of Constraints to Inspire New Thinking and Uplift Your People.* Ensemble Publishing.

Holwell, S. (2000). Soft Systems Methodology: other voices. *Systemic Practice and Action Research, 13*(6), 773-797. https://doi.org/10.1023/A:1026479529130

Homans, G. C. (1958). Social behavior as exchange. *American Journal of Sociology, 63*(6), 597–606.

Horwath, R. (2009). *Deep Dive: The Proven Method for Building Strategy, Focusing Your Resources, and Taking Smart.* Greenleaf Book Group Press.

Horwath, R. (2014). *Elevate: The Three Disciplines of Advanced Strategic Thinking.* Wiley.

Hutton, W. (1995). *The State We're In.* Jonathan Cape.

Hutton, W. (2002). *The World We're In.* Little, Brown.

Hyde, M., & Higgs, P. (2016). *Ageing and Globalisation.* Policy Press.

Jackson, M. C. (2019). *Critical Systems Thinking and the Management of Complexity: Responsible Leadership for a Complex World* (1st edition ed.). Wiley.

Jacques, E. (2006). *Requisite Organization: A Total System for Effective Managerial Organization and Managerial Leadership for the 21st Century* (Second ed.). Cason Hall & Co.

Jensen, M. C., & Meckling, W. (1976). Theory of the firm: managerial behaviour, agency costs and capital structure. *Journal of Financial Economics, 3*(October), 305-360.

Kahneman, D. (2000). Experienced utility and objective happiness: a moment-based approach. In D. Kahneman & A. Tversky (Eds.), *Choices, Values and Frames* (pp. 673-692). Russel Sage Foundation and Cambridge University Press.

Kaplan, R. S., & Norton, D. P. (1992). The balanced scorecard - measures that drive performance. *Harvard Business Review*(January-February), 71-79.

Kaplan, R. S., & Norton, D. P. (1993). Putting the balanced scorecard to work. *Harvard Business Review*(September-October), 135-147.

Kaplan, R. S., & Norton, D. P. (1996a). *The Balanced Scorecard: Translating Strategy into Action*. Harvard Business School Press.

Kaplan, R. S., & Norton, D. P. (1996b). Using the balanced scorecard as a strategic management system. *Harvard Business Review*(January-February), 75-85.

Kaplan, R. S., & Norton, D. P. (2004). *Strategy Maps, Converting intangible assets into tangible outcomes*. Harvard Business School Publishing.

Kaplan, R. S., & Norton, D. P. (2008). *The Execution Premium: Linking Strategy to Operations for Competitive Advantage*. Harvard Business School Press.

Keeley, L., Walters, H., Pikkel, R., & Quinn, B. (2013). *Ten Types of Innovation: The Discipline of Building Breakthroughs*. Wiley.

Kelley, H. H., & Thibaut, J. W. (1978). *Interpersonal Relations: A Theory of Interdependence*. Wiley.

Kim, W. C., & Mauborgne, R. (1997). Value innovation - the strategic logic of high growth. *Harvard Business Review, 75*(January–February), 103-112.

Kim, W. C., & Mauborgne, R. (1999). Strategy, value innovation, and the knowledge economy. *Sloan Management Review, 40*(3), 41-54. http://proquest.umi.com/pqdweb?did=41054993&Fmt=7&clientId=18963&RQT=309&VName=PQD

Kim, W. C., & Mauborgne, R. (2005a). *Blue Ocean Strategy: How to Create Uncontested Market Space and Make the Competition Irrelevant*. Harvard Business School Press.

Kim, W. C., & Mauborgne, R. (2005b). Value innovation: a leap into the blue ocean. *The Journal of Business Strategy, 26*(4), 22-28. http://proquest.umi.com/pqdweb?did=888965931&Fmt=7&clientId=18963&RQT=309&VName=PQD

Kish, K., Bunch, M. J., & Xu, B. J. (2016). Soft Systems Methodologies in action: environment, health and Shanghai's elderly. *Systemic Practice and Action Research, 29*(1), 61-77. https://doi.org/10.1007/s11213-015-9353-4

Kotter, J. P. (2012). *Leading Change*. Harvard Business Review Press.

Kotter, J. P. (2014). *Accelerate: Building Strategic Agility for a Faster-Moving World*. Harvard Business Review Press.

Kübler-Ross, E. (1969). *On Death and Dying*. Routledge.

Kübler-Ross, E., & Kessler, D. (2014). *On Grief & Grieving: Finding the Meaning of Grief through the Five Stages of Loss*. Scribner.

Lafley, A. G., Martin, R. L., Rivkin, J. W., & Siggelkow, N. (2012). Bringing science to the art of strategy. *Harvard Business Review, 90*(9), 56-66.

Lambe, C. J., Wittmann, C. M., & Spekman, R. E. (2001). Social exchange theory and research on business-to-business relational exchange. *Journal of Business-to-Business Marketing, 8*(3), 1-36.

Lewin, K. (1943). Defining the "field at a given time". *Psychological Review, 50*, 292–310.

Lewin, K. (1947). Frontiers in group dynamics: concept, method and reality in social science; social equilibria and social change. *Human Relations, 1*(1), 5–41.

Lewin, K. (1951). *Field Theory in Social Science*. Harper.

Liedtka, J. M. (1998). Linking strategic thinking with strategic planning. *Strategy & Leadership, 26*(4), 30-35.

Locke, E. A., & Latham, G. P. (1990). *A Theory of Goal Setting and Task Performance*. Prentice Hall.

Luffman, G., Sanderson, S. M., Lea, E., & Kenny, B. (1991). *Business Policy: An Analytical Introduction* (Second ed.). Blackwell.

Lyubomirsky, S. (2007). *The How of Happiness. A Practical Way to Getting the Life You Want*. Piatkus.

Lyubomirsky, S. (2013). *The Myths of Happiness*. Penguin Books.

Macaulay, S. (1963). Non-contractual relations in business: a preliminary study. *American Sociological Review, 28*(1), 55–69.

McChesney, C., Covey, S., & Huling, J. (2012). *The 4 Disciplines of Execution*. Free Press.

Medina, J. (2014). *Brain Rules: 12 principles for Surviving and Thriving at Work, Home, and School* (Revised ed.). Scribe Publications.

Miles, R. E., & Snow, C. C. (1978). *Organizational Strategy, Structure, and Process*. McGraw-Hill.

Miles, R. E., & Snow, C. C. (1994). *Fit, Failure, and the Hall of Fame: How Companies Succeed or Fail*. Free Press.

Miller, G. A. (1956). The magical number seven, plus or minus two: Some limits on our capacity for processing information. *Psychological Review, 63*, 81–97.

Mingers, J. (2014). *Systems Thinking, Critical Realism, and Philosophy: a Confluence of Ideas*. Routledge.

Mintzberg, H. (1973). Strategy making in three modes. *California Management Review, 16*(2), 44-53.

Mintzberg, H. (1987). The strategy concept I: five Ps for strategy. *California Management Review, 30*(1), 11-24.

Mintzberg, H. (1994). *The Rise and Fall of Strategic Planning.* Prentice Hall.

Mochon, D., Norton, M., & Ariely, D. (2012). Bolstering and restoring feelings of competence via the IKEA effect. *International Journal of Research in Marketing, 29*(4), 363-369.

Moss Kanter, R. (2004). *Confidence: How Winning Streaks and Losing Streaks Begin and End.* Random House.

National Commission. (2011). *Deep Water: The Gulf Oil Disaster and the Future of Offshore Drilling, Report to the President.* National Commission on the BP Deepwater Horizon Oil Spill and Offshore Drilling.

Norton, M., Mochon, D., & Ariely, D. (2012). The IKEA effect: when labour leads to love. *Journal of Consumer Psychology, 22*(3), 453-460.

Ogilvie, T., & Liedtka, J. (2011). *Designing for Growth: A Design Thinking Toolkit for Managers.* Columbia University Press.

Osterwalder, A., & Pigneur, Y. (2010). *Business Model Generation: A Handbook for Visionaries, Game Changers, and Challengers.* John Wiley and Sons.

Osterwalder, A., Pigneur, Y., Bernarda, G., & Smith, A. (2014). *Value Proposition Design: How to Create Products and Services Customers Want.* John Wiley & Sons.

Peters, T. J. (2018). *The Excellence Dividend: Principles for Prospering in Turbulent Times from a Lifetime in Pursuit of Excellence.* Nicholas Brealey Publishing.

Peters, T. J., & Waterman, R. H. (2004). *In Search of Excellence: Lessons from America's Best-Run Companies* (Second ed.). Harper Business.

Peysha, M., & Peysha, M. (2014). *Strategic Intervention Handbook: How to Quickly Produce Profound Change in Yourself and Others.* Strategic Intervention Press.

Pink, D. H. (2009). *Drive: The Surprising Truth About What Motivates Us.* Penguin.

Pinker, S. (2019). *Enlightenment Now: The Case for Reason, Science, Humanism, and Progress.* Penguin.

Porter, M. E. (1980). *Competitive Strategy: Techniques for Analysing Industries and Competitors.* Free Press.

Porter, M. E. (1985). *Competitive Advantage: Creating and Sustaining Superior Performance.* Free Press.

Prahalad, C. K., & Hamel, G. (1990). The core competence of the corporation. *Harvard Business Review, 68*(3), 79-92.

Purves, D., Augustine, G. J., Fitzpatrick, D., Hall, W. C., & LaMantia, A.-S. (Eds.). (2018). *Neuroscience* (Sixth ed.). Oxford University Press.

Rappaport, A. (1997). *Creating Shareholder Value* (Second ed.). Free Press.

Reason, P., & Bradbury, H. (Eds.). (2001). *Handbook of Action research. Participative Inquiry and Practice*. Sage.

Research and Markets. (2017). *Global Sensors in the Internet of Things (IoT) Devices Market, Analysis & Forecast: 2016 to 2022*. Research and Markets.

Ressler, C., & Thompson, J. (2008). *Why Work Sucks and How to Fix It*. Portfolio.

Rich, B. R. (1996). *Skunk Works: a Personal Memoir of My Years at Lockheed*. Back Bay Books.

Rittel, H. W. J., & Webber, M. M. (1973). Dilemmas in the general theory of planning. *Policy Sciences, 4*, 155–169.

Robertson, D., & Breen, B. (2014). *Brick by Brick: How LEGO Rewrote the Rules of Innovation and Conquered the Global Toy Industry*. Century - Trade.

Robinson, K. (2011). *Out of Our Minds: Learning to Be Creative*. Capstone.

Rodrik, D. (2012). *The Globalization Paradox: Democracy and the Future of the World Economy*. W.W. Norton and Company.

Rumelt, R. P. (1974). *Strategy, Structure, and Economic Performance*. Harvard Business School Press.

Sachs, S., & Rühli, E. (2005). Changing managers' values towards a broader stakeholder orientation. *Corporate Governance, 5*(2), 89. http://proquest.umi.com/pqdweb?did=841941021&Fmt=7&cl ientId=18963&RQT=309&VName=PQD

Sachs, S., & Rühli, E. (2011). *Stakeholders Matter: A New Paradigm for Strategy in Society*. Cambridge University Press.

Schilke, O., Reimann, M., & Cook, K. S. (2015). Power decreases trust in social exchange. . *Proceedings of the National Academy of Sciences of the United States of America, 112*(42), 12950–12955.

Seligman, M. E. P. (2004). *Authentic Happiness: Using the New Positive Psychology to Realize Your Potential for Lasting Fulfillment*. Free Press.

Seligman, M. E. P. (2012). *Flourish. A Visionary New Understanding of Happiness and Wellbeing*. William Heineman.

Seligman, M. E. P., Steen, T. A., Park, N., & Peterson, C. (2005). Positive psychology progress: empirical validation of interventions. *American Psychologist, 60*(5), 410-421.

Shanka, M. S., & Buvik, A. (2019). When does relational exchange matter? Social bond, trust and satisfaction. *Journal of Business-to-Business Marketing, 26*(1), 57-74.

Simon, H. A. (1973). Applying information technology to organizational design. *Public Administration Review, 33*, 268–278.

Smallman, C. (1997). Read all about it - risk trends in the media: a research note. *Disaster Prevention and Management, 6*(3), 160-164.

Smallman, C. (2021). Positive versus toxic leadership in the corporate and political spheres. In A. Waring (Ed.), *The New Authoritarianism. Vol 3: A Risk Analysis of the Corporate/Radical-Right Axis* (pp. 191-224). Ibidem Press.

Smith, N. C., & Rönnegard, D. (2016). Shareholder primacy, corporate social responsibility and the role of business schools. *Journal of Business Ethics, 134*(3), 463-478.

Stajkovic, A. D., Locke, E. A., & Blair, E. S. (2006). A first examination of the relationships between primed subconscious goals, assigned conscious goals, and task performance. *Journal of Applied Psychology, 91*, 1172–1180.

Sterling, J. (2003). Translating strategy into effective implementation: dispelling the myths and highlighting what works. *Strategy & Leadership, 31*(3), 27-34. https://doi.org/10.1108/10878570310472737

Stringer, E. T. (1999). *Action Research* (Second ed.). Sage.

Susskind, R., & Susskind, D. (2015). *The Future of the Professions: How Technology Will Transform the Work of Human Experts*. Oxford University Press.

Temesgen Kitaw, D., & Chris, B. (2017). Analysing information security in a bank using soft systems methodology. *Information Management and Computer Security, 25*(3), 240-258. https://doi.org/10.1108/ICS-07-2016-0053

Thibaut, J. W., & Kelley, H. H. (1959). *The Social Psychology of Groups*. John Wiley & Sons.

Townsend, A. M. (2013). *Smart Cities: Big Data, Civic Hackers and the Quest for New Utopia*. W.W. Norton & Company, Inc.

Trevor, J., & Varcoe, B. (2016). A simple way to test your company's strategic alignment. *Harvard Business Review*.

Tricker, R. I. (2012). *Corporate Governance: Principles, Policies and Practices* (Second ed.). Oxford University Press.

Trimboli, O. (2017). *Deep Listening: Impact Beyond Words*. Oscar Trimboli.

Tsoukas, H., & Chia, R. (2002). On organizational becoming - rethinking organizational change. *Organization Science, 13*, 567-582.

Tuckman, B. W. (1965). Developmental sequence in small groups. *Psychological Bulletin, 63*, 384-399.

Tuckman, B. W., & Jensen, M. A. C. (1977). Stages of small group development revisited. *Group and Organisational Studies, 2*, 419-427.

Tversky, A., & Kahneman, D. (1974). Judgement under uncertainty: heuristics and biases. *Science*(195), 1124-1131.

UNDP & UNIRSD. (2017). *Global Trends: Challenges and Opportunities in the Implementation of the Sustainable Development Goals* United Nations Development Programme and United Nations Research Institute for Social Development.

United Nations. (2006). *The Millennium Development Goals Report*. Retrieved February 27 from http://www.un.org/millenniumgoals/

Vermulen, F. (2017). *Breaking Bad Habits: Defy Industry Norms and Reinvigorate Your Business*. Harvard Business Review Press.

Walsh, B. (2009). *The Score Takes Care of Itself: My Philosophy of Leadership*. Penguin.

Waterman, R. H., Peters, T. J., & Phillips, J. R. (1980). Structure is not organisation. *Business Horizons, 23*(3), 14-26.

Wilson, B. (2001). *Soft Systems Methodology: Conceptual Model Building and Its Contribution*. Wiley.

Wilson, B., & Haperen, K. v. (2015). *Soft Systems Thinking, Methodology and the Management of Change*. Palgrave Macmillan.

Woolley, K., & Fishbach, A. (2015). The experience matters more than you think: people value intrinsic incentives more inside than outside an activity. *Journal of Personality and Social Psychology, 109*(6), 968-982.

Zeldin, T. (1994). *An Intimate History of Humanity*. Vintage.

Zerubavel, E. (2003). *Time Maps: Collective Memory and the Social Shape of the Past* University of Chicago Press.